# The Bully Pulpit

STUDIES IN GOVERNMENT
AND PUBLIC POLICY

# The Bully Pulpit
## The Politics of Protestant Clergy

James L. Guth
John C. Green
Corwin E. Smidt
Lyman A. Kellstedt
Margaret M. Poloma

University Press of Kansas

© 1997 by the University Press of Kansas
All rights reserved

Published by the University Press of Kansas (Lawrence, Kansas 66049), which was
organized by the Kansas Board of Regents and is operated and funded by Emporia
State University, Fort Hays State University, Kansas State University, Pittsburg State
University, the University of Kansas, and Wichita State University

2

Library of Congress Cataloging-in-Publication Data

Guth, James L.
    The bully pulpit : the politics of Protestant clergy / James L. Guth . . . [et al.].
        p.   cm. — (Studies in government and public policy)
    Includes bibliographical references and index.
    ISBN 0-7006-0868-0 (alk. paper). — ISBN 0-7006-0869-9 (pbk. : alk. paper)
        1. Protestant churches—United States—Clergy—Political activity—History—
20th century.   I. Title.   II. Series.
BR516.G87    1997
261.7′0973—dc21                                                          97-35918

British Library Cataloguing in Publication Data is available.

Printed in the United States of America

10   9   8   7   6   5   4   3   2   1

The paper used in this publication meets the minimum requirements of the American
National Standard for Permanence of Paper for Printed Library Materials Z39.48-1984.

Dedicated to clergy who have touched our lives

Leander L. Strodtman
A. Patterson Lee
William H. Willimon
D. Lynn Snider
Esdert Smidt
Tom Stark
Robert Schaff
Arthur Brown
Bill Hybels
John Ortberg
Roger C. Ames
Benno Kornely, S.J.

# Contents

# Preface

When the question of a title for this book came up, the authors—having all sat at the feet of noted preachers—decided to reappropriate Theodore Roosevelt's famous description of the essence of the American presidency. Of course, Americans have always mixed their political and religious metaphors, but TR's use of "the bully pulpit" reminds us of the high power that Protestant clergy have often exercised in our political life—after all, Roosevelt used only muscular images.

TR was not the first, of course, to recognize the power of the pulpit. As in many instances, the most astute observer of this aspect of American life was the French aristocrat Alexis de Tocqueville, who was convinced that American religion was one of "the causes which maintain democracy." Tocqueville warned his European readers to lay aside any images they might have of "otherworldly" American clergy: "If you converse with these missionaries of Christian civilization, you will be surprised to hear them speak so often of the goods of the world, and to meet a politician where you expected to find a priest" (1945, 1:317).

We began seeking the politicians in American Protestant clergy almost two decades ago, when James Guth conducted his first survey of ministers of the Southern Baptist Convention, then experiencing the early stirrings of what became a powerful theological and political movement. Guth repeated this survey in later presidential election years and was joined by John Green, Margaret Poloma, and Corwin Smidt with their studies in 1988, which together provide the basis for this analysis. In the early 1990s, Lyman Kellstedt added valuable material on ministers who were members of national religious activist groups. It took some time and effort to bring these studies together, but this book is the result.

Over the long journey from thousands of questionnaires full of raw data to the finished product, we have incurred more than the usual burden of scholarly debts. None of the studies used here would have been completed without the financial assistance of many organizations. Our own institutions and their academic leaders have supported this project in ways too numerous to count, so we thank Furman University and the Furman Advantage Program; Wheaton College and the Institute for the Study of American Evangelicals; Calvin College and the Calvin Center for Christian Scholarship; and the Ray C. Bliss Institute for Applied Politics at the University of Akron. Other financial assistance, direct or indirect, came from the Lilly Endowment, the Pew Charitable Trusts, and the National Endowment for the Humanities.

We are also indebted to colleagues for their roles in the project. Helen Lee Turner of Furman University not only provided the original stimulus but collaborated with Guth in the collection of the 1988 data on Southern Baptists, Presbyterians, and Disciples of Christ. Professor Turner has been a valuable source of insight into all three denominations. James Penning of Calvin College collaborated with Smidt in several surveys of Christian Reformed and Reformed Church in America ministers. Jim not only is an experienced observer of religious politics in his own right but also provides his own more humorous perspectives when the occasion demands. We also owe a special debt to Richard Dodson for his gracious permission to use the data from his survey of the clergy in the Evangelical Covenant Church.

Of course, we must thank the thousands of clergy who endured repeated blandishments to fill out long questionnaires from distant researchers they did not know. We also had the cooperation of several church agencies, from the Assemblies of God, the Southern Baptist Convention, the United Methodist Church, the Presbyterian Church U.S.A., and the Christian Church (Disciples of Christ).

Along the way we have acquired debts to many other people who make our work much easier: Margaret Crisp at Furman University, Anita Dotson at Wheaton College, and Kimberly Haverkamp, Dana Welch, and Shannon Little of the Bliss Institute performed myriad tasks that let the authors focus on this (and other) work.

Over the years, many undergraduates have cut their survey research and statistical teeth on one or another part of this study: Alicia Lehnes, Mark Taylor, Sarah Moses, Tobin Grant, and Tom Rudolph put in special efforts on this project.

The authors may debate among themselves whether engaging in scholarly activity produces individualistic or communitarian worldviews (see chapter 4), but they are part of a true community of scholars in the field of religion and politics. We want to thank Jeff Hadden for his original encouragement to do this book, which stands on the shoulders of his classic study of Protestant clergy. We also are grateful to many colleagues for trying to dissuade us from making mistakes (although we wish they were better at it): Ken Wald provided many valuable comments on a manuscript that we mistakenly thought was almost completed. For a Catholic, our good friend Ted Jelen has talked to almost as many Protestant clergy as we have, and has always been generous with his insights. David Leege often sees things from a more liturgical perspective than low-church social scientists do, but we value his continuing counsel. Allen Hertzke has also contributed more to this project than even the many references to his fine work would suggest. And many other friends in the American Political Science Association Religion and Politics Division provide frequent inspiration for work such as this.

We also thank Fred Woodward of the University Press of Kansas, who has waited for this volume with unfailing good humor (well, almost unfailing). We hope his confidence is justified. And finally, we thank our families for the love and encouragement that make all our endeavors worthwhile.

# Introduction:
# Clergy in American Politics:
# Some Scenes from the 1990s

## THREE SCENES INVOLVING CASTS FROM THE CHRISTIAN RIGHT

### Scene 1

Michael Cloer is accustomed to controversy. Minister of Siloam Baptist Church in Powdersville, South Carolina, Cloer was thrust into the limelight of the antiabortion movement as head of Pastors for Life, an interdenominational group that drew members primarily from conservative Southern Baptist, Pentecostal, and independent churches. In early 1993, Cloer led hundreds of protesters in "rescue operations" at upstate South Carolina clinics and was arrested several times. Cloer does not keep track of which congregation members participate in his protests but does tell his people that the Bible directs them to save unborn children.

"I have to tell them what the Bible says about repentance and about drinking and about sexual immorality as well. I preach it straight from the pulpit. I'm not intimidating people, I'm just telling them what the Bible says. People who don't understand the Bible would take that as intimidation." Cloer persuaded Pastors for Life to open a crisis pregnancy center next to one clinic, and he helped organize local chapters of the Christian Coalition in 1992. But these are not his only causes. After coming to the area in 1987, he led crusades against pornography, rock music, drugs, and alcohol, and organized boycotts of local convenience stores selling adult magazines or running video poker machines. He has also tried to convince local grocery stores not to sell alcohol. Always, he has counted on support from his 2,000-member congregation (Carnett 1993).

### Scene 2

During the 1992 presidential campaign, the Reverend John Godfrey of the Grandville Assembly of God in Grand Rapids, Michigan, attended rallies for both

1

George Bush and Bill Clinton. And although he did not tell his congregation how to vote, he listed the issues to keep in mind—and offered his endorsement when asked. Godfrey is not afraid to address politics from the pulpit. He has spoken out on abortion, homosexuality, and pornography, and has helped lead abortion protests and boycotts of companies he charged with selling pornography. "I believe people really want and need the church to come out with a strong voice," says Godfrey, who calls himself an independent conservative. "It's one area where the Protestant churches have really fallen behind, and more specifically, the evangelicals. We almost act like we don't dare to even say anything. I think people want to know. Does the Bible have anything to say about that? Or are we just going to let the government feed us everything they want?" (Honey 1995).

## Scene 3

The sanctuary of the First Assembly of God of Des Moines, Iowa, was almost full for the eleven o'clock service. This church of baby boomers and their children attracts 3,000 each Sunday to its joyful Pentecostal services, perhaps the largest congregation in Iowa. John M. Palmer, the forty-three-year-old minister, took the pulpit after the hymns, praise choruses, and special music. Before beginning the sermon, Palmer joked about how his nine-year-old son, in studying how famine and pestilence had afflicted the children of Israel when they departed from God, had reported that Israel's punishment had been "famine and politicians," a natural enough mistake for a nine-year-old in Iowa just days before the 1996 presidential caucuses. The congregation roared with laughter, but the casual observer might have missed a deeper irony. These same churchgoers, with guidance from their pastor, had become a real political force.

Palmer claims, "I am not a political person. The answer for America is not to get a Republican president." But his church has been at the center of the political realignment moving Evangelicals into the GOP. Since the 1980s, Republican politicians have been frequent speakers, and the congregation has helped the Christian Coalition by providing facilities for meetings and publicity. Palmer sees Christian conservatives becoming less reactive: "We're more on the offensive now. Our goal is to strengthen the fabric of society by strengthening families [and] lifting the moral level of our country." Palmer does worry that extensive political activism by Christians and their churches may create problems: "If we allow ourselves to be compromised for the sake of either popularity or pragmatic power, it becomes very dangerous." But, as one parishioner put it, there shouldn't be a problem, "as long as we don't compromise the word of God" (Solomon 1996).

## INTERLUDE

Even casual observers of public affairs will recognize the Reverends Cloer, Godfrey, and Palmer as part of the recent surge of political activity by conservative Protestants. Indeed, clergy in Evangelical churches have been crucial to the Christian Right, a social movement dedicated to restoring "traditional values" in public policy. Scholarly observers might notice that each pastor has entered politics stressing a different clerical role. Cloer's protest activity is a good example of the minister's role as private citizen, exercising constitutional rights to express opinion and influence the government. In contrast, Godfrey stresses his role as religious professional, explicitly connecting the values of his tradition to public affairs. And Palmer is acting as an institutional leader, the head of a local church, mobilizing his congregation—with some caution—into political action. As the scenes make clear, however, none neglects entirely the possibilities inherent in the other roles. In any case, this sort of clerical politics is often controversial even among conservative Protestants, many of whom prefer "Old Breed" pastors, who shun politics and focus on salvation in the next life. Of course, even tougher criticism comes from clergy who oppose the conservative goals of Cloer, Godfrey, and Palmer.

## AND NOW THREE SCENES FROM OTHER CHRISTIAN PLAYERS

### Scene 4

For over three years, workers at the K mart Corporation's Greensboro, North Carolina, distribution center fought for better compensation, claiming that they were paid less than similar workers elsewhere in the country, primarily because so many of them were African-Americans. During the struggle, workers were joined by clergy and other religious activists in boycotts and picketing of a Greensboro K mart store. By early 1996, several clergy had been arrested repeatedly for nonviolent civil disobedience at the store, including ministers from various black Baptist and Methodist churches but also some white pastors from Presbyterian, United Methodist, and other Mainline denominations. In addition to the boycotts and protests, the workers' supporters also sought to mobilize national church action. The annual General Assembly of the Presbyterian Church U.S.A. adopted a resolution expressing concern over the dispute, threatening a national boycott or a sell-off of its K mart stock if the issue was not settled. In July 1996 the corporation and the union reached agreement, ending the strike but not settling all the contested issues. The Greensboro clergy promised to expand their concern with local labor issues, taking a more proactive stance in the future. They also promised to watch the progress of litigation pursuant to the agreement, should their intervention be needed (Shipp 1996).

### Scene 5

Clergy in Bonner County, Idaho, have been mobilized to counter the growing nativist and militia groups that permeate the state. Ministers have been especially instrumental in the Bonner County Human Rights Task Force, including the Reverend

Mary Robinson-Mohr, pastor of the First Presbyterian Church in Sandpoint. The group has sponsored lessons on tolerance in the public schools, brought speakers to community meetings to discuss prejudice, and shown movies like *Schindler's List*. They also sponsored a rally of 500 people in the town of 2,500. Several clergy said they had simply assumed that right-thinking people who understood their Bible would not be misled by the Aryan Nation or other groups, but had concluded that they were wrong. The Reverend Robinson-Mohr observed, "It behooves us to keep our folks biblically literate. Our folks need to determine what is good interpretation and what is ridiculous." She volunteered to be the first chair of the Human Rights Group three years ago but put the decision to the church's elders. "I said, what if it comes down to putting the church building in jeopardy from violence?" After a brief lull, however, the elders supported her. And although she received "some odd phone calls" and had some threatening symbols painted outside her house, no violence occurred.

Many of the same Sandpoint ministers addressed another issue, gay rights, when Proposition 1, an anti–gay rights proposal, was on the Idaho ballot. The Reverend Paul Graves, on sabbatical leave as pastor of the United Methodist Church, preached against the proposal, prompting an angry church member to reproach him for so speaking from the pulpit. "As compassionately as I could, I tried to tell him what I was talking about was justice. I said that has to be a pulpit issue, or the Gospel isn't what it says." Voters narrowly defeated Proposition 1, for which the Bonner County group claims some credit, but the issue remains alive, one that right-wing groups can use to their advantage (Niebuhr 1995).

## Scene 6

At a recent forum sponsored by the Texas Freedom Alliance, one guest speaker railed against the "Christian mess" invading state and local politics. Another blasted the Baptists for blatant self-righteousness. Some people agreed the time had come to don the button: "The Christian Right Is Neither." All were ministers. Formed only in February 1995 and having only two staff members, the alliance quickly drew together a wide-ranging and sometimes surprising coalition of opponents of conservative religious influence in government agencies and public schools. It seeks to represent "moderates" and the "mainstream." The executive director is Cecile Richards, the daughter of former Texas Democratic governor Ann Richards, who was defeated with Christian Right help. Richards and her assistant, Debbie Frank, have debated Christian Right leaders on radio talks shows, organized workshops on combating the Right, and advised PTAs on how to resist censorship in public schools. The group has especially targeted Mainline clergy, claiming a growing number of Methodist, Presbyterian, Episcopalian, and even Southern Baptist ministers.

"I think it's a shameful thing that something like the Texas Freedom Alliance has to be created, but it seems to be necessary," says the Reverend Don Sinclair, pastor of the 500-member Bering Memorial United Methodist Church in Houston. "Religion is getting to be a major social problem. When religious people become intolerant, they do the meanest, strangest, most unconstitutional things, and they think they're doing God's work—they really feel they are. They may have hold of a legitimate issue, but their way to go about it is to deny me the right to disagree." The Reverend Bill Lytle of San Antonio, former moderator of the Presbyterian Church U.S.A., has also joined the fray. "For some time, I've been concerned about the idea that people might think the religious right was speaking for all of the religious community," Lytle says. "Perhaps because we have not been so vocal as we should have been over the past several years, we've allowed a certain position to be expressed that almost seems like the religious position, and that's not true. We're in a place now where we need to be serious about what's happening to the poor, the welfare folks, the immigrants" (Presley 1995).

These clergy may seem somewhat more familiar than their Christian Right counterparts, having a long heritage of Mainline Protestant politics behind them. Indeed, they carry on in the tradition of the "New Breed" of liberal ministers of the 1960s and 1970s who infused the civil rights, antipoverty, and peace movements with much of their moral authority. As with their conservative opponents, these ministers also engaged in political activity in the roles of citizen, religious professional, and institutional leader.

All these scenes may be puzzling to many readers, but they have been drawn from hundreds of similar ones that occur every month in communities all over the United States. Ministers from many political persuasions have long been active in American politics, but in the 1980s and 1990s it seemed impossible to find any political controversy that did not involve clergy—often on both sides of the issue. These examples also illustrate only some of the means clergy use to influence the political process: by preaching to their congregations, lobbying public officials, organizing the dispossessed, supporting political candidates, holding public rallies, and engaging in unconventional political actions such as boycotts, protests, and civil disobedience. How are we to understand this new wave of ministerial activism? We begin our examination of clerical politics in chapter 1 by providing an overview of the critical interpretive issues confronting the puzzled observer.

# 1
# The Politics of the Protestant Clergy: An Overview

Someone coming of age in the late 1980s would surely have taken the political involvement of Protestant clergy for granted. As the foregoing vignettes suggest, one might think that pastors were at home among political activists, not unlike lawyers, journalists, or business owners. And this impression would have been fortified by even a casual reading of American history: the clergy have been a staple of politics since the founding of the nation, from the time colonial preachers blessed (or sometimes cursed) the American Revolution, through the great reform movements of the mid-nineteenth and early twentieth centuries, to the civil rights and antiwar crusades of the 1960s.

It is against this backdrop that we explore the politics of the Protestant clergy at the end of the twentieth century. This book is an inquiry into the political attitudes and behavior of parish clergy across the range of historically white Protestant denominations, including several of the nation's largest, from the Assemblies of God and the Southern Baptist Convention to the United Methodist Church and Presbyterian Church U.S.A. In this chapter, we provide an overview of the literature on clerical politics and of the argument presented in the rest of the book. First, we present a simple explanatory model of the politics of pastors. We then turn to the key elements in that model, considering in turn (1) the theological differences among Protestant clergy; (2) the varieties of social theologies they hold; and (3) the competing agendas of orthodox and modernist clergy. Then we look at the political variables associated with these perspectives, examining (4) ministers' positions on contemporary issues, political ideology, and partisanship, and (5) their attitudes about, and participation in, political activities of all sorts. We then restate the model in more detail and present the plan of the book.

## A SIMPLE MODEL OF PASTORAL POLITICS

Conceptually, the politics of any social group has two basic features: substantive purposes and degree of involvement. "Substantive purposes" refers to the group's goals, typically desired changes in public policy, and the broader values that generate those goals. Fundamentally, such goals motivate political activity. "Degree of involvement" encompasses the level and type of activity that group members direct at achieving these substantive purposes. Put another way, involvement brings substantive purposes into the political process, where they can be acted upon. Participation helps turn political goals into political reality.

Like that of other citizens, the political activity of ministers can be understood in terms of goals and activities. And like most citizens, the clergy's political goals are tied to their personal values, but pastors ground their values in a special way in religious beliefs, including both *theology,* an understanding of the divine and humanity's relationship to it, and what we call *social theology,* beliefs connecting theology to public affairs. On the one hand, such beliefs underlie ministers' political agendas, stances on issues, and more general political attitudes, such as ideology and partisanship, which in turn link clergy to the party and interest group alignments that structure American politics. On the other hand, theology and social theology also define ministers' political role orientations, that is, their assessment of the appropriate level and type of political activity. These role orientations direct clergy toward various forms of political participation—or none at all. The actual translation of beliefs into political goals and activities is also influenced by the clergy's social context, including their personal characteristics, denominational and congregational environments, and political circumstances.

From these definitions, we can posit a simple model of pastoral politics: ministers' theological beliefs, expressed in a social theology and modified by social context, generate political goals and activities. Because ministers' theology, social theology, and social context differ, their goals and activities will vary as well. Now we can fill in this simple model by identifying the theological beliefs, social theologies, and social contexts of contemporary Protestant clergy, and by specifying their connections to political goals and activities.

## THEOLOGICAL ORIENTATIONS

In his seminal article on ideology, Philip Converse defines a belief system as a "configuration of ideas and attitudes in which the elements are bound together by some form of constraint or functional interdependence" (1964, 207). According to Converse, belief systems vary in *range,* with some including beliefs about a relatively few objects, while others encompass a great many. Individual elements in belief systems differ in their *centrality* to the system. Converse argued that the belief systems of most Americans had a narrow range and that attitudes on discrete issues were only weakly associated with each other. Only political and social elites had more "constrained" belief systems, comprising opinions on a broad range of issues, which were closely related empirically (cf. McClosky, Hoffman, and O'Hara 1960). We argue that theology is central to the belief systems of Protestant clergy. Not only does theology cover a wide range of ideas, but it operates at a deeper or more fundamental level than "liberalism" or "conservatism," the terms most familiar to political scientists. In this work we will investigate the strong links between central theological beliefs and a variety of social and political ideas, suggesting that theology not only undergirds ministers' political worldviews but shapes their activity as well. To do this, we begin with an examination of the historical roots of the theological orientations of Protestant clergy.

The political goals and activities of Protestant clergy are still strongly influenced by theological disputes that arose in the late nineteenth century. These profound disagreements ultimately forged what Martin Marty (1970) has called the "two-party system" in American Protestantism, a division between the theologically "orthodox" and "modernist," or, as Marty called them, the "private" and "public" parties. Although the contours of this division have been complex and far from static, by the end of the twentieth century most Protestant denominations fell clearly into either the "Evangelical" tradition, comprising denominations and churches dominated by orthodox forces, or the "Mainline" tradition, in which modernists have been dominant, at least among clergy and denominational leaders (Kellstedt and Green 1993).

This bifurcation of American Protestantism began after the Civil War and resulted in major institutional changes during the 1920s. The split was a reaction to shifting intellectual perspectives among theologians and to new social conditions. Formidable intellectual challenges came in the ideas of Charles Darwin and the "new" German higher criticism of the Bible. Darwin's theory of evolution undermined the Genesis account of Creation, and higher criticism reinforced this assault, arguing that the Bible must be interpreted like other ancient documents, put in social and historical context. These ideas not only threatened literalism in biblical interpretation but also depreciated Scripture's value as science and history. At about the same time, massive social changes such as industrialization, urbanization, and large-scale immigration of Catholics, Jews, and other religious minorities reduced the influence of Protestant churches and increased religious pluralism, producing skepticism about the taken-for-granted tenets of Protestant orthodoxy and prompting at least some theologians, clergy, and even laity to entertain beliefs at variance with traditional creeds, and others to abandon supernatural religion altogether (Abell 1962).

In response to these developments, a new "liberal" Protestant theology arose, seeking to reconcile the historic Christian faith with modern science and social conditions (hence the synonym "modernist"). Although there was much diversity within this new liberalism, adherents shared many perspectives. Rather than regarding the Bible as divine, produced directly by God, liberals were naturalistic, explaining the text and the events it recounted in human terms. And rather than emphasizing God's particular revelation in Jesus Christ, liberals sought a general revelation in nature and history, a "natural theology." Finally, instead of emphasizing God's transcendence and supernatural aspects of the faith, liberals stressed God's immanence, a divine presence in the mundane world.

Liberal theology opened new fissures within Protestantism, often producing cries of heresy from traditionalists, but it did not initially create schisms. Rather, by 1910 liberalism had gradually permeated the most prestigious Protestant seminaries, especially those attached to the new research universities, and had attracted many clergy and sophisticated laity from large, upper-class churches, primarily in the Northeast and Midwest. After World War I, however, the split became too wide to bridge, as conservatives counterattacked, most notably in the northern Presbyterian and Baptist churches. Although comprising a diverse coalition of religious traditionalists, these "fundamentalists" agreed in reasserting historic Christian beliefs ("the fundamentals") challenged by liberals: the centrality of Jesus in achieving personal salvation, the virgin birth, and the Bible's authority, often expressed as "inerrancy." In addition, many fundamentalists preached dispensationalism, a new variant of historic premillennialism, warning that the end times were near, that Jesus' Second Coming was imminent, and that the world would soon face the Great Tribulation. However, the tiny remnant of the true Church would be rescued from this fate by the "Rapture," before the final battle between God and Satan at Armageddon.

Although they mustered considerable support, fundamentalists failed to take control of any major denomination. As a result, by the late 1920s many withdrew from their "apostate" churches, adding the doctrine of separation to their core beliefs. Thus, the character of fundamentalism had changed dramatically (Marsden 1980). No longer located at the center of organized Protestantism and with no prospect of capturing the historic denominations, this movement of staunch traditionalists regrouped outside, sometimes within a few schismatic denominations, but more often in independent congregations, parachurch agencies, and institutions. The denominations they deserted became part of the modern Protestant Mainline, usually incorporating a range of theological orientations, but with a theological tone set by liberal or modernist elites.

Not all of American Protestantism was immediately troubled by the fundamentalist-modernist controversy. Methodism, especially its southern branch, had witnessed little of the infighting. Although Methodist seminary professors were drawn to modernist ideas, the clergy as a whole were affected only gradually, as most Methodist pastors were still not seminary trained (Chiles 1965). Even in the North, where the new theology made inroads, the accommodating Wesleyan theology, grounded in "Scripture, tradition, reason, and experience" rather than strict creeds, and the church's historical emphasis on personal piety rather than doctrine, allowed competing groups to coexist. Nevertheless, as denominational leaders experimented with the new liberalism and Methodist laity moved up the social class ladder, some traditionalist Wesleyans, often working-class people, deserted the church for the Holiness movement. They often shared orthodox tenets with fundamentalists but were preoccupied with regaining the spiritual fervor of the Wesleys' early converts. Like the Methodists, the Disciples of Christ also had a mixed experience with liberalism: they had a growing coterie of clergy educated at "modernist" schools, such as Yale and the University of Chicago, but were still a predominantly rural and small-town denomination, with many other clergy trained only in Bible colleges. Their congregational polity also muted conflict, as critics of modernist trends could (and did) "go independent" (Williams 1991).

Other Protestant churches were even more isolated, a least for a time, from the full impact of this controversy. The traditionalist Southern Baptist Convention (SBC) was preserved by regional isolation in its rural homeland, protecting its modest seminary from inroads by German higher criticism in two skirmishes in the late nineteenth century but also ejecting fundamentalist followers of Texan J. Frank Norris in the 1920s. Many ethnic churches also ignored the emerging Evangelical and Mainline camps. Dutch Calvinists in the Christian Reformed Church resisted conscription into the new Evangelical armies, as did the pietists in the predominantly Swedish Evangelical Covenant Church, who nevertheless maintained their traditional beliefs. As we shall see, most of the denominations not experiencing the full brunt of the controversy eventually gravitated to one side or the other.

At the same time that the fundamentalist-modernist struggle was reshaping the theological boundaries of historic Protestant communions, the new Pentecostal movement further complicated the American religious picture. Convinced that the end times were near, Pentecostals experienced a renewal of New Testament "gifts of the Spirit," such as speaking in tongues (like the first Christians at Pentecost), healing the sick, and other manifestations. Attracting millions of rural and blue-collar Americans, Pentecostalism drew adherents from many religious backgrounds, but especially from the Holiness movement, and quickly congealed into two loose alliances, the Assemblies of God (predominantly white) and the Church of God in Christ (primarily African-American), and a myriad of smaller denominations and independent churches.

Although fundamentalists and Pentecostals shared many beliefs, especially traditional orthodoxy and variants of dispensational theology, their early relationships were tense. Fundamentalists rejected Pentecostal claims about the "gifts," especially speaking in tongues and faith healing, making cooperative relationships difficult. Not until the 1940s did joint ventures get off the ground, when moderate fundamentalists (who had revived the old term "Evangelical" to describe their movement) invited Pentecostals to join the new National Association of Evangelicals (Spittler 1994). More recently, social mobility among Pentecostals and a shared perception among orthodox Christians that they are fighting common enemies—proliferating theological liberalism and a secularizing culture—have led to additional cooperation, at least among denominational leaders. Although tensions persist at the grass roots (see Jelen 1991), most leaders in both communities now regard themselves as part of a single Evangelical tradition.

Indeed, today more than ever before, many observers see Protestantism divided into two coherent traditions, one consisting of Evangelical denominations dominated by orthodox theology, and the other made up of Mainline churches, characterized by modernist or liberal theology, at least among denominational leaders and most clergy. As our profiles in the next chapter will show, each party now includes denominations or groups isolated or immune from the earliest confrontations. The exact extent to which theological alignments coincide with denominational lines is still subject to dispute: some analysts see theological cleavages cutting right through many church bodies, but others claim that most denominations are moving into one or the other camp, depending upon their dominant theological perspective (cf. Wuthnow 1988; Warner 1993). In any case, in an era when fundamental values and "policy predispositions" increasingly dominate political choices and activity (Miller and Shanks 1996, 383–388), these basic theological ideas provide a firm foundation for ministerial politics.

## SOCIAL THEOLOGY

Almost from the birth of this two-party system, the orthodox and the modernists had divergent perspectives on the role of the church in the world, or what we call *social theology*. Although these competing social theologies have been given various names (see Warner 1988, 51), they are best thought of as examples of *individualist* and *communitarian* worldviews (Leege and Kellstedt 1993, 216–231). Individualists see the essential problems of religion as "vertical," in the relation of the individual soul to God, the disciplined transformation of believers through the cultivation of personal morality, and the preaching of the gospel to bring others into the faith (cf. Thomas 1989). Communitarians, in contrast, stress the "horizontal" aspect of religion: community building among interdependent individuals. Religion is about the redemption of society in this world, not individual salvation in the next (cf. Benson and Williams 1982, 148–166).

For many theological liberals at the turn of the twentieth century, the Social Gospel was the answer to the problems of the new industrial civilization, such as the marginal existence of the working class, widespread and abusive child labor, and the squalor of the burgeoning city (May 1949). This perspective abandoned the historic revivalist emphasis on spiritual conversion and personal sanctification as the only sure route to social change, stressing instead the structural reform of society. For Social Gospelers, the sorry state of urban civilization was the result not simply of human depravity but rather of social injustice. Reflecting turn-of-the-century optimism, the Social Gospel espoused a positive view of human nature; sin was something that education could mitigate or social reform prevent (Hoge 1976, 21). Although many Social Gospelers saw churches as the primary instruments for reform—in part by persuading wealthy and powerful members to act more justly—they soon formulated more ambitious roles for government in building the Kingdom of God on earth, a vision captured in the social creed of the new Federal Council of Churches in 1908 (Schneider 1989). As much as anything, this commitment to social and political action elicited Marty's classification of Mainline Protestantism as the "public party."

Although wounded by the horrors and disillusionment of World War I and by the postwar "return to normalcy," the Social Gospel was kept alive by the Great Depression and the activism of the New Deal until the 1960s, when it was again revived by the civil rights, antipoverty, and peace movements. By this time, social reform had become the primary mission of the church for a new generation of liberal clergy, who abandoned otherworldly religion altogether in favor of social transformation (Quinley 1974). And soon, liberation theology, with its "preferential option for the poor" and ambitious political role for religion, moved out of its Latin American Catholic birthplace and had "a nearly incredible impact" (Hunt 1987, 94) among Protestant theologians, clergy, and religious activists (see, for example, Hessel 1993, 21–38). Today, a communitarian theology of reform is still a defining element of Mainline churches; indeed, sociologist Stephen Warner has argued that liberal Protestants are united not by religious doctrine but by "an optimistic, socially responsible attitude" (1988, 56).

Not surprisingly, most traditionalists saw the Social Gospel as just another liberal heresy (cf. Ahlstrom 1972, 2:788). Fundamentalists, Pentecostals, and other orthodox Protestants continued to preach the "individual gospel" (Marty 1970, 179), and for much of the twentieth century their successors rejected political action as a task for the church. Still emphasizing salvation in the next life, they focused on converting sinners. From this perspective, the only true reform came from above, through transformation of the converted individual, not from "getting involved in politics." Of course, not all traditionalists agreed precisely on the limits of political effort. The strictest fundamentalists, convinced that the world was inevitably deteriorating and the end imminent, saw evangelism as the only responsibility of faithful Christians, but expected no improvement in social conditions. Other conservatives held out more hope for social change through evangelism. If the hearts of individuals were purified, social problems would either dissipate (for those of Wesleyan bent) or at least be ameliorated (a more somber Calvinist assessment). Thus, some traditionalists entered the political fray to preserve opportunity for preaching the gospel, to protect moral standards, and to assist converts in living the Christian life. In this sense, the orthodox contingent was not entirely apolitical, but Marty's term the "private party" does capture their preoccupation with individual salvation, personal morality, and skepticism about politics.

By the 1960s, the conflict between these rival social theologies reached full boil. First the civil rights movement and the War on Poverty, then the Vietnam War, and finally other cultural conflicts stimulated a bitter debate over the role of religious values in public affairs. Indeed, these controversies prompted social scientists to conduct the first systematic studies of pastoral politics, culminating in several now-classic works, most notably Jeffrey Hadden's *Gathering Storm in the Churches* (1969); Rodney Stark et al.'s *Wayward Shepherds* (1971), and Harold

Quinley's *Prophetic Clergy* (1974). In addition to providing the first extensive data on clerical politics, all of these studies portrayed religious modernists as the "relevant" political force, pushing for fundamental social and political change, while traditionalists remained on the sidelines, obsessed with otherworldy salvation and personal morality, thereby buttressing the status quo.

The conservative Protestant resurgence in American politics after 1976 demands that we revisit such conclusions. Critical changes in conservative social theology, some scholars argue, have facilitated this new political engagement (see Wuthnow 1983). On one extreme, a few observers insist that Evangelicals have jettisoned their social individualism, now believing that poverty and other social problems are "the result of structural or systemic barriers," adopting "faith and social justice perspectives" like those of Mainline Protestants (Dudley and Van Eck 1992). Other scholars argue that there have indeed been real changes in Evangelical social theology but that these ultimately preserve the tradition's individualism (see Guth et al. 1994). In this view, individualist social theology has been slowly infused by a new "civic gospel," envisioning a crucial role for politics in sustaining the moral order and protecting religion, families, and individuals. This new version of individualism thus identifies a broader set of political goals, although many involve reversing past "reforms" and social experiments. As we shall see, neither communitarian nor individualist social theology is inherently political or apolitical, but each is associated with radically different political agendas.

## POLITICAL AGENDAS

As political scientists increasingly recognize, decisions to participate in politics often depend in part on the "political agenda," the policy questions currently receiving serious attention from decision makers, whether because of visible problems or threatening events, changes in public opinion or "national mood," or the actions of elected officials, interest groups, and other political elites (Rosenstone and Hansen 1993, 101–117; Kingdon 1984). While the national agenda is quite variable, the personal agendas of religious leaders are much more stable, rooted as they are in deep-seated theological perspectives and their associated social theologies. Thus, the extent of clergy activism often depends upon the mesh between the current national agenda and those issues that their own worldviews identify as vital.

Throughout this century, the basic political and social concerns of orthodox and modernist clergy have shown considerable continuity. Modernist and communitarian clergy in Mainline Protestant churches have held a *social justice agenda,* while orthodox, individualist religious leaders in the Evangelical tradition have advanced what we call the *moral reform agenda* (cf. Beatty and Walter 1989). We will consider each in turn.

With the advent of the Social Gospel, modernist leaders began to address a vast array of social welfare issues, participating first in the Progressive movement, then in the New Deal of the 1930s, and later in the antipoverty campaigns of Lyndon

Johnson's Great Society. These concerns persisted into the 1990s, as Mainline churches lobbied vigorously for wider access to child care for working mothers, higher minimum wages, federal aid for the homeless, and preserving benefits for the poor in "welfare reform." In the 1990s environmentalism was added to the social justice agenda, with liberal Protestant elites responding to the cause with striking alacrity (Fowler 1995). As Daniel Hofrenning has observed, Mainline lobbyists perceive all these stances as a prophetic witness against the wealthy and selfish economic elites dominating American society (1995, 100).

Mainline church bodies also claim a continuing commitment to civil and human rights. In the 1960s they supplied much of the moral impetus and lobbying pressure that finally elicited critical Republican support for civil rights bills in Congress (Findlay 1993). Such concerns persisted into the 1980s and 1990s, as religious liberals condemned Reagan-Bush policies on school desegregation, employment discrimination, and voting rights. Support for civil rights extended to related issues, including the rights of women and of gays and lesbians. Mainline leaders have also defended human rights abroad, although their voices have been loudest when violators are right-wing or racist regimes, such as the former Afrikaner government of South Africa, rather than Marxist or leftist ones (Billingsley 1990).

Finally, Mainline leaders have usually reflected contemporary liberal priorities on international issues. Reluctantly supporting American military action in the two world wars, their more characteristic posture has been to deplore militarism. Many Protestant pastors joined the antiwar movements of their era, demanding peaceful settlement of international disputes in the 1930s, criticizing American use of nuclear weapons against Japan in 1945, and insisting on withdrawal from Vietnam. During the 1980s, Mainline churches condemned Reagan's aid to the contras in Nicaragua, opposed his defense buildup, and demanded strategic arms pacts with the USSR. Later, prominent Mainline figures attacked President Bush's military response to Saddam Hussein's invasion of Kuwait, calling for a negotiated settlement (Hertzke 1991; Murphy 1992).

Although it might appear less ambitious than the Mainline social justice agenda, the Evangelical churches have also had a list of critical concerns, what we call the *moral reform agenda*. The most ancient cause, fighting alcoholic beverages, persists from the heyday of nineteenth-century revivalism. Although the Prohibition movement actually held together the emerging fundamentalist and liberal camps as "the last crusade for Protestant civilization," after ratification of the Eighteenth Amendment liberal zeal waned, and conservatives were left to battle Demon Rum alone. With the repeal of national Prohibition, the fight reverted to the states, where antiliquor (and antidrug) legislation remained a principal concern of traditionalists (Meier 1994). Conservatives have also fought gambling, long associated with the saloon, but transformed into a national political controversy in the 1980s, as historic legal restrictions fell and as state governments used lotteries to fill public treasuries. To conservative critics, this amounts to state-sponsored immorality (see, for example, Rozell and Wilcox 1996, 44).

Another central component of the moral reform agenda involves the regulation of sexuality and family matters. Conservative Protestants have continually sought public policy fostering "traditional" sexual mores: maintaining laws against easy divorce, legal prohibition of pornography, and, by the early 1970s, strict limitations on abortion. Indeed, the first contemporary Christian Right groups emerged from campaigns opposing the Equal Rights Amendment, the *Roe v. Wade* decision, and the gay rights movement. Most analysts have argued that issues of sexuality, sometimes summarized as "pelvic politics," were central to the rise of conservative Christian activism, much of it led by pastors.

Education issues have long been a salient point on the moral reform agenda, reflecting the proliferating conflicts between traditionalist values of conservative Protestant parents and the perspectives of educational professionals. From the time of the antievolution movement in the 1920s, conservative parents have sought to make sure that public schools reflect their values. The religious exercise cases decided by the Supreme Court in the 1960s revived one facet of the struggle, but contemporary conservative Protestants have even deeper worries that beliefs and values taught at home are demeaned in public institutions, whether through evolutionary theories of human origins, which to many orthodox Christians undercut the first two chapters of Genesis; or through sex education classes, which sometimes endorse practices or relationships many conservatives regard as immoral; or through the curricular innovations and educational "reforms" such as outcome-based education (OBE), a kind of bête noire to many Evangelicals. To evade these dangers, many conservatives formed Christian schools or home-schooled their children, leading to yet other conflicts with education authorities. Some have sought public support for religious education, while others have fought to "take back" the public schools and their curricula through political mobilization (Bates 1993; Martin 1996).

Finally, foreign policy has also attracted the attention of many conservative Protestants, especially since World War II. The anti-Communist movement of the 1950s drew avid support from many religious conservatives, who feared not only the "godless" Marxist philosophy but also the militantly antireligious Soviet and Chinese regimes. The return of thousands of Evangelical missionaries from the Far East after the 1949 Communist "takeover" certainly fed these sentiments. Indeed, for dispensationalists both countries soon figured as allies of the Antichrist in imaginative scenarios leading up to the end times (Weber 1987, 214–215). As a result, conservative Protestants were often quite supportive of the American military establishment and defense spending, and drank deeply at the well of patriotism. In a related vein, many in the Evangelical tradition also had a special fascination with the state of Israel, as their dispensational beliefs told them that the Jews' return to Palestine was a marker of the end times and that support of Israel was a responsibility of true Christians, an attitude that persists in the 1990s (Guth et al. 1996).

In some respects, then, the *moral reform agenda* has also shown a good bit of continuity over time. Although policy concerns over alcohol, gambling, sexual behavior, and education were often dismissed by earlier analysts of clerical politics as being irrelevant to the great public issues of the 1960s that mobilized liberal clergy and attracted sympathetic academics, they were nonetheless salient public concerns for many orthodox Protestants and, especially, their clergy. As Theodore Lowi (1995) has cogently observed, in the 1970s and 1980s these questions became not so much politicized as *nationalized,* removed from the safe confines of local and state control by the Supreme Court, Congress, and other forces, and put onto the national policy agenda, drawing religious conservatives onto new and more competitive political terrain.

## IDEOLOGY AND PARTISANSHIP

Our discussion of the historic beliefs and issue agendas of the two Protestant "parties" leads naturally to analysis of two key characteristics of all political activists and elites: ideology and partisanship. Both concepts have received much attention from political scientists but have played only minor, supporting roles in studies of clergy.

An early discovery of the new behavioral political science in the 1950s was that most Americans have only vague notions about politics: they care little about most public policy questions, have very modest information about them, and often hold only superficial attitudes (Zaller 1992). Nor do most citizens connect ideas about different issues in any systematic way; in other words, most Americans are "non-ideological" (Campbell et al. 1960). At the same time, studies found that political activists and elites had much firmer political beliefs and exhibited more *attitudinal constraint;* that is, they connected their opinions on different issues in a more comprehensive conservative or liberal worldview (Converse 1964). Thus, elites often play a vital role in opinion leadership, eliciting the support of other citizens for candidates and causes that embrace their ideological positions.

Ministers not only share many traits of other social and political elites, but by definition are in the business of opinion leadership. Their views not only inform their own activity but also may shape the perspectives of their congregations. Previous studies reveal that ministers who hold orthodox theological views generally express conservative political beliefs, while modernists hold more liberal positions (Hadden 1969; Quinley 1974). Some scholars have argued, however, that these tendencies hold only on the issues of greatest import to each group: traditionalists are conservative only on moral issues, while modernists are liberal primarily on the social justice agenda. Of course, issues have changed, political alignments have altered, and the religious balance of power has shifted in the three decades since the classic works, calling for a reevaluation of the linkage between theology and ideology found in that research.

Like ideology, partisanship is a potent influence on political activists and elites, and is even more directly related to many political choices. Partisanship is particularly important in the United States, given the dominance of the two-party system;

most Americans feel some partisan attachment and are likely to vote for candidates of "their" party. Indeed, other criteria for political judgment are often encapsulated in partisanship, connecting citizens' values to electoral politics in a direct and efficient fashion. Despite the centrality of party identification to American political behavior, studies of clerical politics have seldom given it much attention. In his Oregon case studies, sociologist Benton Johnson (1966) discovered that "ascetic Protestant" clergy identified as Republicans, while theological liberals leaned Democratic, a finding confirmed by Hadden (1969, 82–85). Quinley reported the same tendency but emphasized that a majority of California clergy were Republicans, reflecting their middle-class backgrounds. He noted, though, that many had deserted their ancestral party, usually in a direction befitting their own theological perspective: offspring of Republicans who became theological liberals moved toward the Democrats, while Democratic scions who held conservative theologies were drawn toward the GOP (1974, 83–87).

Despite consistent results, these studies devoted little further attention to partisanship, or to its causes and effects. All had other concerns: Johnson focused on the ideological consequences of theological orientations; Hadden documented the "gathering storm" between liberal clergy and conservative laity over civil rights; and Quinley (like Hadden) was fascinated by the unconventional political tactics of a new generation of modernist clergy. As these pastors were far more visible in demonstrations, on picket lines, and committing civil disobedience than in election campaigns, scholars passed lightly over their partisan lives. Quinley concluded that their "moral resources" were unsuited to electoral politics and that, with the passing of the great causes of the 1960s, clergy would lose their leadership role (1974, 4). In fact, there is little evidence that liberal clergy shunned party politics in the 1960s, or that they abandoned politics altogether in the 1970s. Indeed, liberal ministers were probably overrepresented among Democratic party activists in the early 1970s (cf. Kirkpatrick 1976, 65–66), and with the rise of conservative electoral activity in the early 1980s, both groups of clergy were quite numerous in partisan campaigns (Beatty and Walter 1989, 137–138). Thus, the partisan location of pastors becomes crucial. Not only are clergy themselves a significant bloc of potential party activists, but if American party coalitions are restructuring along religious lines, as many observers contend (Green et al. 1996), the partisan preferences of clergy may explain one source of that realignment: the cues provided to churchgoers (Miller and Shanks 1996, 231).

## ROLE ORIENTATIONS AND POLITICAL ACTIVITIES

What prompted the classic studies of pastoral politics was certainly not interest in the clergy's ideology or party ties but rather a striking "theological" imbalance in political activity. Simply put, modernists not only approved of activism but engaged in much more of it than did traditionalists. Liberal clergy joined the 1960s reform movements with great enthusiasm, an upsurge unusual enough to elicit Harvey

Cox's label for them, the "New Breed" (Garrett 1973). Their involvement in the politics of protest was every bit as controversial as their broad agenda and liberal ideology. Some "Quiescent" modernists disagreed with New Breed tactics, if not their goals, but the loudest objections came from "Old Breed" traditionalists, who argued that clergy should simply stay out of politics—at least on the issues and in the ways favored by the New Breed. And, according to many analysts, orthodox clergy practiced what they preached. Indeed, Stark et al. (1970) caricatured their politics as "the sounds of silence," and the minuscule number of active traditionalists were often dismissed as far-right curiosities (Jorstad 1970). Of course, Hadden, Stark, and Quinley may have inadvertently distorted the clergy's role by focusing on liberal causes and unconventional activity, as Stark (1980) himself later admitted. And they assumed that the liberal bias in activism (which characterized the mass public as well) was an eternal fixture of ministerial life, rooted in theology, rather than a reflection of the agendas, incentives, and opportunities presented by the politics of the 1960s (Beck and Jennings 1979).

As prophecy, of course, the classic studies failed. Within a decade the New Breed was in retreat, and the "Christian Right" was pioneering a new wave of activism, led by staunchly orthodox pastors exemplified by Jerry Falwell, James Robison, Charles Stanley, Tim LaHaye, D. James Kennedy, Pat Robertson, and many others. As the Christian Right grew, political activism spread to other traditionalists, including many skeptical of the movement itself (Guth 1996). Today, clergy from both sides of the political spectrum engage in a wide range of actions. Nevertheless, there is little systematic data about the activities of either traditionalist or modernist clergy in contemporary politics, nor have social scientists explored a full range of explanations for such activism.

Our final questions, then, address the nature and extent of clerical participation: How do different groups of ministers see their role in politics? What kinds of activities do they approve or disapprove? How active are contemporary Protestant clergy in politics? In what kinds of activity? What factors account for the level and kinds of participation? To answer these questions we will draw on several strands of the political science literature on political participation. We focus here on perspectives that help explain activism in the mass public, among professional elites, and by members of organizational networks. Each may add something to our portrait of clerical politics.

First of all, ministers are private citizens who have the same kinds of opportunities, motivations, and resources as other citizens in the political process. Thus, factors that influence participation by the mass public should affect clergy as well. The central perspective here is Verba and Nie's (1972) "socioeconomic status," or "SES," model, which showed that citizens with greater wealth, higher social class standing, and especially advanced education participate more in politics. This advantage may derive not so much from SES itself, however, as from accompanying cognitive and psychological traits, such as interest in politics, concern about political outcomes, a sense of civic responsibility, and feelings of political efficacy.

Despite the great impact of Verba and Nie's theory on studies of participation

(Jankowski and Strate 1995), it has not influenced work on clerical politics, largely because scholars assumed that ministers share roughly equal status as well-educated professionals. Therefore, differences in activism could not be explained by variation in socioeconomic factors. Although Quinley did note some minor exceptions in his California sample (1974, 84–85), he did little analysis of the effects of SES differences, nor did he consider the cognitive and psychological traits encouraging participation (cf. Beatty and Walter 1989). In reality, however, Protestant clergy are not uniformly middle-class but often come from working-class or farm backgrounds and have modest educational attainments and incomes. Thus, if Verba and Nie's findings hold among clergy, perhaps some of the participatory edge of modernist clergy is attributable to class and educational advantages, or to associated psychological resources. And, perhaps, the conservative upsurge after 1980 owes something to the recent social and educational mobility of many orthodox clergy.

Of course, ministers are religious professionals as well as citizens. As Verba, Schlozman, and Brady have observed, professional groups may display "different configurations of participatory factors and levels of activity" (1995, 414). Indeed, the classic works on ministerial politics were dominated by discussions of the professional role orientations of clergy. Quinley discovered large disparities between the New and Old Breeds in their approval of political activism by clergy: modernists were much more supportive of almost every type of political activity by ministers, while traditionalists were generally opposed to most clerical involvement. These role orientations were, of course, tied closely to theological beliefs. Modernists' "this-worldly" theology impelled them toward political involvement, while traditionalists' inactivity followed from their orthodox, "otherworldly" doctrine, which emphasized the clergy's evangelistic role and deplored wasting resources in politics. But there is some evidence that such role expectations may have changed in the 1980s, with the constant mobilizing efforts of the Christian Right, the appearance of moral and cultural issues on the national agenda, and the adoption of the "civic gospel" by many conservative clergy.

Another reason to revisit the findings of earlier studies is their inadequate conceptualization and measurement of participation. Although the classic studies found modernist clergy much more approving of clerical involvement, and more engaged as well, they usually regarded "pastoral activism" as a single dimension, consisting of a mélange of acts within the pulpit, the church, or the public realm. For example, Quinley constructed a single activity scale for analysis, although he did observe in passing that a factor analysis produced three modes of behavior: *church leadership, public leadership,* and *protest leadership* (1974, 157 n. 7). On the whole, however, his discussion, like Hadden's a few years earlier, was dominated by protest and unconventional tactics rather than more conventional acts. In fact, Quinley neglected many channels, both inside and outside the church, by which pastors, especially orthodox ones, might enter the political process. Similarly, the most recent studies have also used single scales, incorporating items on either electoral politics or conventional pastoral acts, ignoring other types of participation (Beatty and Walter 1989).

Students of clerical politics should take seriously Verba and Nie's (1972) early discovery that many citizens specialize in different participatory modes, such as "voting," "campaigning," "communal activities," and "contacting." Indeed, previous studies have seldom considered that orthodox and modernist clergy might be drawn to different kinds of activity. Ironically, only on a mode neglected by Verba and Nie — demonstrations, protest rallies, and civil disobedience — did the classic studies provide much guidance, echoing studies of the mass public which found that unconventional politics in the 1960s was the province of young, well-educated, politically liberal, and religiously nontraditional or secular citizens (Barnes and Kaase 1979; Quinley 1974, 141–146). If clerical activism does, in fact, occur in several distinct modes, it may well be that each mode is preferred by distinct groups of clergy, influenced by unique constellations of socioeconomic, theological, ideological, and contextual factors.

Finally, parish ministers not only are citizens and religious professionals, but are leaders of important institutions as well. Thus, their activities are influenced by their organizational context. In this respect, the recent "mobilization" model of political participation is especially relevant. Rosenstone and Hansen (1993) and Verba, Schlozman, and Brady (1995) have argued that citizens may have all the requisite personal traits and attitudes for participation but remain passive in the absence of external stimuli. Both works stress two kinds of mobilization. The first is *issue* or *ideological mobilization,* in which the appearance of controversial issues on the political agenda activates people, either directly or, more often, through intermediaries. The second form of mobilization is *organizational,* in which groups activate citizens by fostering skills and capacities useful in politics, providing members and others with political information at minimal cost, stimulating political interest, and even directing and channeling that activity (cf. Verba, Schlozman, and Brady 1995).

Obviously, ideological and organizational mobilization often go hand in hand. Both have clear implications for clergy. First, as highly educated, politically interested citizens, clergy respond to many issues. We expect that clergy who stress either the moral reform or social justice agendas should be more active. In a slightly different vein, theology and social theology themselves may serve as functional equivalents of the strong liberal political ideology that motivated more secular activists in the great movements of the 1960s and early 1970s. And perhaps the recent development of the civic gospel may help account for the rise of conservative activism, emulating the impact of libertarianism or other secular ideologies for "movement conservatives" in the 1980s. Whatever the direct effects of theology and social theology, we expect that ministers who, like other citizens, take more extreme ideological stances, or who are strong partisans, will also be more engaged in political life.

Organizational mobilization perspectives may also help explain clerical activism. Clergy who affiliate with political organizations are likely to be more active, as are those who live where party and interest group organizations are well developed. With respect to such organizational factors, of course, clergy should react like other citizens with similar social traits. But more important, clergy are also part of formal religious institutions and informal networks, and confront unique incentives and constraints within the church. In fact, the classic studies were preoccupied with identifying organizational and institutional influences on pastors. For both Hadden and Quinley, parishioners were the most potent constraint on activity, but neither attempted any comprehensive assessment of congregational impact, while controlling for other influences. Nor did either scholar consider the possibility that parishioners might serve as agents of mobilization, a role they reserved for denominational elites and ministerial colleagues.

## THE SIMPLE MODEL RESTATED AND THE PLAN OF THE BOOK

We can now restate our simple model of pastoral politics, clothed with the key characteristics of the contemporary Protestant clergy. Ministers' beliefs are crucial in determining their political goals and activities. Those who are theological traditionalists and are influenced by individualist worldviews and the civic gospel are likely to have a moral reform agenda, hold conservative attitudes, and identify with the Republican party. In contrast, theologically modernist clergy, who hold communitarian worldviews, are more likely to advance a social justice agenda, hold liberal attitudes, and identify as Democrats. With respect to activism, we see parallel results. Traditionalists who adhere strongly to the civic gospel will be more active in politics, particularly in their role as religious professionals, making pronouncements in religious settings. Similarly, to the extent modernists partake of communitarian social theology, they will also be more active in politics, particularly in their role as private citizens, engaging in a wide variety of conventional and unconventional activities. As with other citizens, ministers with extensive personal and psychological resources and strong ideological and partisan motivations should participate most extensively. Finally, ministers subject to intense organizational stimuli, whether inside or outside the church, should be more involved in political life.

Thus, we ought to find four "ideal types" of ministers based on the combination of political goals and activity level. First, we expect to discover the New Breed, modernists with liberal goals and high activism, and their opposites in politics, the Christian Right, traditionalists with conservative goals and high activism, holding down opposite ends of a continuum. We also expect to find what we might call "Quiescent Modernists," who share theological orientations with the New Breed but exhibit low levels of activism, as well as the "Old Breed," traditionalists who persist in rejecting politics in favor of otherworldly priorities. Of course, not everyone will be captured by these ideal types; consequently, there will also be more conventional liberals and conservatives, who combine theological and political moderation with similarly moderate levels of activism.

In the rest of this book, then, we analyze the nature, extent, and manifestations of clerical political activism across denominational lines, assessing explanations for the variation in contemporary ministerial activism. In particular, we test
whether generalizations about clerical activism in the 1960s and early 1970s
apply today: Is ministerial activism still largely limited to theological liberals
from Mainline churches? Or has ministerial activism expanded across theological
boundaries since the 1960s? Has there perhaps been a reversal in patterns of clerical activism, so that theological conservatives now dominate? Has the "gathering
storm in the churches" (Hadden 1969), in which conservative laity rejected the
liberal activism of their clergy, muted the political voice of theological liberals in
Mainline churches? Is there, perhaps, a new "gathering storm" in which moderate laity in Evangelical churches resist the politicization of the church by clerical
conservatives?

In chapter 2 we describe the surveys that provide the basis for our examination
of clerical politics and then give brief profiles of the eight denominations that are the
primary target of our investigation, providing thumbnail sketches of their histories,
theological tendencies, and political involvement. We then turn to an examination
of the foundations of clerical worldviews in chapter 3, starting with theological orientations, including commitment to Christian orthodoxy, adherence to dispensational eschatology, and affiliation with religious movements. We find rather stark
differences in the distribution of orthodox and modernist clergy among, and sometimes within, these church bodies, and consider the roles that religious socialization,
socioeconomic factors, and professional training have in producing theological perspectives. In chapter 4 we look at the rival social theologies of individualism and
communitarianism, and the perspectives on church priorities that link the theologies
of orthodox and modernist clergy to the political world. We find that the Social Gospel is alive and well among liberal clergy, and that a new civic gospel has taken root
among many orthodox ministers, providing a firmer basis for countervailing political activism.

In chapter 5 we move on to the explicitly political orientations of clergy. First,
we consider the competing political agendas of orthodox and modernist clergy,
identifying the issues on the *moral reform* and *social justice agendas.* We find these
agendas are quite distinct; only on a few issues do the competing camps share concerns. Then we address in chapter 6 the critical question of ministerial ideology:
what kinds of political worldviews do ministers possess? Although we find a certain
residual political liberalism among orthodox ministers on a few issues, a single
liberal-conservative dimension subsumes ministers' views on most questions,
whether drawn from the moral reform or social justice agenda. Thus, for most
clergy, the structure of ministerial ideology has become more "constrained" over
time. We also assess the degree to which clergy match their congregations in ideological terms, confirming the finding of earlier studies that orthodox clergy are a
better "political match" with their congregations than are modernists, often distinctly more liberal than their people. In chapter 7 we study the distribution of cleri-

cal partisanship, showing that a minister's party identification is now largely determined by ideology rather than by older factors such as ethnicity, region, social class, or even denominational tradition. Among contemporary clergy, partisanship represents a critical political distillation of ministerial theology, social theology, and ideology, one that has led to a match between the theological and political "two-party systems."

In the remainder of the book, we turn to political activism itself. In chapter 8 we report the evaluations of different political acts by clergy and the factors that influence their approval of *direct action* and *cue-giving* activities. Although modernist clergy still have an edge in their approval of direct action, orthodox clergy have pulled even with respect to cue-giving. In addition, we discuss clergy's perception of their congregations' potential reaction to these same activities, finding that pastors perceive much support for ministerial activism from their congregations, although not at the level they themselves would prefer. In chapter 9 we review the modes of ministerial political participation and the types of clergy who prefer each. When this is done, we find that modernist clergy have clung to their advantage on some modes of activity at which they excelled in the 1960s, primarily in direct action, but that orthodox clergy match their performance on others and probably dominate a few modes of pastoral cue-giving not considered by the classic studies. Thus, not only do the orthodox and modernists have competing agendas, ideologies, and partisan affiliations, but they differ in participatory orientations and modes of activism. As we shall see, the factors influencing participation vary from mode to mode, but psychological resources, professional role orientations, ideology, and mobilization factors all have important effects.

Finally, in chapter 10 we summarize our findings on the goals and activities of the Protestant clergy with a typology of ministers, revealing the structure of a true "two-party system" in ministerial politics. We find that two polar groups of New Breed liberals and Christian Right conservatives have reached rough equivalence in numbers but may very well exhibit rather different participatory agendas and styles. We then speculate, with some trepidation, about the future role of ministers in American politics and offer some ideas about what that role should be.

# 2
# Eight Protestant Denominations: Theology, Organization, and Politics

The classic studies of clerical politics paid relatively little attention to denominations as a distinct influence on ministers. Much of our analysis confirms that choice by demonstrating the waning vitality of denominational "distinctives" in the face of the solidifying "two-party system." In the real world, of course, Protestant clergy are still more than theologically "orthodox" or "modernist," politically "liberal" or "conservative," partisan "Republicans" or "Democrats." They are "Southern Baptist," "United Methodist," or "Disciples of Christ," and, as such, part of historic institutions, with special theological doctrines, polities, traditions, and, sometimes, regional or ethnic identities. Most clergy, whether Evangelical or Mainline, are brought up as members of their denomination, are educated in its colleges and seminaries, are trained in its theology and history, read its official publications, attend its meetings, and even obtain pastoral positions with its blessing. No one who has spent any time at denominational meetings can fail to appreciate the variations in religious style, language, and climate that still characterize American Protestantism.

This wonderful diversity raises some problems for the scholar, however. Probably no small group of denominations could ever provide a perfectly representative cross section of clergy. Indeed, the very task of identifying the universe of Protestant clergy and drawing a sample has vexed a good many analysts, who have solved (or more often avoided) the problem in several ways: (1) by focusing on ministers in one denomination (Guth 1996; Luidens and Nemeth 1989); (2) by looking at a single tradition, such as Mainline Protestants (Hadden 1969) or Evangelicals (Langenbach and Green 1992); (3) by using local (Olson 1994) or statewide samples (Quinley 1974; Koller and Retzer 1980); or (4) by employing a purposive sample, with clergy from a national commercial or political mailing list (Beatty and Walter 1989; Shie 1991).

To study clergy in their denominational context and at the same time make our findings as representative as possible of white Protestant clergy, we pursued two separate strategies. The core of our analysis is based on national surveys of more than 5,000 clergy in eight church bodies. These include four from the Evangelical tradition (the Assemblies of God, Southern Baptist Convention, Evangelical Covenant Church, and the Christian Reformed Church) and four from Mainline Protestantism (the Reformed Church in America, the United Methodist Church, the Presbyterian Church U.S.A., and the Disciples of Christ). Although these churches are not a true cross section of all American Protestantism, they provide ample scope for study. They include the two largest American Protestant bodies (the Southern Baptist Convention and the United Methodist Church) and two others with "top dozen" status (the PCUSA and Assemblies). The other four are quite small, although two of these, the Reformed Church in America and the Disciples of Christ, have often wielded influence all out of proportion to their size. Some are quintessentially American in culture, while three represent distinct European immigrant traditions. All are predominantly white, but each has growing contingents of African-American, Hispanic, and other "new ethnic" congregations, although these groups are not widely represented as yet in their clergy.

Although denominational surveys conducted in 1989 provide most of our data, we also make frequent use of several other clergy surveys. (See Appendix A for details on the surveys and methods.) In addition to a 1992 survey of Evangelical Covenant clergy, which we usually incorporate directly into the analysis, we also have 1992 and 1996 studies of Southern Baptists and a 1992 survey of Christian Reformed Church ministers, valuable in confirming the persistence of patterns found in the earlier years. For this purpose, we also draw on earlier surveys of Southern Baptists, which provide time series data for all the presidential election years from 1980 through 1996 (Guth 1996). Because Southern Baptists constitute a critical case for the new wave of ministerial activism in the Evangelical tradition, this series is very instructive.

To confirm or elaborate upon findings from the denominational surveys, we often turn to another study, the Wheaton Religious Activist Survey, which we conducted in 1990–91. This survey elicited responses from 5,002 activists in eight religious interest groups: Bread for the World, JustLife, Evangelicals for Social Action, the National Association of Evangelicals, Prison Fellowship, Focus on the Family, Concerned Women for America, and Americans for the Republic (Guth et al. 1995). Although most respondents were laity, approximately one-fifth were clergy, including over 700 Evangelical and Mainline Protestants. Many of the former come from Evangelical churches and subtraditions not represented by the denominational surveys, especially the large, growing, and politically activist "nondenominational" Evangelical churches; the latter include Lutherans, Episcopalians, United Church of Christ, and other Mainline churches not studied in a denominational survey. We must remember, however, that these clergy are by definition organizational and/or political activists, and use these data with care. Nevertheless, the Wheaton study not only enriches our findings but also confirms that these are not simply an artifact of the specific denominations chosen for study. All in all, we use the responses of over 8,000 clergy, perhaps the largest clergy database since Jeffrey Hadden's survey in 1965.

These studies, then, provide the material for this book. As a backdrop for our analysis, we describe the Evangelical and Mainline denominations we studied, offering a profile of their histories, predominant theological perspectives, and political characteristics. We introduce them in the order of general theological conservatism, describing first the four churches from the Evangelical tradition, followed by the four Mainline denominations.

## THE ASSEMBLIES OF GOD (AG)

The Assemblies of God grew out of the Pentecostal revivals of the early 1900s, in which participants recovered the "gifts of the Spirit," such as glossolalia (speaking in tongues), faith healing, and prophetic powers. Despite its apparent novelty, early Pentecostalism drew on several American religious movements: restorationism, the impulse to re-create the primitive Christian community; premillennialism, the belief that Jesus will return to earth and rule for a thousand years; revivalism, an emphasis on the sudden conversion of sinners; and, holiness teachings, on the necessity of living a pure Christian life (Blumhofer 1993; Poloma 1989).

Emerging from the Pentecostal ferment of the first decade of the century, the General Council of the Assemblies of God was formed in 1914 to provide guidance to the new movement. The council eventually pushed out theologically heterodox elements, and the Assemblies began a long period of expansion. By the 1990s, the AG's continuing evangelism had produced a North American membership of 2.5 million, making it the nation's twelfth-largest denomination, and achieved even more impressive growth abroad, with over 25 million members, most notably in Latin America and Africa. In the United States today, the AG's 13,000 churches are located in virtually every county but are especially concentrated west of the Mississippi.

Although early Pentecostals regarded established Protestant churches as apostate, they felt much closer to the contemporaneous fundamentalist movement, which had also rejected modernist theology. Most fundamentalists did not reciprocate, however, rejecting Pentecostal revivals as false or even satanic. Nevertheless, by the 1940s moderate fundamentalists invited the Assemblies to join the new National Association of Evangelicals (NAE), created to assist conservative Protestants hoping to exert a greater impact on American society and culture. Still, during most of the twentieth century, the Assemblies concentrated on saving souls and avoided social and political activism. A few AG leaders joined the Prohibition, Christian Zionist, and antievolution movements in the 1920s and 1930s, and by the late 1940s closer ties with other Evangelicals led to a strong anticommunist stance, but their premillennial theology and "outsider" mentality dampened enthusiasm for politics

(Poloma and Green 1992). In any case, the Assemblies' early membership was made up largely of farmers and blue-collar workers, with modest education and status, often located in the least politically competitive regions of the country.

This apolitical stance began to change in the 1970s and 1980s, as evangelism brought in many middle-class converts, and second- and third-generation Pentecostals enjoyed upward social mobility. This new constituency of well-educated technical, professional, and businesspeople was more interested in politics than their Pentecostal predecessors. Some Assemblies laypeople moved into political life, with several members elected to Congress (all Republican), most notably United States Senator John Ashcroft of Missouri. As AG clergy also benefited from additional education and higher status, many reexamined the church's social and political role (Richardson 1996). Above all, the 1988 candidacy of charismatic religious broadcaster Marion G. "Pat" Robertson for the GOP presidential nomination energized many clergy and laity alike. Robertson focused on the AG's proliferating large suburban churches, many of which were already quite active politically (Johnson 1990). By this time, as well, some denominational leaders were participating in campaigns against abortion, pornography, media violence, and other "moral" evils. In 1989 the Assemblies' General Council even passed a resolution implicitly endorsing civil disobedience on the abortion issue but leaving "to the discretion of individual ministers the extent to which they may participate in non-violent and peaceful acts of intervention to prevent the killing of the unborn" (Frame 1989). Some clergy joined abortion clinic protests, but others, such as Patrick Mahoney of Operation Rescue, left the Assemblies because of what they considered a lack of commitment to the pro-life cause.

In recent years the Assemblies have enjoyed some continuing organizational success but have confronted problems as well. Internal debate continues over whether the Assemblies is a "movement" or a "denomination," while many current members have not experienced the "gifts of the Spirit," the Assemblies' doctrinal and experiential distinctives. Scandals involving television evangelists Jim Bakker and Jimmy Swaggart, both AG ministers, brought unwelcome public scrutiny and lower internal morale. The denomination's recent growth has slowed and derives primarily from minorities, especially Hispanics, quite different from the Assemblies' original constituency. And political activism remains controversial, as some leaders stress evangelism and church growth, while others envision a sustained public role, often in conjunction with Christian Right organizations. Thus, the Assemblies of God's approach to politics remains "a study in ambiguity and ambivalence," but in the context of staunchly conservative views (Poloma and Green 1992).

## THE SOUTHERN BAPTIST CONVENTION (SBC)

The Southern Baptist Convention is not only part of the biggest "family" of American Protestants—Baptists—but is also the nation's largest Protestant body, with over 15 million members in almost 40,000 congregations. In most of the American South the SBC is the "established church" because, as the ancient witticism has it, "There are more Baptists than people." But the SBC is now also a national body, as migration and evangelism have taken it to every state. In fact, a 1992 study showed Southern Baptists to be the largest single denomination in 42 percent of America's counties (Cornell 1992).

This success is remarkable, given Baptists' origin as religious outcasts. Emerging from the Reformation's radical wing, colonial Baptists faced persecution not only in Puritan New England but also in Anglican Virginia. Ardent friends of the American Revolution, Baptists later joined Madison and Jefferson in the fight for the separation of church and state. Their emphases on believer's (adult) baptism, individual competence to interpret Scripture, congregational autonomy, and a called, rather than professional, clergy were shaped by, and in turn fostered, American democratic culture (Hatch 1989). In one sense, however, the SBC itself began in a less democratic vein when Southern Baptists left their Yankee brethren in 1845, following a quarrel over financial support for slaveholding missionaries. This first regional split in a major church body was a harbinger of the Civil War; unlike later schisms among Presbyterians and Methodists, it has never been repaired.

Following the Civil War, Southern Baptists began a steady expansion that accelerated after World War I. During the 1920s the SBC centralized its structure, replacing a multitude of agencies, each raising money, with the Cooperative Program, in which churches would merge funds for mission agencies, seminaries, and other institutions. Long regarded as a model of denominational organization, the Cooperative Program provided a focus for mission work and institutional loyalty, encouraging Baptists to ignore minor theological differences. The program also buttressed SBC expansion by planting new churches, training thousands of religious workers (by 1981, four of the five largest American seminaries were SBC-run), and providing standardized materials for almost every church function. Indeed, the program's success reduced any need for the SBC to cooperate with other denominations, and, with few exceptions, Southern Baptists strenuously avoided ecumenical entanglements, even with other conservative Protestants (Thompson 1982).

For most of the twentieth century, Southern Baptist politics combined varying proportions of church-state separationism, premillennialist passivity, and activism on "moral" issues such as Prohibition, gambling, and the teaching of evolution. On the whole, though, Southern Baptist ideology was deeply conservative, encouraging acceptance of the social and political status quo, a posture clearly seen in resistance to the civil rights movement of the 1960s (Eighmy 1972). Nevertheless, by the 1970s the SBC leadership was inching to the center on issues ranging from abortion and civil rights to the emerging environmental and women's movements, a tendency epitomized by the 1976 election of Jimmy Carter, a Baptist Sunday school teacher.

This shift toward the center did not go unchallenged. By 1980 the SBC was torn by bitter factional warfare (Ammerman 1990). After sidestepping theological quagmires for decades, the SBC faced a campaign by hard-line conservatives or "fundamentalists" to eject its "moderate" leaders, who had supposedly allowed infiltration of the denomination by theological and political "liberals." After fifteen years of massive mobilization, countermobilization, strident confrontations, and narrow elections at annual meetings, the SBC's "two-party" competition ended, as victorious conservatives purged officials with suspect theologies or, sometimes, simply too much sympathy for the losers. They also moved the SBC out of its religious isolation into greater cooperation with other orthodox groups, as several conservative leaders were personally active in groups such as the National Association of Evangelicals.

The conservative triumph had enormous political implications. All the movement leaders were either prominent Christian Right figures or fellow travelers, and they worked to put the SBC behind a staunchly conservative political agenda, often in close cooperation with Republican party officials. Throughout the 1980s, political debates often garnered as much attention at SBC meetings as the theological strife, but the 1991 convention was a symbolic ratification of the conservative victory. Attended by over 23,000 "messengers" from local churches, the meeting had all the trappings of a "God and Country" rally. At the preliminary pastors' conference, messengers heard pleas for political action from Lieutenant Colonel Oliver North, SBC leaders, and other Christian Right figures. Then the convention's featured speaker, President George Bush, won repeated ovations after his calls for restrictions on abortion, a school prayer amendment, school vouchers, and parental choice in education, as messengers waved 15,000 American flags distributed earlier at the pastors' conference.

The Baptists did more than applaud and wave flags. They condemned departures from traditional sexual morality, opposed abortion and fetal tissue research, expressed concern for religious liberties, criticized the National Endowment for the Arts for funding obscene art (asking Bush to fire NEA chief John Frohnmeyer), attacked alcohol ads, proposed tax breaks for families, endorsed parental choice in education, and applauded Bush's conduct of the Gulf War. They also "defunded" the Baptist Joint Committee on Public Affairs (BJC), long the SBC's voice on religious liberty issues and a staunch defender of church-state separation, but broadened the responsibilities of the Christian Life Commission (CLC), once the SBC's "liberal social conscience" and now under conservative control (Parry 1996). Over the next few years, the CLC built a well-staffed Washington office, led by its new chief, Richard Land, and moved into a vigorous political role, sometimes on the liberal side, as on racial bias and hunger, but most often in alliance with the Christian Right on abortion, gay rights, and other moral issues. During the 1992 presidential election, CLC voter guides for Baptist churches were less partisan than the Christian Coalition's, but they favored the Bush-Quayle ticket over fellow Southern Baptists Bill Clinton and Al Gore. Similarly, growing numbers of Southern Baptists in Congress were found on the GOP side of the aisle, including party leaders such as Newt Gingrich, the Speaker of the House, and Trent Lott, the Senate majority whip and, later, majority leader.

And despite initial pledges of cooperation from SBC leaders, the Clinton administration's early actions reversing Reagan-Bush abortion limitations, proposals on gays in the military, and stances on many other issues quickly soured relations. At the 1993 SBC meeting almost half the forty resolutions introduced were critical of administration policies; they were finally combined in a strong resolution admonishing Clinton and Gore to "affirm biblical morality in exercising public office" (Harwell 1993). An abortive attempt was even made to "withdraw fellowship" from both men, and messengers from Immanuel Baptist, Clinton's home church in Little Rock, were required to state their personal opposition to homosexuality to the credentials committee before being seated. Ed Young, whose Second Baptist Church of Houston was famous for its extensive program of political activity, was reelected SBC president without opposition.

Outsiders and insiders alike were impressed by this new wave of activism. One Southern Baptist moderate looked ruefully back at his modest efforts to mobilize the SBC on behalf of more liberal causes in the 1970s and lamented the changed political landscape:

> What a shift! A sea change! A revolution! In a relatively short period of time, a sizable segment of the Christian community in the United States completely reversed its position on political involvement. In light moments, I laughingly claim great success for my efforts to get Christians involved in the political process. At more sober moments, though, the thoughtless plunge into politics on the part of many in the Christian community made me feel like a complete failure. . . . Within my own denomination, many ministers now set aside a long-standing tradition of professional silence on partisan political issues and personalities to endorse (or condemn) both candidates and issues-positions via church stationary [*sic*] emanating from their offices and sermons preached from their pulpits. It is a new day for Christians and politics, but the dangers of the present are as grave as those created by Christians' complete absence from politics in another day. (Gaddy 1996, 5)

Greater political activity coincided with new institutional challenges. The SBC's growth slowed in the 1990s and was concentrated among minorities, especially Hispanics and African-Americans. Contributions stagnated, in part because some moderate churches diverted mission funds to alternative agencies such as the Cooperative Baptist Fellowship, while SBC seminaries suffered from changes in leadership and faculty. Despite these internal problems, the SBC seems likely to remain a consistent voice for conservatism in national politics.

## THE EVANGELICAL COVENANT CHURCH (ECC)

The Evangelical Covenant Church, founded by Swedish immigrants in 1885 as a "voluntary covenant" of congregations, now has over 600 churches in the United

States and Canada, with close to 100,000 members. The ECC's original theology combined traditional Lutheran doctrine, evangelical revivalism from America and Britain, and strong pietistic and missionary emphases, all incorporated in a free church structure.

The ECC's contemporary theology preserves these strands, falling closer to American evangelicalism than to religious liberalism but allowing considerable diversity (Dodson 1995). The ECC is not creedal, but it values historic Christian confessions, especially the Apostles' Creed. The Bible, however, is the ultimate authority, providing "the only perfect rule for faith, doctrine and conduct." The ECC cherishes "the pietistic restatement of the doctrine of justification by faith as basic to the dual task of evangelism and Christian nurture, the New Testament emphasis upon personal faith in Jesus Christ as Savior and Lord, the reality of a fellowship of believers which recognizes but transcends theological differences, and the belief in baptism and the Lord's Supper as divinely ordained sacraments of the church." Although the ECC practices infant baptism, it also recognizes believer's baptism, in conformity with the principle of personal freedom. The ECC is nonhierarchical, with congregations free to call ministers, but the denomination does control entry to the ministry and ministerial discipline (Evangelical Covenant Church Website 1996).

Over its history, there have been repeated attempts to move the ECC toward some fundamentalist doctrines, such as dispensationalism, often coming from the ECC's western wing and from conservatives elsewhere. Such theological revisionism has often been directed at the ECC's sole seminary, North Park in Chicago, which plays a crucial role in maintaining the delicate balance between orthodoxy and religious freedom in which Covenant leaders take pride. As the strength of the ECC's ethnic tradition has waned, theological polarization has become a greater threat to denominational unity (Olsson 1985, 2:321–328). Perhaps for this reason, the ECC has not aligned with either the National Association of Evangelicals or the National Council of Churches.

The ECC has historically avoided political as well as theological entanglements. The denomination has had a considerable "social ministry," operating a hospital and many retirement homes, but has been less engaged with explicitly political questions. Nevertheless, national issues have troubled the denomination in recent decades. During the 1960s and 1970s, for example, civil rights and the Vietnam War evoked sometimes heated discussions at ECC meetings, as in other denominations. The question of selective conscientious objection was especially controversial; ultimately, the ECC officially supported the idea. More recently, attention has turned back to "moral issues," with the annual meeting adopting resolutions urging that ministerial pension funds not be invested in companies dealing in alcohol, tobacco—or weapons. Abortion has been the most hotly contested issue of the 1990s, however, raised repeatedly by conservatives. After several attempts to push the denomination into a strong pro-life stance, in 1994 the ECC adopted a very carefully modulated statement, emphasizing the sinfulness of abortion but also stressing exceptions for maternal health, rape, and incest, and the need for pastoral understanding. In some ways, however, the resolution was unsatisfactory to protagonists on both sides and was sure to be revisited (Evangelical Covenant Church Website 1996; Dahlstrom 1996).

Although Evangelical Covenant laity are predominantly conservative politically, some liberalizing forces influence many pastors. The ECC's expansion beyond its Swedish-American base into ethnic communities, especially African-American and Asian, has led to a certain amount of social activism by ethnic churches, which may then expect more action from the denomination itself. Another liberalizing influence is North Park Seminary, where future pastors confront the realities of urban problems and often study urban ministry. This experience, combined with a certain theological diversity among the faculty, produces a leaven of social activism among denominational leaders and clergy. Many congregations, however, are still located in rural areas and small towns; these obviously have a different political agenda and, perhaps, less opportunity for pastoral involvement. On balance, ECC politics can be characterized as cautious and moderate, with a conservative tilt.

## THE CHRISTIAN REFORMED CHURCH (CRC) AND THE REFORMED CHURCH IN AMERICA (RCA)

Both the Christian Reformed Church and the Reformed Church in America are offshoots of Dutch Calvinism, but they have come down on opposite sides of the Evangelical-Mainline divide. The RCA dates to the settlement of New Amsterdam by the Dutch in the early 1600s; at the time of the American Revolution there were ninety-eight Dutch Reformed Church congregations, with 45,000 parishioners (Luidens 1993). Although there were constant struggles over "Americanization," in 1869 the Dutch Reformed Church was officially renamed the Reformed Church in America, signaling (perhaps prematurely) its transformation into an American denomination. The RCA had spread slowly through the Middle Atlantic States in the early 1800s but gained new strength with midcentury waves of Dutch immigrants to the Midwest, especially Michigan and Iowa, many of whom were religious "Seceders" from the Reformed Church of the Netherlands. The less separatist elements affiliated with the RCA, eventually becoming its conservative western wing, while others rejected what they saw as an Americanized and theologically lax RCA leadership and established the precursors of the Christian Reformed Church. Most Dutch immigrants after 1880 joined the CRC, rather than the RCA, because of its greater similarity to their dissenting congregations back home (Bratt 1984). Despite the historical divergence, there is still much interchange between the two denominations, each of which currently claims about 200,000 active members.

Although the Christian Reformed Church is best classified as part of the Evangelical tradition, its relationship to other Evangelicals has always been ambivalent.

Both ethnic differences and adherence to a strict variant of confessional Calvinism long separated the CRC from American Evangelicals, usually Arminian in doctrine and indifferent to rigorous theology. In addition, the CRC has always had a high but less literalist view of biblical authority than its American theological cousins. Still, the biblicism, pietism, and moralism common to both groups made the CRC an attractive target for proponents of American "heresies" such as premillennialism and revivalism (Bouma 1984, 9–10). And although CRC leaders fought off such innovations, they have long recognized their family resemblance to other orthodox Protestants. In 1943 the CRC joined the new National Association of Evangelicals, but withdrew in 1951, only to return in 1988 when assimilation had reduced the power of ethnic (and perhaps theological) differences and the American "culture wars" encouraged choosing up of religious "sides."

Historically, the CRC has also differed from other conservative Protestants in its approach to politics. The CRC always emphasized Christian education and construction of a Christian worldview, with implications for all human endeavors, including social and political life (Bouma 1984). Indeed, one Dutch hero of CRC leaders, the neo-Calvinist Abraham Kuyper (1837–1920), was simultaneously a theologian, journalist, party leader, and finally, prime minister of the Netherlands. Factions might quarrel over the proper orientation ("positive" Calvinists favored engaging the social and political world aggressively, while "antitheticals" more often wanted to withdraw), but unlike some American Evangelical groups, the CRC was never dominated by advocates of abstention from the (sinful) political world.

The nature of CRC political concerns has varied, however. During the Progressive Era, CRC leaders focused on alcohol, sexual licentiousness, and other "moral" evils, but they sometimes contributed to broader reform movements, especially in heavily Dutch areas. Indeed, Teddy Roosevelt's Bull Moose Progressives carried the CRC vote in 1912, no doubt helped by his Dutch heritage. The CRC initially fought women's suffrage but later relented; similar vacillation marked its attitude toward non-Christian labor unions. The denomination's supportive, but critical, attitude toward American entry into World War I was not enough to avert some hostility from nativists, however. The 1920s saw continued CRC moral preoccupations, scarcely shaken by the Great Depression or the New Deal, which most CRC leaders either rejected or accepted selectively. (Teaching or supporting socialism was a sin under the CRC's 1935 Rules of Order, along with theater attendance, dancing, and card playing.) After World War II, the denomination became fervently anti-Communist and free enterprise–oriented. The upheavals over civil rights and the Vietnam War also left the CRC largely unmoved, despite some activity by younger intellectuals (Watson 1982; Bratt and Wells 1997). During the 1980s, however, the CRC did pressure sister Reformed churches in South Africa to help liberalize that country's racial policies.

Ideologically, then, the CRC was always "conservative," but its partisan coloration evolved somewhat over time. During the late 1800s, the CRC's constituency was slightly less "anti-Democratic" than the RCA's, perhaps because of its ethnic character (Kleppner 1970), but by 1900 its leaders were solidly Republican. More-over, by 1945 the CRC was well represented among the political elites of Michigan and Iowa, mostly by Republicans but with a few prominent Democrats as well. Overall, however, the evidence suggests that both CRC clergy and laity were con-sistently conservative in ideology and very Republican in politics, although the church's explicitly political pronouncements are few (Menendez 1977, 134–135; 1996, 38–41; Ellingsen 1993).

Despite its seeming theological and political homogeneity, the CRC has re-cently been buffeted by the same controversies afflicting other conservative Protes-tant communities, battles that pit theological and cultural conservatives against more "progressive" factions and that have important social and political implica-tions. The first skirmish involved "creationism," and was sparked by accusations that the science faculty at the denomination's Calvin College espoused "theistic evolution." The CRC has also experienced protracted turmoil over female clergy, eventually authorizing a kind of local option plan for such ordinations. Finally, the CRC joined other denominations in confronting the relationship of homosexuals to the church. As a result of such controversies, some conservatives, including several Korean congregations, left the CRC to protest its "liberal" drift. As historian James D. Bratt has noted, these struggles confirm "the belated emergence of a two-party system" in the CRC (1992, 805).

In contrast to the CRC's reluctant adherence to the Evangelical camp, the Re-formed Church in America moved steadily toward Mainline Protestantism, led by its dominant eastern wing. With a long history of cooperation in the mission, tem-perance, and antislavery campaigns of the nineteenth century, the RCA has readily joined most twentieth-century ecumenical movements. The Reformed Church was a charter member of the National and World Council of Churches, and RCA execu-tives have held leadership posts in both. That such affiliations arouse some contro-versy, however, is suggested by the fact that two regional RCA bodies are part of the National Association of Evangelicals. Indeed, the RCA has experienced incessant and often bitter struggles over its extensive ecumenical cooperation. And although often viewed as more traditionalist than other Mainline churches, the RCA also faces a crisis of theology (Luidens 1993). The old Calvinist confessions hold little attraction, even for the declining membership with Dutch ancestry, and there is much internal diversity. Regional RCA bodies are the final judges of theological standards and vary from quite liberal (in the East) to very conservative (in Iowa, for example). In recent years, a theological cause célèbre has involved Michigan pastor Richard Rhem, an outspoken religious pluralist, who has argued that Christianity is not the only way to salvation. This resulted in his expulsion by the Muskegon Clas-sis (regional governing body), an action that probably would not have occurred in the East. Fueled by continuing membership decline, the RCA's debate over doc-trinal issues promises to continue (Niebuhr 1996).

Politically, the RCA usually joins in the liberal pronouncements of other Main-line churches, although these positions are often adopted at the annual General

Synod only by narrow margins and after heated discussion. In recent years, for example, the synod has ratified wide-ranging resolutions, including opposition to deforestation in the tropics, the greenhouse effect, apartheid in South Africa, the return of Haitian boat people without asylum proceedings, nuclear testing, economic embargoes against Cuba, and use of tobacco products (National and International Religion Report 1993; Ellingsen 1993). The RCA has also made symbolic statements of political importance by electing its first African-American president in 1988 and the first woman to that office in 1992. RCA politics are thus characterized by liberal commitment at the top, subject to fierce conservative resistance from a substantial minority of clergy and laity.


## THE UNITED METHODIST CHURCH (UMC)

Although President Theodore Roosevelt was active in the RCA, when he wanted to find a typical American audience, he went to a Methodist church (Hudson 1961, 128). As the "most powerful religious movement in American history," early Methodism was spread after 1784 by hundreds of itinerant "circuit riders." Sometimes poorly educated, they preached the gospel all over the frontier, often in revivals of great emotional intensity. With the "breathtaking message of individual freedom, autonomy, responsibility, and achievement" (Hatch 1994, 177), Methodism held out the promise of personal reform and social mobility. Tight organization allowed Methodism to overtake older denominations to become, for many years, America's largest Protestant church. Like the Baptists, Methodists were divided by the Civil War but reunited in 1939 and were joined by the Evangelical United Brethren in 1968–69. The UMC remained the largest Protestant denomination until it was surpassed in 1967 by Southern Baptists. But even after three decades of declining membership, in 1996 the UMC still claimed 8.6 million adherents in 36,000 churches, found in virtually every county in the United States, and was the largest denomination serving Mainline Protestants.

Despite their lowly origins, by 1880 many Methodists had become middle-class, influential citizens in virtually every state and community. Indeed, in that year more governorships were held by Methodists than by members of any other church, and in 1896 a former Methodist Sunday school superintendent, William McKinley, was elected president, the last of five chief executives from the church. Until 1960 Methodists consistently had more members of Congress than any other Protestant denomination (Menendez 1977, 145).

Although historians have neglected Methodism as "representing the bland, uninspired middle" of American religion (Hatch 1994, 186), this "centrist" position reflects diversity as much as moderation, as the UMC spans the theological and political spectrum. (In statistical jargon, the "church of the golden mean" is also "the church of the large standard deviation.") In part, this diversity reflects the UMC's geographical, social, and ethnic range. In addition, although early Methodism was theologically orthodox, it shunned the rigid doctrinal formulations of the Christian Reformed or Presbyterian churches; Methodists were always more interested in practical piety and personal holiness than in doctrinal rigor.

In recent decades, however, theological squabbles have become a larger part of denominational life. The UMC's first General Conference after the 1968 merger, held in 1972, adopted "theological pluralism," declaring that many points of view were acceptable as long as they resulted from application of the "Wesley quadrilateral," using Scripture, tradition, experience, and reason as theological tools. In the years since, dissenters have mounted several campaigns, ranging from the evangelical "Good News" organization (active since 1966) to the more centrist "Confessing Movement" of the 1990s, bringing together varying combinations of traditionalists and moderates favoring a more orthodox confessional stance. In 1988 these forces had modest success, as the General Conference dropped references to theological pluralism from the *UMC Book of Discipline* in favor of the primacy of Scripture, with tradition, experience, and reason "as creative vehicles of the Holy Spirit." This did not settle much, however, as factions still competed, with liberals dominating the seminaries, denominational bureaucracies, and leadership posts, and conservatives proportionately more numerous among parish clergy and, especially, among observant laity (Green and Guth 1996; Reichley 1985, 271–272).

Methodists have also had a long tradition of political involvement, which has escalated in recent decades. Early Methodists stressed "social holiness," as well as the personal kind, and thus spearheaded many reform movements, such as the nineteenth-century temperance, prison reform, and antislavery endeavors. In 1908 the Methodist Episcopal Church (North) adopted a "Social Creed" that put the church into the Social Gospel battle for Prohibition, workers' rights, women's suffrage, world peace, and a host of other causes (McEllhenney et al. 1992). The creed was virtually copied by the new Federal Council of Churches in the same year, and by other Methodist bodies later. After the 1968 merger, the UMC adopted and continually revised new "Social Principles," providing the basis for liberal stances on birth control, population limitation, abortion, civil disobedience, civil rights, social welfare, defense policy, gay rights, and the environment. The UMC's Council of Bishops issued a pastoral letter in 1986 condemning nuclear war and rejecting the theory of nuclear deterrence, going even further than the U.S. Catholic bishops' celebrated 1983 letter, and the 1988 General Conference approved an economic justice statement quite critical of free-market economics.

As part of the National Council of Churches, the UMC's direct political activities have been closely aligned with liberal forces. The Methodist Board on Church and Society is central to most liberal religious lobbying coalitions in Washington, D.C. Indeed, several religious lobbies are housed in the United Methodist Building itself, just across the street from the Capitol. In addition, political and social causes are represented within the UMC by "caucus" groups, most of which seek to elicit denominational aid. The Methodist Federation for Social Action, a venerable liberal pressure group, has been joined by various ethnic, feminist, and gay rights caucuses.

On the other side, the Good News movement has usually coupled theological conservatism with critiques of the UMC's unrelenting liberal stands, especially assailing Methodist affiliation with the Religious Coalition for Abortion Rights. By the mid-1990s the role of homosexuals in church and society constituted another flash point, as the UMC reaffirmed its traditional position that homosexuality was "incompatible with Christian teaching" but by narrowing margins at successive General Conferences, and rejected ordination of practicing homosexuals, a policy that was also challenged by many within the church.

By the 1980s, UMC General Conferences increasingly resembled political party conventions, with extended debate, fierce lobbying, press conferences, and news releases on all sides (Bellah et al. 1991, 179–219). If the 1996 General Conference mimicked a party convention, however, it was a *Democratic* convention: First Lady Hillary Rodham Clinton, a lifelong Methodist and member of the Foundry United Methodist Church in Washington, one of the UMC's most liberal congregations (which Elizabeth and Robert Dole had recently left because it was *left*), received a boisterous standing ovation from the delegates, most of whom were Democrats, especially among the clergy (Witham 1996). Of course, even conservatives angered by the UMC's defection from "biblical Christianity" may have joined in the applause because, as one lay delegate noted, "She quoted more scripture, sounded more like a preacher, and converted more souls than anybody else who's preached here this week" (quoted in Willimon 1996, 534). Thus, politically the UMC has become a quintessential "caucus" church with a strong "two-party system," where liberals and conservatives contend but liberals have the organizational advantage.


## THE PRESBYTERIAN CHURCH
## IN THE UNITED STATES OF AMERICA (PCUSA)

If the Methodists have long represented the "solid center" of American religious life, Presbyterians deserve the appellation of America's religious elite. From the early 1700s, Presbyterians played a major role in American religious, social, and political history. Predominantly middle-class from the start, they have also contributed a disproportionate share of America's political leadership. In 1967, for example, 12 percent of U.S. senators, 17 percent of U.S representatives, and 10 percent of the nation's governors were Presbyterians (Piepkorn 1978, 2:303). As the largest contemporary expression of this multifarious tradition, the PCUSA resulted from mergers of smaller Presbyterian churches, first in 1958 of the "northern" Presbyterian Church in the United States of America with the United Presbyterian Church in North America, to form the United Presbyterian Church in the United States of America (UPCUSA), then in 1983 with the southern Presbyterian Church in the United States (PCUS) to form the present denomination.

Each regional wing of Presbyterianism had followed a different theological and political course. As part of the great nineteenth-century evangelical reform movement, the northern churches were increasingly influenced by liberal currents after 1900. As a result of deep fissures between theological factions in the 1920s and 1930s, fundamentalists left the denomination after failure to gain control (Longfield 1991). Influenced in the 1940s and 1950s by neo-orthodoxy, which for many Presbyterians permitted at least a symbolic obeisance to traditional doctrines, northern Presbyterian leaders moved to the religious and political left during the 1960s and 1970s, as theological pluralism prevailed and many clergy and denominational leaders joined the civil rights, antiwar, and antipoverty movements. These trends did not engage laity as strongly; indeed, some Presbyterians in the pews, organized by the *Presbyterian Layman,* demanded greater orthodoxy and a more conservative political stance (Coalter, Mulder, and Weeks 1992).

Although southern Presbyterians had long been more conservative theologically and politically, the 1983 merger did not dramatically transform the Mainline Presbyterian profile. At one time, the old PCUS was more traditional in doctrine and its political position still reflected the old southern doctrine of "spirituality of the church," which argued that while Christians could be active as citizens, the church and clergy had no business participating as such in social and political affairs. Although this view gradually lost favor after 1935, PCUS conservatives always opposed political action and especially disliked the Federal (later National) Council of Churches, which the PCUS joined and abandoned several times. In 1973 many conservatives left to form the Presbyterian Church in America, an action that paved the way for reconciliation of the PCUS with the northern church (Alvis 1994).

The 1983 merger prompted additional secessions among PCUS churches, while the membership decline experienced by both branches continued in the unified church as well, reducing the denomination to about 2.8 million members in 11,500 churches in 1994. The merger did bolster conservatives' leverage slightly, as they formed caucuses to restore theological orthodoxy in the denomination. And although the PCUSA bureaucracy was firmly in liberal hands, some caucus groups appeared on the left as well, prodding the church to take even more progressive stances on religious, social, and political questions. The mobilization on both sides led to extended controversy. The new 1991 PCUSA creed was designed to encourage consensus, reasserting some traditional doctrines by using new concepts and language, but in the 1990s, two bitter theological and social controversies threatened to deepen internal divisions. Both struggles involved gender. The first was set off by a long-awaited 1991 report on sexuality, which proposed to replace traditional "biblical" sexual mores with "justice-love," an affirmation of committed sexual relationships of many sorts, including homosexual ones. This report was rejected but was followed by intensification of the continuing struggle over homosexuality, especially concerning ordination of gays and lesbians. PCUSA leaders ran into another firestorm with their sponsorship, with several other Mainline churches, of the feminist-dominated 1993 "Re-imagining God" conference, which stimulated thousands of letters of protest and prompted many churches to withhold funds from the PCUSA treasury.

As in other Mainline churches, the PCUSA's annual General Assembly often spent considerable energy dealing with political issues. From its very advent in 1983, the new denomination was at odds with the Reagan administration: the PCUSA opposed a school prayer amendment to the constitution, supported a pro-choice position on abortion (though not without annual confrontations), and backed civil rights for racial minorities and for gays and lesbians. On domestic policy issues, the denomination repeatedly disapproved cuts in social welfare programs, demanded stronger defense of the environment, and supported economic justice for women. In foreign policy, the PCUSA condemned Reagan's large defense budgets, Central American policy, and nuclear weapons buildup, while supporting the nuclear freeze movement, sanctuary for Central American refugees, and a homeland for Palestinians.

These policies clearly aligned the PCUSA with Reagan's Democratic critics. In 1985, twenty of the fifty-seven PCUSA members in the U.S. House issued a public letter criticizing their denomination for its liberal politics. After several other confrontations, the Reverend Donn Moomaw, the pastor of President Reagan's Presbyterian church in California, arranged for PCUSA officials to meet directly with the president to exchange views. Despite some temporary softening of the rhetoric, the PCUSA remained extremely critical, a posture that persisted into the Bush administration, when many leaders condemned American involvement in the Persian Gulf War. Such political preoccupations led John Leith, a veteran Presbyterian theologian and observer of the denomination, to reflect about the 1992 General Assembly:

> The General Assembly was preoccupied not with the ground and sources of the church's life but with derivative issues. A commissioner who has attended many Democratic conventions could have closed his eyes at various times during the Assembly, even during prayer, and imagined that he was at the Virginia State Democratic Convention. The attention of the Assembly was not on the commission of the risen Christ to preach, to teach, and to baptize or on the origin of the church in the hearing of the word of God, but on its social agendas and its organizational structures. (Quoted in Neuhaus 1992, 67)

Conservative criticism had little impact on the PCUSA political witness, however. In 1996 PCUSA's Washington office maintained ten "action networks," whose issue agendas still resembled those of other liberal interests in the nation's capital.

## THE CHRISTIAN CHURCH (DISCIPLES OF CHRIST)

As part of the Christian restoration movement of the early 1800s, the Disciples sought Christian unity by returning to the beliefs and practices of New Testament Christian communities. Led by Barton Stone and Thomas and Alexander Campbell, they emphasized "no creed but Christ," believer's baptism, and weekly observance of the Lord's Supper, and they rejected central organization and educated clergy.

With a simple theology and congregational structure suited to the American frontier, the Disciples avoided schism during the Civil War, growing rapidly for the rest of the century. A preacher in the movement, James A. Garfield, was elected president in 1880 (Williams 1991).

By 1900 several issues split the movement. Many rural congregations, especially in the South, rejected instrumental music and missionary societies as foreign to first-century Christianity. This faction became the Churches of Christ (noninstrumental), leaving the remaining Disciples more open to ties with other Protestants, a gradual transition to an educated clergy, and greater institutionalization. Over the following decades, the Disciples' leadership moved toward modernist views, driving off another wave of theological conservatives, who eventually became the Independent Christian Churches and Churches of Christ. In 1968 the Disciples formally adopted a modern denominational framework, abandoning their loose "brotherhood" status, rationalizing their institutional structures, and adopting their current name (which we will abbreviate to Disciples of Christ). At the same time, they intensified ecumenical work with both Protestant and other Christian churches, although their perennial effort to merge fully with another predominantly liberal denomination, the United Church of Christ, was constantly frustrated by stubborn conservative resistance.

Since their 1968 "restructure," the Disciples have often exemplified advanced theological, social, and political liberalism. The General Board's 1981 statement that "God has never in any time or place been without witness," implicitly rejecting Christian exclusivism, was continuously challenged unsuccessfully by more orthodox factions. The 1987 General Assembly, for example, debated at length whether Jesus was the only way to salvation. The Disciples' political liberalism also intensified. In the 1960s and 1970s, their leaders favored civil rights for African-Americans, ending the Vietnam War, equal rights for women, choice on abortion, international human rights, aid to the poor at home and abroad, opposition to the death penalty, and equal rights for homosexuals. The General Board's 1981 faith statement formalized this political commitment, arguing that "Christ calls the church to identify with the oppressed, the prisoners, the poor, and the sick." And the General Assembly's own 1981 "Peace with Justice" statement signaled a renewed push for disarmament, protection of the environment, education, social welfare programs, and opposition to apartheid in South Africa and to Reagan administration Central American and defense policies. (Reagan, ironically, was brought up in the Disciples and attended a denominational college.)

Indeed, through this entire era the Disciples' annual meetings were dominated by "social witness" issues; some, such as gay rights, created considerable internal rancor (Friedly and Cummins 1987). As one conservative delegate said in 1979, "I know where this assembly stands on about everything, but not where it stands on personal morality." Such dissidents organized Disciples Renewal as a pressure group for greater theological, social, and political conservatism. Although a small minority within the denomination, on questions such as gay rights and sexual morality their forces were buttressed by Hispanic and black Disciples congregations, also quite traditionalist. The activities of liberal caucuses such as the Disciples Peace Fellowship and the Gay, Lesbian and Affirming Disciples also evidenced a growing politicization of the denomination.

Many conservative dissidents feared that political activism by denominational agencies and clergy contributed to the precipitous membership decline that reduced the Disciples' participating membership from 950,285 in 1971 to 603,235 in 1995, in about 4,000 churches. Although reassured by scholars that such losses were unrelated to the church's "prophetic" witness, not all clergy and laity agreed, lamenting that political action often diverted resources away from evangelism, spiritual nurture, and congregation building. All these issues were the backdrop in 1991 to the unprecedented failure of seminary professor Michael Kinnamon to gain the necessary two-thirds majority for election as general minister and president at the General Assembly. Kinnamon, who favored ordination of homosexuals, was pro-choice on abortion, and believed that salvation is possible outside of Christ, reported later that his extensive campaign meetings had convinced him that "the Disciples of Christ, like other mainline churches, comprises fundamentally divergent conceptions of what it means to be Christian," and that it was also "clear that people in the pews are less and less committed to general programs of social action" (1992, 646). By the mid-1990s, Disciples leaders sought more balance in emphasis, but they also clung steadfastly to a staunchly liberal political agenda.

## CONCLUSIONS

Our quick review of the history of these Protestant denominations reveals common elements as well as denominational distinctives. For churches in the Evangelical tradition, we see the historic and continuing strength of doctrinal concerns, an early tendency to ignore or withdraw from at least some political involvement, and more recent propensities for internal doctrinal disputes and mounting political activity. The Mainline churches exhibit another set of common themes: greater openness to theological variation or "pluralism," the vigorous social and political liberalism of denominational elites, often contested by conservative minorities—especially among the laity—and the internal trauma attendant upon declining membership and lowered institutional morale. Of course, these "organization-level" characteristics may or may not be reflected in the religious beliefs, political attitudes, or behavior of the parish clergy. In the next chapter, then, we begin our analysis of pastoral politics with the foundation stone of their goals and activities: theology.

# 3
# Theology and the
# "Two-Party System"
# in American Protestantism

The dominant theme of the literature on clerical politics is that theological perspectives shape political orientations. As religious professionals, ministers take theology very seriously: it influences their social values, political agendas, attitudes on issues and candidates, and, not least, feelings about political activity. Any assessment of ministerial politics must, therefore, come to terms with theology. Earlier studies emphasized different aspects of clergy belief. Theologians and historians have stressed the historic divisions among Protestant denominations, based on ancient creeds and doctrines. Social scientists have more often focused on another sort of division, that between "orthodox," "traditionalist," or "conservative" clergy on the one hand and "modernist," "nontraditionalist," or "liberal" ministers on the other. Certainly the classic studies by Hadden (1969) and Quinley (1974) fall into this tradition.

In this chapter we introduce some important measures of theological perspective that will be used throughout the book, examine denominational differences on these measures, and consider the factors that influence ministers' adherence to these perspectives. To map fully the beliefs of clergy in our sample, we followed three strategies. First, we assigned the eight denominations to the appropriate Protestant tradition, either Evangelical or Mainline. Although there is obviously much diversity within each tradition, especially among Mainline Protestants, our classification comports with widely recognized alignments (Kellstedt and Green 1993), and our results show commonalities among Evangelical pastors on the one hand and among Mainline ministers on the other.

Second, we asked clergy about the core beliefs of the historic Christian faith and, in addition, about issues distinctive to their own denomination. Thus, we have not only a set of identical questions across the eight denominations to assess the strength of Christian orthodoxy but also additional items that tap particular theological issues within each. We are especially interested in one constellation of ideas held by many Evangelicals, which address eschatology, or the doctrine of the end times. Premillennial beliefs have often been blamed for the political passivity of some conservative Protestants, a claim we wish to test. Third, we also asked whether ministers identified with various well-recognized religious movements within Protestantism, such as fundamentalism, evangelicalism, or liberalism, to name a few. Of course, the relevant labels differ somewhat by denomination, but self-conscious identification with a religious movement may have a vital impact on a minister's religious and political beliefs, sometimes at variance with traditional denominational doctrine and practice (Green et al. 1996, chap. 10).

## CHRISTIAN ORTHODOXY

Given the history of Protestant theological controversies in the past century, it is not surprising that asking ministers about the tenets of classic Christian orthodoxy has been the measurement strategy most often used by social scientists. And the strategy works: clergy who adhere to orthodox belief are usually quite different politically from those who hold a more modernist or liberal version of the faith (Hadden 1969; Quinley 1974). Based on these earlier studies and our own denominational sketches, we have very clear expectations. Clergy from the Evangelical denominations should be the most orthodox, with the Assemblies of God holding down the traditionalist pole, followed by Southern Baptists, the Evangelical Covenant, and finally the Christian Reformed. On the other hand, Mainline pastors should deviate more often from orthodoxy, especially as one moves from the Reformed Church through the United Methodists, to the Presbyterians and Disciples. With rare exceptions, this pattern is what we found.

To tap the core of Christian orthodoxy, we used three items long at the center of controversy between the orthodox and modernists: the exclusivity of Jesus' role in bringing salvation to humanity, the literal existence of the Devil, and the inerrancy of the Bible in all matters, historical and scientific, as well as religious. As Table 3.1 shows, clergy differ dramatically in their adherence to these basic doctrines. Assemblies ministers are fiercely orthodox, followed by the Southern Baptist, Evangelical Covenant, and Christian Reformed pastors. The strength of orthodoxy drops noticeably among the RCA clergy and reaches the lowest level among Presbyterians and Disciples, who are especially likely to reject the literal existence of Satan ("the Devil exists—metaphorically," said one liberal pastor) and the doctrine of inerrancy. When other questions on traditional Christian orthodoxy are available in the individual surveys, they buttress the general pattern: clergy from Evangelical denominations believe in the virgin birth of Jesus and hold that Adam and Eve were real historical personages but reject the symbolic interpretations of the Scriptures favored by many Mainline pastors, especially the Presbyterians and Disciples.

To summarize these differences, we calculated a Christian orthodoxy scale by

Table 3.1
Religious Beliefs and Orthodoxy Among Clergy by Denomination (Percent "Strongly Agree")

| | AG | SBC | ECC | CRC | RCA | UMC | PRES | DOC |
|---|---|---|---|---|---|---|---|---|
| Beliefs | | | | | | | | |
| Jesus only salvation | 97 | 83 | 74 | 73 | 58 | 40 | 30 | 32 |
| Devil actually exists | 95 | 79 | 69 | 72 | 48 | 32 | 18 | 15 |
| Scriptures inerrant | 88 | 60 | 33 | 21 | 14 | 19 | 5 | 6 |
| Virgin birth of Jesus | * | 82 | * | 69 | 47 | * | 22 | 17 |
| Adam actual person | * | 72 | 44 | 61 | 31 | * | 9 | 8 |
| Myth/symbol in Bible | * | 19 | 28 | 30 | 37 | * | 42 | 41 |
| Orthodoxy scale | | | | | | | | |
| Most orthodox | 87 | 58 | 29 | 21 | 13 | 15 | 5 | 6 |
| Orthodox | 11 | 26 | 45 | 45 | 31 | 25 | 14 | 11 |
| Modernist | 2 | 14 | 20 | 30 | 35 | 22 | 34 | 21 |
| Most modernist | 1 | 3 | 6 | 4 | 21 | 38 | 48 | 63 |
| | 100% | 100% | 100% | 100% | 100% | 100% | 100% | 100% |

AG = Assemblies of God; SBC = Southern Baptist Convention; ECC = Evangelical Covenant Church; CRC = Christian Reformed Church; RCA = Reformed Church in America; UMC = United Methodist Church; PRES = Presbyterian Church in the U.S.A.; DOC = Christian Church (Disciples of Christ). These abbreviations will be used in tables in the rest of this book.
* Item not available in this survey.

adding ministers' scores on the three items common to all the surveys: on Jesus' role, the Devil, and biblical inerrancy. The scale runs from a score of 3 (strong agreement with the orthodox position on each item) to 15 (strong disagreement with all three). The scale is highly reliable (alpha = .84), and correlates strongly with other doctrinal questions included in some of the surveys, such as the virgin birth ($r = .76$) and the historicity of Adam and Eve ($r = .82$). Thus, we have a great deal of confidence that the scale is a strong measure of supernaturalist Christian orthodoxy. For purposes of presentation at the bottom of Table 3.1 and in subsequent chapters, we have divided the ministers into four approximately equal groups, ranging from the most orthodox to the most modernist. In multivariate analyses, however, we will use the full thirteen-point scale.

Thus, clergy in these Protestant denominations differ systematically in their adherence to traditional Christian tenets. The Evangelical pastors hold to these doctrinal "fundamentals" in a very direct, literal sense, while dominant forces in the Mainline churches attempt, in the words of a Disciples pastor, "to develop a spiritual life that allows freedom and diversity" in theology. This difference in understanding the very nature of Christianity is widely recognized on both sides; many respondents see a deep gulf between the orthodox and the modernist. One dissident conservative Disciples pastor put it bluntly, "Historical Biblical Christianity emphasizes the existence of a personal God and a supernatural realm; leadership in the

Disciples does not." On the other side, a Presbyterian liberal observed that there are two fundamentally different conceptions of the deity: "Fundamentalists and charismatics do not worship the same God that Christians do."

## CONSERVATIVE ESCHATOLOGY

In addition to historic Christian orthodoxy, we also inquired about issues that have shaped the specific theological traditions of only some denominations. Perhaps the most important of these is conservative eschatology, in the form of dispensationalism. This mid-nineteenth-century revision of historic Christian premillennialism is characterized by high supernaturalism (reinforcing traditional orthodoxy in this regard), belief in the imminence of the "end times" and the Second Coming of Jesus, and emphasis on evangelism: "Save all you can while you can" (Marsden 1980; Boyer 1992). Dispensationalism and other forms of premillennialism—which are often hard to distinguish, even for the theological cognoscenti—are deeply imbedded in American religious movements such as fundamentalism and Pentecostalism, and in some denominations in the Evangelical tradition. Historically, these doctrines encouraged believers to separate themselves from apostates in "liberal" denominations, forswear futile social and political reform efforts, and focus instead on "soul winning" and building moral bulwarks against "the evils of this world." It is certainly in this vein that one Assemblies of God pastor admonished us that no matter what Christians do, "the world is still under the dominion of Satan until Christ's return."

Whatever the historic depoliticizing effects of this eschatology, there is prima facie evidence that dispensationalists may be playing a new political role. Many Christian Right activists of the 1980s were dispensationalists, apparently no longer restrained from political involvement. Indeed, astute observers such as Jeffrey Hadden (1987) and Helen Lee Turner (1992) have seen a tentative return to the "postmillennialism" of nineteenth-century Protestants, who thought the Kingdom of God could be brought in through the efforts of Christians *before* the Second Coming of Christ. Susan Harding (1994) has argued, however, that premillennial ideas remain prevalent among conservative Protestants but that heterodox theorists have introduced very subtle new elements, making dispensationalism much more compatible with political activism. Indeed, among religious activists dispensationalist beliefs in the cosmic struggle between God and Satan may now contribute to Christian militancy, conservative social and political beliefs, and political involvement (Wilcox, Jelen, and Linzey 1991; Guth et al. 1994). If the same effect appears among clergy, conservative eschatology may no longer lead to political abstinence.

Table 3.2 lists three items tapping the extent to which clergy adhere to the complex of ideas surrounding dispensationalism. First, we asked whether they believed in the "rapture of the church," a core dispensational doctrine, but one common to other premillennial interpretations as well. We also asked whether "the Bible clearly teaches a 'premillennial' view of history and the future," and, finally, whether they accepted "a dispensational interpretation of Scripture." (Ministers in the two Dutch Reformed churches were asked only the second question because their theological tradition has adamantly rejected all forms of premillennial theology.) As the upper section of Table 3.2 demonstrates, the doctrine of the rapture is the most popular eschatological measure, followed by premillennial theology, and with dispensationalism strong only in the Assemblies of God and among Southern Baptists. To summarize our findings, we created a highly reliable scale of conservative eschatology from the three items (alpha = .83). As the lower section of Table 3.2 shows, such beliefs are strongest in two Evangelical denominations, the Assemblies of God and the Southern Baptists; the former have been premillennial since their origins in the Pentecostal revivals of the early 1900s (Blumhofer 1993, 15–16), with their firm expectations that believers were living in the end times, while the Southern Baptists have always had a premillennial element, which became almost normative after 1945 (Turner and Guth 1989). The Evangelical Covenant Church, with its Lutheran and pietist heritage, has resisted frequent eschatological "invasions" by some Americanized adherents, without total success (Olsson 1985), and all three denominations in the Calvinist or Reformed tradition, with their historic "postmillennial" or "amillennial" doctrines, reject premillennial notions, although all three have had to fight off incursions of this common American theological "virus" (see, for example, Bratt 1984, 131–134).

The Methodists and Disciples, on the other hand, have been open to most theo-

Table 3.2
Religious Beliefs and Eschatology Among Clergy by Denomination
(Percent "Strongly Agree" or "Agree")

|  | AG | SBC | ECC | CRC | RCA | UMC | PRES | DOC |
|---|---|---|---|---|---|---|---|---|
| **Eschatology** |  |  |  |  |  |  |  |  |
| Rapture of church | 98 | 83 | 50 | 0* | 0* | 36 | 20 | 20 |
| Premillennialism | 81 | 61 | 23 | 2 | 10 | 21 | 8 | 12 |
| Dispensationalism | 54 | 40 | 10 | 0* | 0* | 11 | 3 | 11 |
| **Eschatology scale** |  |  |  |  |  |  |  |  |
| Very high | 33 | 23 | 4 | 1 | 3 | 4 | 0 | 2 |
| High | 43 | 29 | 9 | 1 | 6 | 12 | 4 | 9 |
| Neutral | 13 | 15 | 11 | 4 | 20 | 18 | 9 | 17 |
| Low | 9 | 17 | 36 | 47 | 38 | 40 | 35 | 41 |
| Very low | 2 | 16 | 40 | 47 | 33 | 26 | 52 | 31 |
|  | 100% | 100% | 100% | 100% | 100% | 100% | 100% | 100% |

* The questions on the "rapture of the church" and dispensationalism were not asked of ministers in the Christian Reformed Church and the Reformed Church in America. Given their long-standing official opposition to these premillennial concepts, it is safe to assume that the number of clergy agreeing with these beliefs is low, closely resembling those for the premillennial item itself, which meets with very little agreement and much rejection among CRC and RCA clergy.

logical innovations with a significant following, and thus from the beginning have had some premillennial traces among their clergy, albeit confined today to the conservative side of the ministerial corps and among the laity. Like other grassroots Protestants, these Mainline church people have been influenced by the strong premillennial elements in popular religious culture and by best-sellers such as Hal Lindsey's *Late Great Planet Earth* (Boyer 1992). As one liberal Methodist pastor from Mississippi told us, "There's a lot more 'end times' stuff out there in the pews than the United Methodist leadership wants to recognize." Indeed, our own 1992 study of the mass public found that 43 percent of United Methodists and 47 percent of laity in the PCUSA agreed with the premillennialist doctrine that the world would end with a great battle between God and Satan at Armageddon (Guth et al. 1996, 350–353). Thus, eschatology may bolster the impact of theological orthodoxy in the most conservative denominations and influence a scattered but dedicated corps of conservatives in others. In subsequent analyses we will often use this conservative eschatology score to help predict ministerial attitudes and activities.

We also investigated a large number of other beliefs *within* denominations that might reflect a distinct doctrinal heritage. Almost none added much to the analysis. For example, knowing that a PCUSA pastor favored inculcating historic Calvinist doctrines such as "election" or that a Disciples minister wanted strict adherence to "believer's baptism" or a return to other restorationist beliefs did not differentiate either pastor politically from colleagues of similar orthodoxy but different views on denominational "distinctives." Only in the Assemblies of God did the doctrine of speaking in tongues as a manifestation of the Spirit add much to our ability to predict other variables, once orthodoxy is taken into account. This is due in part to the absence of variation in orthodoxy, but it also reflects the fact that this doctrine is still a defining theological tenet of the Assemblies, although many current members have not had the experience. For the most part, though, adherence to historic denominational "distinctives" is strongly associated with general Christian orthodoxy in all eight denominations; in other words, those who honor the ancient denominational landmarks are much more orthodox than their colleagues who do not. Among Mainline churches the failure of denominational doctrines to have much impact is not surprising: theological liberalism is specifically the rejection of orthodoxy of any sort, a kind of ecumenical absence of dogma. Of course, only when the possibility of essential Christian doctrine is maintained can any group insist on historic denominational creeds. Ironically, then, even denominational "distinctives" now buttress the orthodox bulwarks in their battles with religious modernists.

## RELIGIOUS MOVEMENT

Many clergy also identify with *theological movements* such as fundamentalism, Pentecostalism, liberalism, or "evangelicalism" (used here in a different sense than in our reference to the Evangelical tradition). As we have seen, these movements represent conscious efforts to change the religious status quo by those dissatisfied with existing denominations and churches. Sect movements reject the accommodations that existing religious institutions have made with the culture and are exemplified by the fundamentalist and Pentecostal movements described earlier. Church movements, on the other hand, such as religious liberalism or modernism, seek to accommodate religious faith to contemporary life and culture. Identification with both kinds of movements cuts across denominational lines, and even the boundaries of religious traditions. Thus, a pastor in the PCUSA, a Mainline denomination, may identify as an "evangelical," while a Southern Baptist, in an Evangelical denomination, may call herself a "liberal." These identifications differ from simple theological beliefs by involving a clear sense of attachment to a broader constituency, often represented by organizations and institutions outside the denomination and, usually, by factional alignments inside. The former may take the shape of organizations such as the World Congress of Fundamentalists, the National Association of Evangelicals, or the National Council of Churches; the latter are sometimes officially recognized as denominational caucuses or institutionalized in other ways, with their own leaders and historical continuity.

Although some movement labels are commonly used across denominations, others have special meaning within a single church body. For example, we asked Southern Baptists whether they identified with "fundamentalist," "conservative," "moderate," or "liberal" theological movements. For many Southern Baptists, such terms represent a sense of affiliation with a broader national movement; this is especially true of fundamentalists. But because the SBC has often been quite insulated from national theological trends, for other pastors these terms signify internal factions. As Nancy Ammerman (1990) has noted in her pathbreaking study, the SBC's "fundamentalist" movement coalesced in organizations such as the Baptist Faith and Message Fellowship, led by the "Patterson-Pressler crowd" and mobilized annually in the SBC's Pastors' Conference, while "moderate" opposition organized in the Baptist Alliance and Cooperative Baptist Fellowship, begun and led by the "Gatlinburg Gang" and brought together by the SBC Pastors' Forum. In the PCUSA, on the other hand, an "evangelical" faction has clear ties to outside groups such as the National Association of Evangelicals, various mission groups, and seminaries in the Evangelical tradition, such as Fuller in California, but has also had many internal caucuses, such as Presbyterians United for Biblical Concerns, to influence denominational policy. In recent years, such evangelical "renewal movements" have arisen in all Mainline churches and have often linked arms across denominational boundaries. Most Mainline churches also have internal caucuses identified with more liberal theological movements, some of which have spread into Evangelical churches as well, resulting in many of the controversies described in chapter 2.

This mix of widely recognized common affiliations, cutting across denominational boundaries, with other ties available only within one or two denominations, creates some problems for measuring movement attachments. After considerable experimentation, we assembled a fourfold classification or scale that captures movement affiliation in a common metric across denominations. For the sake of simplicity, we call the most ardent traditionalist group "fundamentalist," the next, "evangelical," then "moderate," and finally, "liberal." Although the "evangelical" and "moderate" categories include various "evangelicals," "conservatives," "centrists," and "loyalists," often using denomination-specific labels, the overwhelming majority of those we have put in the fundamentalist category, and all those assigned to the liberal camp, actually use those labels. And the classification is validated by the fact that each group has the expected attitude toward the national and denominational representations of their cause: fundamentalists and evangelicals rate highly the National Association of Evangelicals, while liberals laud the National Council of Churches. Similarly, the scale predicts with impressive accuracy ministers' attitudes toward the myriad pressure groups within their denominations, left and right. As the top part of Table 3.3 reveals, the theological movement measure shows that denominations have different centers of gravity: Assemblies pastors are uniformly on the right, the ECC is almost monopolized by evangelicals, and Southern Baptists have a solid majority of evangelicals (with fundamentalist and moderate wings), while the balance shifts somewhat to the left in the CRC and the RCA. The tenuous theological standoff among Methodists gives way to liberal dominance among Presbyterians and, especially, Disciples, many of whom are quite vocal about their adherence to "card-carrying" religious liberalism.

Although the theological movement scale does not measure religious beliefs

Table 3.3
Religious Movement Self-Identification and Religious Change
Among Clergy by Denomination (Percent)

|  | AG | SBC | ECC | CRC | RCA | UMC | PRES | DOC |
|---|---|---|---|---|---|---|---|---|
| Religious movement | | | | | | | | |
| "Fundamentalist" | 75 | 15 | 5 | 9 | 3 | 9 | 1 | 2 |
| "Evangelical" | 24 | 68 | 83 | 77 | 78 | 40 | 26 | 15 |
| "Moderate" | 1 | 26 | 11 | 14 | 13 | 35 | 28 | 27 |
| "Liberal" | 1 | 2 | 1 | 1 | 5 | 16 | 45 | 56 |
|  | 100% | 100% | 100% | 100% | 100% | 100% | 100% | 100% |
| Religious change | | | | | | | | |
| Much to right | 5 | 4 | 4 | * | * | 4 | 5 | 4 |
| To right | 6 | 15 | 10 | | | 17 | 14 | 11 |
| Have not moved | 79 | 65 | 73 | | | 53 | 56 | 58 |
| More liberal | 10 | 14 | 13 | | | 21 | 17 | 18 |
| Much more liberal | 0 | 3 | 1 | | | 5 | 9 | 9 |
|  | 100% | 100% | 100% | | | 100% | 100% | 100% |

*The question on theological movement affiliation at age 21 was not asked of the CRC and RCA clergy.

directly, it does permit us to make a crude, but useful, assessment of probable theological change among ministers during their adult years. We asked clergy in six denominations (the CRC and RCA pastors are missing here) how they would have identified with these theological movements at age twenty-one, at a point when most were completing college. By comparing this information with pastors' current attachment, we can gain some insight into patterns of theological change. As college education no doubt had some impact by this point (see later discussion), our estimates should be conservative; if we err, it is probably by understating change during early adulthood.

Has there been systematic theological change among ministers? As the second section of Table 3.3 shows, over two-thirds of the ministers in Evangelical denominations report that their movement identification has not changed since they were twenty-one, while only about half the Mainline clergy make the same claim. The direction of change also varies somewhat. Evangelicals report about equal (but modest) movements in both conservative and liberal directions, while the UMC, Presbyterian, and Disciples clergy are prone to shift in a liberal direction, despite their more liberal starting points. A closer look at who has moved modifies the picture somewhat—or, perhaps, changes the interpretation. Splitting the pastors into those who were brought up in their current denomination's tradition (Evangelical or Mainline) and those who were not shows that the largest changes come from those leaving an Evangelical background for a Mainline affiliation, or vice versa. Not surprisingly, such shifts are accompanied by substantial changes in attachments to theological movements. Thus, pastors raised in Mainline churches who have switched to the Assemblies of God or Southern Baptist Convention have become much more conservative in their attachments; conversely, Evangelicals who defect to the Presbyterians or Disciples report much more "liberalization" than those raised and, presumably, socialized religiously within those faiths. So, among clergy as well as laity, Americans are finding denominational homes compatible with their emerging theological beliefs, resulting in clearer distinctions than ever between the two Protestant "parties" (Green and Guth 1993).

Although such change is not the only factor influencing the theological composition of the clergy (selective recruitment and differential retention are also important), this evidence suggests that the theological divide among Protestant clergy is probably widening, as Evangelicals remain relatively stable in their attachments while Mainline clergy drift in a more liberal direction, at least by their own estimates. These sorts of changes suggest that Mainline ministers' adherence to orthodox theology may be declining over time. The long-term results are shown by a comparison of data for United Methodists and Presbyterians from Hadden (1969) and the present surveys. On two items in both surveys, the virgin birth and existence of the Devil, about half of these Mainline clergy took the "orthodox" position in both 1965 and 1989, but the "strength" of agreement with the belief statements had declined dramatically. For example, 36 percent of the 1965 Presbyterian clergy "definitely agreed" with the statement on the virgin birth, but even after the 1983 merger with the more conservative Southern Presbyterians, only 22 percent of the 1989 sample did, indicating increased theological modernism among Mainline clergy.

By this point the reader may accuse us of theological overkill. The distributions of all three theological measures by denomination look quite similar, ranging from conservative dominance in the Assemblies to liberal hegemony among Disciples. And yet the measures are distinct: true, the correlation between theological orthodoxy and identification with theological movements is quite strong ($r = .74$), but they are not identical measures, contrary to the assertions of some previous analysts (Jeffries and Tygart 1974), and, as we will see, adding the latter usually bolsters the statistical power of our results. The relationship between conservative eschatology and the other variables is weaker ($r = .56$ with orthodoxy, .45 with theological movement), but like religious movement affiliation, eschatology shapes ministerial politics in a somewhat different fashion than does theological orthodoxy. As our orthodoxy measure is usually most powerful, we shall use the recoded four-category version for illustrative purposes, and much of the succeeding analysis will focus on its impact. Nevertheless, we shall have frequent occasion to make use of the theological movement and conservative eschatology measures as well.

## SOURCES OF THEOLOGICAL DIVERSITY

Where does this great diversity of theological perspective come from? Why do ministers from different denominations—and, for that matter, within some denominations—hold such different beliefs? While we cannot address this issue in all the detail it deserves, we can test some explanations offered by social scientists. Some scholars have emphasized religious socialization, others demographic factors; still others have stressed the role of professional socialization. As we shall see, each plays a part in explaining theological orientations, but professional socialization is the major influence.

The most obvious way that ministers come to differ is that they are socialized in varying theological traditions, which in the United States have been encapsulated in denominational institutions. Thus, most Assemblies clergy have been brought up in AG churches, perhaps attended Assemblies educational institutions, and presumably became part of the clergy by demonstrating adherence to Pentecostal theology and practice. Or, as one Southern Baptist theologian and historian has described the denominational connection, there was until recently "a Baptist ethos—you'd be reared in a Baptist home, attend a Baptist church, go to a Baptist college, and then network in the convention" (Mooney 1995, A13). And, in fact, such patterns are characteristic of the clergy in most denominations. For example, 73 percent of the Southern Baptists, 72 percent of the DOC clergy, 68 percent of the Presbyterians, and 67 percent of the Methodists were raised in their denomination, and additional numbers come from "close cousin" churches. Many attended denominational colleges (67 percent of the Assemblies clergy, for example, and 51 percent of the Disciples), and the great majority attend denominational seminaries.

An alternative perspective stresses social class, region, and other demographic variables as explanations for ministers' theological perspectives (cf. Niebuhr 1929; Lerner, Rothman, and Lichter 1989). According to this view, ministers from rural, working-class, and southern origins should be more traditionalist in belief than those from middle-class, urban, and nonsouthern backgrounds. Obviously, our clergy differ substantially on these traits, especially on social class origins, with a large majority of Assemblies and Southern Baptist pastors coming from farm and working-class homes, and the Mainline clergy more likely to have middle-class families of origin. Mainline pastors are also likely to come from the city rather than from rural areas, where many of the Evangelicals start life. In the same vein, age and sex may have some impact on a minister's theology. Hadden (1969) and Quinley (1974) demonstrated that the New Breed clergy in the 1960s were disproportionately liberal; while this may still be the case, some observers have pointed to a new conservatism among younger clergy. And as more women have entered the Mainline clergy, especially, many scholars anticipate a "liberalizing" of theology, arguing that women are distinctly more nontraditional (Hunter and Sargeant 1993; but cf. Lehman 1993), a suggestion certainly buttressed by popular perceptions of feminist activism at the 1993 "Re-imagining God" conference, sponsored by the Mainline churches.

Finally, other observers argue that professional socialization, especially in the form of higher education, accounts for theological differences (cf. Carroll and Marler 1995; Goldman 1991). Whatever the ministers' social background, their educational experiences are even more diverse. Among the Assemblies and Baptists a significant number represent the old tradition of the "called" clergy, who respond to a supernatural summons; they are often pastors without benefit (or hindrance) of formal theological training or, sometimes, even a college degree. (Only 43 percent of AG clergy have college diplomas, and only 19 percent have seminary degrees; the comparable figures for Southern Baptists are 69 and 62 percent.) Clergy in these denominations who have attended both college and seminary have usually matriculated at less selective institutions, often tied to the denomination. Their college degrees are often in "Bible" or an applied discipline, such as education or business administration. On the other side, Mainline clergy are usually the products of more routine career decisions (they are less likely to enter the ministry because of a supernatural "call") and are shaped by college and, frequently, graduate study, often in the social sciences and the humanities. Almost invariably they also have seminary degrees or advanced theological training, most often from denominational seminaries but sometimes from the most prestigious and selective interdenominational divinity schools, such as those at Harvard, Yale, Chicago, or Union (New York City), all noted for their avant-garde theologies.

How do these factors influence theological perspective? We constructed several measures to summarize these influences. To capture religious socialization, we used the tradition in which the minister was brought up (Evangelical or Mainline), along with his or her own theological affiliation at age twenty-one. To this we added social background measures: the size of the community and whether the minister grew up in the South, the social class of his or her family, gender, age, and years in the ministry. Finally, to measure professional socialization we included several items on education. The first two variables measure the extent of college and seminary education, ranging from none at all to work beyond the bachelor's degree, such as master's or doctorate programs. Major incorporates course of college study in the order of the disciplines' "liberalizing" influence (Ladd and Lipset 1975), with the social sciences followed by the humanities, at one end of the scale, and applied disciplines at the other. College prestige measures the selectivity (and presumably quality) of the college attended. Seminary prestige is a scale with ministers without theological training at one end and those attending the most selective and prestigious divinity schools at the other.

A quick review of the bivariate relationships between all these variables and our theological measures offers support for each set of hypotheses (data not shown). Not surprisingly, ministers' theological outlooks are strongly associated with their childhood denomination and early theological identification. In addition, those from rural areas, working-class and farm families, and the South are, as expected, more likely to be orthodox, hold conservative eschatology, and identify with fundamentalist movements, as are male clergy. Age has a mixed effect, with both younger and very senior ministers more conservative. Finally, all three theological measures are related to education: the higher the level of secular and seminary education, the more prestigious the college and seminary, and the more liberal the major, the greater the likelihood that a minister adopts less orthodox positions, disagrees with conservative eschatology, and identifies with liberal movements. Thus, key variables from the theories stressing religious upbringing, socioeconomic factors, and professional socialization all exhibit more or less the expected relationships to the theological variables.

Of course, these variables are interrelated. Ministers from Evangelical homes are most likely to come from working-class backgrounds and less likely to have extended education than those from Mainline churches. Older clergy have less education as well, often grew up in smaller communities, and so on. To sort out the most important direct influences on theology, then, we used multiple regression, which isolates the impact of each variable in the analysis while holding all the others constant. The results for orthodoxy, conservative eschatology, and religious movement identification are reported in Table 3.4. As we see in the first column, orthodoxy is influenced primarily by the pastor's early theological perspective on the one hand and by the prestige of the college and seminary attended on the other. Ministers with Bible college training are the most conservative theologically—even more so than those without any formal theological training whatever (data not shown), while those attending the major interdenominational divinity schools are most liberal, with those graduating from denominational seminaries in between. A few other educational variables, such as length of seminary education and a liberal arts major (especially in the social sciences or the humanities), also push ministers toward a more liberal theological stance, as does longer experience in the ministry.

Unlike the religious and professional socialization variables, however, socio-economic and demographic factors have little direct impact. Men and scions of working-class and farm families are slightly more orthodox, and, as predicted, women are more modernist even when all other factors are accounted for. (Indeed, the significant minority of women in the UMC, PCUSA, and Disciples of Christ are distinctly more modernist than their male counterparts in each church.) Most other demographic factors, such as urban origins and age, have very modest effects, not statistically significant even in this very large sample. Southern birth and being raised in an Evangelical denomination have no statistically significant independent

Table 3.4
Explaining Theological Diversity among Protestant Pastors: Multiple Regression Analysis

|  | Orthodoxy | Conservative Eschatology | Conservative Movement ID |
|---|---|---|---|
| Religious socialization |  |  |  |
| Early theological affiliation | .23** | .16** | .36** |
| Childhood denomination |  |  |  |
| Evangelical | −.05 | −.09** | −.05 |
| Mainline | −.06* | −.01 | −.01 |
|  |  |  |  |
| Demographic and personal |  |  |  |
| Size of community | −.03 | −.05** | −.01 |
| Raised in South | .02 | .05** | −.02 |
| Working class | .04** | .04* | −.01 |
| Male | .07** | .01 | .05** |
| Age | .03 | −.01 | .08** |
| Years in ministry | −.11** | .00 | −.10** |
|  |  |  |  |
| Education |  |  |  |
| College prestige | −.34** | −.18** | −.33** |
| Seminary prestige | −.26** | −.18** | −.20** |
| Years of education |  |  |  |
| Secular | .06** | .00 | .04* |
| Seminary | −.04* | −.25** | −.07** |
| Liberal college major | −.04** | −.09** | −.01 |
| Adjusted $R^2$ | .58 | .43 | .61 |

*$p < .05$; **$p < .001$.
Coefficients indicate the relative influence of each variable on ministers' orthodoxy, eschatology, or movement identification once the impact of all the other variables in the analysis is taken into account. The adjusted $R^2$ measures the proportion of variation in each variable explained by all the independent variables combined.

effects (and the sign for Evangelical upbringing runs in the wrong direction). And when all else is accounted for, longer secular education produces modestly more orthodoxy. All measures together explain a substantial 58 percent of the variation in orthodoxy.

The pattern changes slightly in the second and third columns of Table 3.4 for both conservative eschatology and theological movement identification, but early socialization and education still dominate. Early fundamentalist identification, along with rural and southern origins, predisposes some toward premillennialism, but such tendencies are eroded by attendance at selective colleges and prestigious seminaries, extended theological training, and a liberal arts major. For fundamentalist affiliation, once again liberal early identification combines with the quality of college and seminary to reduce conservative affiliations, while length of formal theological training and the number of years in the ministry also make significant contributions. Men and older ministers are also slightly more likely to identify with a conservative movement, once other factors are in the equation.

These patterns all point in the same direction: although clergy are obviously shaped by the religious context in which they were raised, the most important influence on a pastor's theological beliefs, movement affiliations, and eschatology is professional training, both in college and at the graduate level. In all denominations, more conservative orientations are produced by a combination of childhood conservatism; attendance at less selective colleges and universities; studies in business, education, the applied sciences, or other "practical" disciplines; and attendance at less selective theological institutions—or having no seminary training at all. Although demographic factors may exercise a modest direct influence at times, their major impact is indirect—by influencing the path of a minister's educational career. Thus, the instincts of many a conservative pastor are correct: the most selective and prestigious American educational institutions are still "dangerous" to the orthodox faith of the young, as are the "relativizing" disciplines of the social sciences and the humanities.

Of course, education has other significant effects, producing political interest, enhancing personal resources, both intellectual and financial, and constraining ideologies into coherent systems. These results, in fact, are produced even by the kind of education favored by most Evangelical denominations, which like their Mainline counterparts long ago, have decided in favor of a professionally trained clergy. Although this decision may ultimately threaten the viability of their churches (cf. Finke and Stark 1992), it also has enormous implications for the role of conservative ministers in politics, producing the attitudes and resources necessary for effective participation.

## CONCLUSIONS

Thus, the broad contours of the old cleavage between the orthodox and their modernist opponents still characterize the theological landscape of American Protestantism. Each denomination has a distinctive mix of these contending factions; some, like the Assemblies, are overwhelmingly orthodox; others, like the Disciples, have a distinctly modernist hue. And we discover that other theological notions, especially conservative eschatology, also influence pastors within at least some churches. Finally, ministers do identify with particular theological movements, which in many church bodies are institutionalized in various caucuses and more or less formal movement organizations. All in all, we may be witnessing another stage in the historic shift of Protestantism away from primary divisions rooted in ethnicity and religious particularism toward a systematic alignment based on theological orthodoxy, incorporating denominations and movements left largely untouched by the controversies of the 1920s. Distinctive denominational traits have been subsumed, and perhaps overridden, by the larger theological divide between orthodoxy and modernism (Wuthnow 1988). In any event, these competing theological perspectives provide the sure foundation for differences in ministerial perspectives on politics. In the next chapter, we turn to the respective social theologies of the two parties of American Protestant clergy.

# 4
# The Public Church:
# The Social Theologies of
# Protestant Clergy

Close observers of American religion have long noticed the striking difference between the individualist social theology of Evangelical Protestants and the communitarian perspective of Mainline Protestants. As we saw in chapter 1, these social theologies follow closely from the fundamental doctrinal perspectives of orthodoxy and modernism, respectively, and in turn link these theological beliefs with contemporary political ideologies, such as liberalism and conservatism. And yet we are not sure whether these historic social theologies still suffuse the belief systems of Protestant clergy today. Some observers think they have lost none of their original force (Gamwell 1996), while others see important changes occurring, especially in the Evangelical party, but disagree on the nature of that change. A few claim that orthodox Protestants are adopting more communitarian perspectives, drawing closer to the fundamental worldviews of their Mainline sisters and brothers (Dudley and Van Eck 1992), while others find new elements that provide a rationale for collective political action, while preserving the basic individualism of the Evangelical tradition (Lienesch 1993).

Are any of these reports true? Have Evangelical Protestant clergy adopted a new understanding of the church's role in social change? In what ways do Evangelical and Mainline pastors still differ in their contemporary views of the role of the Christian church in the city of man? We find that Evangelical Protestants have indeed formulated a new social theology, one that incorporates the old individualist model of social change but superimposes on it new (or perhaps renewed) expectations for government's role in fostering moral transformation. For their part, Mainline Protestants still persevere in the old Social Gospel tradition, without the illusions of their Progressive Era predecessors or of the New Breed of the 1960s, but with even greater expectations about the role of government in bringing about social justice.

## SOCIAL THEOLOGIES OF THE PROTESTANT CLERGY

We asked ministers how Christian faith should relate to the social and political world, using a large number of items designed to tap the competing social theologies of individualism and communitarianism. The results are reported in Table 4.1 by orthodoxy category. (As we shall note, the results by denomination, by theological movement, and by eschatology exhibit comparable patterns.)

What can we conclude? First, the old dispute over social theology between the Evangelical and Mainline camps is clearly alive, at least in formal terms. The first section of Table 4.1 shows that orthodox clergy still insist that social reform comes from the changed hearts of individuals, not from alteration of social institutions. As one Assemblies of God pastor put it, "Our problems are not drugs, divorce, abortion, greed, etc. These are but the symptoms of a much larger problem, that of alienation from God." The orthodox remain firmly convinced that widespread conversion to faith in Jesus Christ will lead directly to social improvement. Few themes were so frequently reiterated:

I strongly believe that with the Power of the Spirit of God flowing over our land, and the people humbling themselves before God, the social problems would soon dissolve and disappear. (Assemblies of God)

I personally believe and actually proclaim from the pulpit that Christ was apolitical. Save souls, and the rest will take care of itself. (Southern Baptist)

Individual changes, personal changes, for better or worse, always affect the social order. (Christian Reformed Church)

Churches should transform society with transformed people. (Assemblies of God)

Many social and moral issues could easily be handled if we would only trust in God. (Southern Baptist)

Jesus is the answer to all problems: social, financial, health, national, international, civil, moral, and educational . . . but folks must be saved first. (Southern Baptist)

As Ted Jelen discovered in his intensive conversations with Evangelical clergy, "the transformative nature of coming to Christ" is viewed by many of these ministers "as highly radical in nature" (1993, 45).

True, not every conservative is quite so convinced that spreading the gospel automatically brings about social transformation. One Southern Baptist dissented in part, arguing that individual change must go beyond simple conversion: "Although I consider myself very conservative, I question the traditional assumption that changed lives will change society. We must encourage true believers to live out their

Table 4.1
Social Theologies of Protestant Clergy (Percent)

| | Most Orthodox | | | Most Modernist |
| --- | --- | --- | --- | --- |
| | 1 | 2 | 3 | 4 |
| **Individualist** | | | | |
| Reform by changing hearts, not institutions* | 91 | 79 | 58 | 19 |
| People not innately good in good environment | 75 | 67 | 60 | 49 |
| Christians must keep separate from the world* | 72 | 51 | 31 | 8 |
| If enough are saved, social ills will disappear | 68 | 47 | 29 | 19 |
| Church should focus on personal morality* | 60 | 35 | 25 | 5 |
| Christian faith is primarily spiritual | 52 | 37 | 13 | 5 |
| **Communitarian** | | | | |
| Social Gospel at heart of New Testament | 36 | 60 | 79 | 82 |
| Causes of poverty primarily structural* | 29 | 35 | 58 | 80 |
| Liberation theology gets to heart of the gospel | 8 | 20 | 48 | 75 |
| Church should emphasize social transformation | 4 | 10 | 22 | 46 |
| Church focus on social justice, not morality* | 6 | 7 | 15 | 42 |
| Kingdom of God can be built now in this world | 22 | 25 | 34 | 31 |
| **Summary of individualism/communitarianism** | | | | |
| Most individualistic | 53 | 26 | 6 | 1 |
| Individualistic | 36 | 42 | 16 | 9 |
| Mixed | 7 | 16 | 21 | 12 |
| Communitarian | 4 | 14 | 33 | 36 |
| Most communitarian | — | 2 | 14 | 42 |
| | 100% | 100% | 100% | 100% |

*Data from the clergy in the 1990–91 Wheaton Religious Activist Study.

discipleship and become agents of change." Other orthodox pastors, especially Calvinists in the Christian Reformed Church, are even more cautious, warning that not "enough" people will be brought to Christ to transform "a fallen world." Even they added, however, that saving more souls "sure would help." In any case, outside the Calvinist fold even such minor skepticism about this historic tenet of Evangelical social theology was rare.

Whatever the putative relationship between individual salvation and social change, for some conservative clergy the relationship is immaterial, as Jelen discovered, for "politics is simply irrelevant to the important task of spreading the word of God, and to the occasioning of individual religious conversions" (1993, 46). Indeed, religion is ultimately spiritual and not about temporal things. As one Southern Baptist minister reminded us, "Our nation and government are part of the world. I cannot waste God's time by trying to influence for God that which is irreparably set against God and His Kingdom." Thus, the church should continue to focus on individual salvation and personal morality, not social transformation, by whatever means it might be achieved. Even clergy sympathetic to some Christian political activity warned of limits to its efficacy. A Christian Reformed pastor identified the theological errors implicit in social and political reformism:

> Since believers are creatures who still are part of this sin-cursed creation, they are involved in all aspects of life, including the political. I think that believers may work together to affect the political process. But it is a mistake to think that Christ's kingdom comes through the political process of using power and law. The laws established and enforced by the state can effect change only from the outside of the person. They can never effect a change of heart. Only the gospel, proclaimed by the church, is the tool, the means used by Christ himself through the Holy Spirit to change hearts and transform life from within the person.

Another conservative Southern Baptist pastor also had some sympathy for Christian political involvement but was concerned about the "opportunity costs" attendant upon such activism:

> I suppose my main concern with all the energy put into political issues by many Christians . . . is what would happen if those same dollars and that same energy were put into personal witnessing for Christ and prayer. For me as a citizen— a Christian citizen—I have a responsibility to take a stand, but I cannot legislate "Christianity." I must allow the Holy Spirit to do his work in lives, for we must be a constant, open witness to others of a living faith. A country will only change and people will only change when Christ is Lord—not when legalism becomes our God.

Ultimately, for many orthodox clergy, the limitations and dangers of political involvement militate against it. Christians must still maintain the old distance from "worldly" things, including political machinations. One Southern Baptist sang the old separationist refrain: "I think a true Christian has no place in politics. Politics and religion don't mix."

As modernists' responses to the communitarian items in Table 4.1 show, they are clearly on the other side, still seeing the "Social Gospel at the heart of the New Testament message." Most regard poverty and other social problems as primarily structural, caused by social, economic, and political discrimination against the poor, not by personal inadequacies or failures. Indeed, this perspective on social injustice leads many modernists, especially young clergy fresh out of seminary or possessing advanced degrees, to express sympathy for liberation theology, with its "preferential option for the poor." As one Methodist admonished us, "I'm a little concerned about your questions. I am a progressive and not a liberal. Liberals want to reform society. Progressives are interested in transforming structures from their very roots." As Table 4.1 confirms, this more radical communitarian faith is almost universally rejected by the orthodox. Thus, despite some claims that Evangelicals have adopted a more structural interpretation of social problems, the old dividing lines are not only intact but even appear to have been reinforced, at least on many of the ancient issues.

Of course, individual clergy do not always adopt a position at either the individualist or the communitarian extreme. A careful look at Table 4.1 shows that some orthodox clergy recognize the structural facets of social problems and sympathize with the Social Gospel. A conservative Southern Baptist pastor, for example, argued that fostering spirituality was not enough: "I try to get the church values moved outside the church walls. We need to get Christ into the community." Conversely, some modernists remain concerned with individual transformation. A Reformed Church minister insisted that juxtaposing conversion and social change produced a false dichotomy: "Individual sanctification and transforming society are always interlinked." Clergy on both sides also share a good bit in their views of human nature and the direction of society. Although modernists have a somewhat rosier picture of humanity than the orthodox do, few exhibit the social optimism of their Progressive Era progenitors. The evil committed by human beings during this century has no doubt precluded such sentiments, even without Reinhold Niebuhr's warnings or liberation theologians' admonitions about institutional evil. They are reluctant to claim with the firm conviction of early Social Gospel enthusiasts that the Kingdom of God can be built here and now, but they almost unanimously reject the idea that "the world is growing worse and worse and there is not much Christians can do about it" (data not shown). The orthodox, of course, resist all optimistic assessments of human nature and the possibility of this-worldly accomplishment of all God's purposes, but four-fifths also reject the gloomy assessment of the world characteristic of classic dispensationalists; only a tiny remnant high on the eschatology index hold such views. More characteristic is the Christian Reformed minister who told us—true to both historic Calvinism's pessimism about society *and* its reformist bent—"I do believe that the world is getting worse; however, as Christians we have been called to do our part in changing the world for Christ."

Despite some overlap in worldviews, in the final analysis the natural tendencies of the orthodox and modernists are still far apart. As the summary measure in the last section of Table 4.1 shows, the most orthodox clergy are strongly individualistic, while the most modernist are overwhelmingly communitarian. The denominational distribution of social theologies should present no surprise. In the Assemblies of God, 87 percent of the clergy fall into one of the individualistic categories, with a majority in the most individualistic camp. From that point the individualist totals decline from the Southern Baptists (81 percent), through the Evangelical Covenant (59 percent), Christian Reformed (42 percent), Reformed Church (48 percent), Methodists (49 percent), the Presbyterians (29 percent), to the Disciples of Christ (22 percent). Communitarian totals, of course, run the other way, with only 6 percent among the Assemblies but 66 percent among Disciples. Denominations in the middle of the scale—the CRC, RCA, and UMC—are all deeply divided, with substantial numbers of pastors in each category. We should also note that the three denominations with recent ethnic heritages—the Swedish Evangelical Covenant and the two Dutch Reformed churches—have more communitarians than their orthodoxy would suggest, perhaps reflecting residual ethnic communalism.

Thus, we have found that historic Evangelical and Mainline social theologies persist, although not without some change. Clearly, the modernists are chastened communitarians, bereft of the liberal illusions of their predecessors at the turn of the century but still affirming the old Social Gospel and, for many, the even more radical tenets of liberation theology. As Dieter Hessel argues, "In a century that began with the social gospel and is concluding with the flowering of various liberation theologies, a continuity of commitment to social ministry is quite evident" among modernist Protestants (1993, 19). Similarly, while orthodox clergy recite the verities of nineteenth-century revivalist social theory, a distinctly individualistic worldview, most disavow the pessimistic dispensationalist rejection of the "world" and its political order. That rejection in itself, of course, does not constitute a new social perspective. Indeed, the attitudes portrayed in Table 4.1 would suggest that orthodox clergy persist in the "otherworldly," apolitical preoccupations of which they were accused by Hadden, Quinley, Jelen, and a host of other analysts. Without additional developments, these ideas would not seem to provide a strong basis for political activism.

## A NEW "CIVIC GOSPEL"?

In fact, there are innovations in orthodox social theology that may, at least in part and among some clergy, offset the antipolitical impact of social individualism or perhaps incorporate it in a new, politically activist amalgam. As Bruce Nesmith has noted, by the late 1970s, "Many evangelical preachers began to see the world, or at least their role in the world, very differently. They presented Christianity as an alternative, in one's political as well as personal life, to a liberalism which was socially pervasive but morally bankrupt" (1994, 21). Few elements of this new perspective are entirely novel: in some cases, they reassert elements long present in American Protestant civil religion (cf. Manis 1987 for the Southern Baptist case). Although shared to an extent by modernist clergy, these elements together represent the emergence of a new and distinctive orthodox perspective, one promulgated over the past two decades by Christian Right leaders such as Jerry Falwell, Pat Robertson, James Dobson, and Tim and Beverly LaHaye, among others (for a fine analysis, see Lienesch 1993). As several analysts have noted, these ideas have met strong objections from some theological conservatives but have been vital components of the new Christian activism on the right. We asked ministers in both the denominational and Wheaton activist studies a number of questions designed to tap the component elements of this new conservative social theology. Table 4.2 reports the results.

How has this new Christian Right "civic gospel" been received by conservative clergy? On the whole, the answer is "quite well." First, we find an almost universal orthodox conviction that the Bible not only is authoritative for theology but also is the only sure basis for ethics; it must be at the center of the nation's moral system, as demanded by the Christian Right (Jelen 1993). And, for orthodox clergy, national well-being depends on faithfulness to God. Theological conservatives believe that the United States was founded as a Christian nation, on religious principles, but has moved far from that starting point, threatening its political health. Indeed, religion itself is now under attack by hostile organizations, which seek to remove faith from the public square. These enemies of religion have been so successful that religious people may actually require protection by government action (cf. Olson 1994). Most of the orthodox perceive that the antireligion campaign is succeeding, agreeing that religion is indeed losing influence over American life, despite its ancient heritage. Thus, some conservative clergy may have come to see

Table 4.2
New Conservative "Civic Gospel" (Percent)

| | Most Orthodox | | | Most Modernist |
|---|---|---|---|---|
| | 1 | 2 | 3 | 4 |
| New conservative "civic gospel" | | | | |
| Bible only reliable ethical guide for society | 91 | 75 | 42 | 14 |
| Nations will prosper if faithful to God | 87 | 68 | 38 | 25 |
| U.S. was founded as Christian nation | 79 | 59 | 35 | 21 |
| Antireligious groups threaten freedom of religion | 79 | 64 | 42 | 17 |
| Religious people now need protection in U.S.* | 68 | 59 | 46 | 27 |
| Hard to be a true Christian and political liberal | 66 | 29 | 9 | 4 |
| Religion is losing influence in America | 59 | 58 | 54 | 48 |
| One correct Christian view on most issues* | 52 | 37 | 16 | 6 |
| Government must back religion to sustain morality | 48 | 35 | 16 | 8 |
| God works through the election process | 48 | 27 | 13 | 4 |
| Free enterprise only Christian economic system | 46 | 22 | 10 | 6 |
| U.S. needs Christian political party* | 23 | 16 | 9 | 4 |
| Proximity to Christian Right groups | | | | |
| Close to Focus on the Family | 90 | 83 | 54 | 21 |
| Close to Moral Majority | 48 | 23 | 5 | 0 |
| Summary of conservative "civic gospel" | | | | |
| Highest quintile | 49 | 21 | 5 | 0 |
| High | 32 | 33 | 11 | 2 |
| Moderate | 14 | 27 | 27 | 10 |
| Low | 3 | 14 | 35 | 33 |
| Lowest quintile | 2 | 5 | 23 | 55 |
| | 100% | 100% | 100% | 100% |

*Data from clergy in the 1990–91 Wheaton Religious Activist Study.

political involvement as "a regrettable necessity in the modern world" (Jelen 1993, 130–131).

For many orthodox ministers, the opponents are obvious: political liberals. Indeed, two-thirds of the most orthodox insist that it would be "hard to be both a true Christian and a political liberal." While some might take this assertion (perhaps rightly) as a mark of orthodox intolerance, it also reflects widespread consensus on the enemy's identity. Among the most orthodox pastors in the Wheaton study, for example, fully 47 percent replied to an open-ended query about the "most dangerous" political group in America by naming the American Civil Liberties Union (ACLU), while another 15 percent listed other advocates of strict church-state separation. Many orthodox clergy insist on evaluating politicians and political ideas in a religious context. For example, the most orthodox clergy see a candidate's religious views as a crucial basis for their own vote. And, although this is still a minority opinion, many orthodox pastors think that government should support religion—to maintain social order, public morality, and harmony. One Southern Baptist pastor, politically quite moderate, put it this way: "On politics—there is an absolute and profound difference between our Constitutional separation of church and state and our historic commitment to the state's awareness and appreciation of our diverse religious and moral values."

Finally, a substantial number of the most orthodox clergy confidently expect to see God's hand working in the nation, perhaps through elections. Even most conservative clergy, however, reject one vehicle through which God might work: a Christian political party. This option is occasionally discussed by some intellectuals in the Christian Reformed tradition and by a few militant fundamentalists who have toyed with a possible alliance with the U.S. Taxpayers' Party, but it is supported here by only a small minority, even among the most orthodox. One nondenominational fundamentalist pastor gave us his objections: "The idea of a Christian political party is very dangerous for several reasons: (1) Society is not changed permanently by political means, and (2) Christianity would be seen as another political party and not as a life-changing experience that crosses cultural, ethnic, and political boundaries." Thus, even the most militant clergy on the right seem unlikely to foster this kind of Christian politics.

Another component of the new civic gospel is a theological preference for free enterprise. Not only has the Christian Right tried to inculcate such beliefs, but religious conservatives in other traditions, especially the Roman Catholic, have made similar efforts (Novak 1982). Table 4.2 suggests that free-enterprise enthusiasts have made inroads among orthodox clergy but still have a long way to go. When we asked ministers whether "free enterprise is the only economic system compatible with Christian values," a plurality concurred only among the most orthodox; other clergy were often undecided or, in the case of the modernists, in strong disagreement. No doubt a somewhat more moderate phrasing might have elicited more agreement on the preferability of free economic systems, but the results are still indicative of the limits of Christian Right success.

On all these elements of the civic gospel, modernists hold views dramatically different from those of the most orthodox. They do not see the Bible as the sole guide to ethics, reject connections between religious faithfulness and national well-being, do not accept theories about the Christian origins of the Constitution, and see no dangers to religion from hostile liberals. Nor do they think that they should examine candidates' religious attitudes as a way of assessing their worth as potential office-holders. In fact, a good many perceive not-so-subtle dangers in the new conservative civic gospel. One Disciples minister worried about these developments:

> I strongly feel that in our society, with so many different religious backgrounds, the Christian faith should not impose its views in political areas—not because I do not have confidence in our faith solutions but because I believe the Christian faith is a matter of personal choice. I believe the church should teach its people to become involved in political issues and participate in the democratic process *but do not use the ploy of "Christian America" to coerce citizens who may not accept Jesus as their Savior.*

A Presbyterian put it more bluntly: "Religious freedom in the United States is threatened by Christian fundamentalists: 'our way or no way.'" Modernists abjure government support of religious faith, informal religious "tests" for office, and a religious political party as a vehicle for Christian social values. Only in their assessment that religion may be losing influence—although through different mechanisms than those blamed by conservatives—is there substantial agreement with their orthodox counterparts.

Another way of tapping clergy's reaction to the new civic gospel is through their evaluation of Christian Right groups that are the chief disseminators of these ideas. Table 4.2 reports reactions to two such organizations, James Dobson's Focus on the Family and Jerry Falwell's Moral Majority, which constitute the high and low water marks for the Christian Right, respectively. Quite clearly, Focus on the Family emerges as much more popular, with overwhelming support from the orthodox, considerable backing even among moderate modernists, but very little among the most modernist. By denomination, Focus had massive approval from all Evangelicals: the Assemblies (90 percent), the Baptists (84 percent), the Evangelical Covenant (67 percent), and the CRC (80 percent). Even among the Mainline RCA and Methodists, Focus did quite well (66 percent and 55 percent, respectively), falling off sharply only among Presbyterians (39 percent) and Disciples (37 percent), where Dobson has support only among conservatives. Falwell, on the other hand, divides even religious conservatives, gaining approval from only half of the most orthodox. The denominational data show that the Moral Majority had strong backing only from the Assemblies (41 percent) and Southern Baptist pastors (47 percent), and relatively little from other churches, even the Evangelical ones.

To summarize support for the new civic gospel, we computed a score using three items available in all eight surveys: theological preference for free enterprise and proximity to the two Christian Right organizations. To determine whether this measure captures belief elements tapped in only some surveys, we calculated several indices from the items in Table 4.2 available in each study (seven for the Baptists, Presbyterians, and Disciples, and four in the Assemblies, Evangelical Covenant, and Methodist studies). Invariably, the three-item scale correlated very strongly ($r = .83$ or better) with those based on more items, giving us a great deal of confidence in our measure. As the last section of Table 4.2 shows, the new civic gospel is quite appealing to the orthodox, less convincing to the moderately orthodox, and not accepted by the more moderate modernists. The most modernist pastors, naturally, are strongly opposed.

Although this new civic gospel is in many ways an extension of the old Protestant individualist social theology, its tenets clearly suggest a new justification for political action by orthodox Christians. In the following analyses, we find that this new set of ideas is indeed associated with the new wave of conservative activism among some clergy.

## TRADITIONAL MORALITY: THE LINK BETWEEN INDIVIDUALISM AND THE CIVIC GOSPEL

The new orthodox vision for the public role of religion is rooted in a critique of social decay in American society. As the Christian Right's preoccupation with morality suggests, these concerns center on family life, sexuality, and moral relativism. For a fuller assessment of moral traditionalism, we turn to the Wheaton study. We asked the pastors there a variety of items about moral issues, most of them drawn from the moral traditionalism battery in recent American National Election Studies (Conover and Feldman 1986) or from Ronald Inglehart's "Postmaterialism" battery (Barnes and Kaase 1979, 308–342). As Table 4.3 demonstrates, orthodox and modernist clergy diverge widely on such items. While there is a solid consensus (except among the most modernist) that bolstering traditional family structures would ameliorate social problems, that newer lifestyles break down American society, and that moral diversity is not healthy, clergy divide over whether there is only one correct moral philosophy, whether believers should tolerate other moralities, and whether preserving traditional moral standards and maintaining social order are the most important functions of government. An overall index of moral traditionalism shows that orthodox clergy are strong adherents of traditional moral codes and public order—to be preserved by government—while modernists tolerate diversity and, often, actually affirm moral pluralism (or what critics would call ethical relativism). The most modernist clergy are, in fact, quite distinctive in this respect. In any case, few modernists put maintenance of moral order at the top of their expectations for government.

These issues not only divide pastors in Evangelical churches from Mainline ministers but also create tensions within denominations. Although we lacked identical items on traditional morality across all the denominational surveys, we did ask pastors in several churches whether more emphasis should be put on "traditional values." The results are highly consistent with the Wheaton study evidence. In each denomination we found much diversity on moral traditionalism, based on theological differences. For example, in the Christian Reformed Church 60 percent of the most orthodox thought Christians should shun "worldly activities" such as drinking and dancing, compared with fewer than 10 percent in the two modernist categories (who, admittedly, are few in the CRC). Similar figures obtained in the CRC's Mainline cousin, the Reformed Church in America, with merely a difference in the number of ministers in each theological category. Similarly, in both the CRC and the RCA over 90 percent of the most orthodox "strongly" agreed that "when it comes to sexual morality, some things are simply right or wrong, not matters of individual preference." Fewer than 15 percent of the most modernist agreed, with a substantial minority regarding sexual ethics as purely an individual choice. And, although the historic Methodist moralism persists in all theological groups, 62 percent of the most orthodox "strongly" favored more church emphasis on personal morality, compared with only 6 percent of the most modernist. Even in the liberal PCUSA and

Table 4.3
Orthodoxy, Moralism, and Political Tolerance (Percent)

| | Most Orthodox 1 | 2 | 3 | Most Modernist 4 |
|---|---|---|---|---|
| Moral traditionalism* | | | | |
| Emphasis on traditional family, fewer problems | 97 | 90 | 90 | 49 |
| Diverse moralities don't lead to healthy society | 92 | 84 | 66 | 25 |
| New lifestyles are breaking down American society | 91 | 88 | 80 | 34 |
| Setting moral standards top government function | 81 | 73 | 68 | 26 |
| Only one correct moral philosophy in world | 79 | 72 | 49 | 11 |
| Should not tolerate moralities other than our own | 66 | 54 | 28 | 11 |
| Maintaining social order a top government function | 53 | 46 | 23 | 10 |
| Summary index of moral traditionalism* | | | | |
| Very traditionalist | 42 | 22 | 11 | 1 |
| Traditionalist | 27 | 31 | 14 | 2 |
| Moderate | 20 | 24 | 24 | 3 |
| Nontraditionalist | 9 | 18 | 29 | 20 |
| Very nontraditionalist | 2 | 6 | 22 | 74 |
| | 100% | 100% | 100% | 100% |
| Political tolerance for "dangerous groups" in American politics* | | | | |
| High tolerance | 39 | 50 | 52 | 70 |
| Low tolerance | 61 | 50 | 48 | 30 |
| | 100% | 100% | 100% | 100% |

* All data in this table from the clergy in the 1990–91 Wheaton Religious Activist Study.

Disciples of Christ, orthodox ministers are much more committed to traditional moral standards than their modernist colleagues. As Ted Jelen observed in his study of ministers: "Issues of personal behavior, which are central to the politics of evangelicalism, are viewed with tolerance, ambivalence, or as symptoms of more general maladies" by Mainline clergy (1993, 77).

A final aspect of the new civic gospel is a reluctance to allow groups that threaten cherished social values to exercise the full range of civil liberties. In the Wheaton study we used a technique pioneered by Sullivan, Piereson, and Marcus (1982) to tap Americans' political tolerance. After allowing the pastor to name "the most dangerous" political group in America, we asked whether its members should enjoy democratic privileges, such as running for office, holding rallies and meetings in the local community, or teaching in public schools, among others. We summed the six responses and divided the sample into quartiles for presentation. As the last section of Table 4.3 demonstrates, orthodox pastors are most reluctant to admit un-popular and sometimes radical groups to participation in the political process. This reflects, as the orthodox see it, the serious threat such groups pose to social tradition-alism, as well as to traditional religion (Green and Guth 1991a).

To sum up, then: the competing social theologies of contemporary Protestant clergy reveal some very old and some very modern features. Quite clearly, orthodox and modernist clergy have different social and political worldviews. The orthodox still hold to the individualist reformism of revivalism, which stressed individual conversion, self-discipline, and morality. In this view, the church does transform so-ciety, but primarily through saving souls and, to a lesser extent, by creating an atmo-sphere conducive to individual sanctification. Modernists, on the other hand, cling to an updated Progressive Era Social Gospel, shorn of its easy optimism but still full of hope that structural injustices in American society can be rectified by the church, by faithful congregations—and by Christian efforts in the political process. And al-though the contours of the dispute may seem familiar, both social theologies have incorporated new elements. The orthodox are increasingly disturbed both by Amer-ican society's desertion of its religious roots and traditional moral systems and by the accompanying threat to Christian faith itself. They want government to act on those dangers. Modernists not only fail to see such threats but often rejoice in the diversity of American culture. And many have adopted an even larger ideal role for government in rectifying social, economic, and political injustices, often reflecting the more radical insights of liberation theology.

## THE TASK FOR THE CHURCH

Social theology should influence the way pastors envisage the role of the church. In-dividualists, who see salvation in the next life and personal sanctification as the most important aspects of religion, should want the church to focus on evangelism, spreading the gospel to those who have not yet accepted it; communitarians, for whom the essence of religion is the building and fostering of human solidarity, should put higher institutional priorities on those tasks. Roozen, McKinney, and Carroll (1984) see the former tasks characterizing churches with "sanctuary" and "evangelistic" mission orientations, while the latter describe churches with "civic" and "activist" orientations. McKinney and Olson's (n.d.) study of denominational leaders finds a similar division, with Evangelicals occupied with evangelism and church-planting, and Mainline leaders with social and political witness, often in ecumenical venues. Other studies of denominational elites, ranking clergy, and lay leaders have discovered similar variation among Protestants on the role of the church and clergy (Schuller, Strommen, and Brekke 1980).

Even more than these denominational professionals, parish clergy must allocate scarce time and energy among the many tasks performed by their institutions, with important implications for their political activity. Hart Nelsen and Sandra Baxter (1981), for example, found that ministers taking (1) *traditional,* (2) *community problem-solving,* and (3) *counseling* roles differed in their political agendas, preferences, and activities. The first group emphasized evangelism, the second, social witness, and the third, traditional morality. Although ministerial role might be distinguished from attitudes on *church* priorities, we expect that the two concepts should be closely related empirically and exhibit many of the same tendencies. So to gauge ministers' ideas about the church's most critical responsibilities, we asked them to rank ten functions from highest priority to lowest. Some clergy resisted, contending that they simply could not rank the functions: "I and my congregation regard all these ministries as part of a single ministry," objected one Methodist. A Christian Reformed pastor couched his rejection in a culinary metaphor, noting that the ingredients of ministry could not be ranked in importance: "Do you like the beans, tomatoes, spices, or what in a chili recipe?" Nevertheless, most pastors were quite forthcoming about the tasks deserving greatest attention, and some produced detailed and explicit rationales for their choices — even if they thought their church failed to perform those functions adequately.

As we expected, clergy with different theological perspectives had quite dissimilar visions for the church. As Table 4.4 shows, local evangelism was ranked first by the clergy as a whole, but the orthodox gave it highest priority, while modernists were less enthusiastic. National evangelism and world missions are both endorsed by the orthodox but are downrated by modernists. These choices are, of course, consistent with both the beliefs and the social theologies of each group. Evangelical Protestants still maintain extensive local, national, and international organizations designed to convert sinners to the only true faith, while Mainline churches have long since redefined missions away from proselytizing and toward social and economic development. As Presbyterian theologian and historian John M. Mulder puts it, Mainline Protestantism long ago "just reduced its commitment to evangelism," shifting emphasis "away from 'word evangelism'—testifying to your faith—to 'deed evangelism'—the social justice agenda of the church" (quoted in Hessel 1993, 6).

There are fewer differences between groups on charity and counseling, with only a slight tendency for modernists to put a higher priority on both. Charity has

Table 4.4
Pastors' Views on Priorities for the Church

|  | All | Most Orthodox | | Most Modernist | | |
|---|---|---|---|---|---|---|
|  |  | 1 | 2 | 3 | 4 | $r=$[*] |
| Evangelistic priorities |  |  |  |  |  |  |
| Local evangelism | 2.8[†] | 2.0 | 2.3 | 2.8 | 4.3 | .37 |
| National evangelism | 4.0 | 2.5 | 3.1 | 4.0 | 5.8 | .46 |
| World missions | 5.4 | 3.6 | 4.9 | 6.1 | 7.5 | .48 |
| Charitable activities |  |  |  |  |  |  |
| Charity to individuals in need | 4.9 | 5.1 | 5.2 | 4.8 | 4.6 | −.10 |
| Guidance and counseling | 4.8 | 4.8 | 5.2 | 4.7 | 4.4 | −.08 |
| Moral concerns |  |  |  |  |  |  |
| Work for Christian morality in U.S. | 6.0 | 4.5 | 5.9 | 6.8 | 7.2 | .33 |
| Social and political priorities |  |  |  |  |  |  |
| Local social change | 5.5 | 6.5 | 5.9 | 5.1 | 4.0 | −.41 |
| Self-help in local community | 6.2 | 6.8 | 6.5 | 5.8 | 5.2 | −.26 |
| Oppose injustice and oppression | 6.2 | 7.6 | 6.9 | 5.7 | 4.2 | −.45 |
| National social reform | 7.4 | 8.0 | 8.0 | 7.5 | 6.0 | −.32 |

[*] Pearson correlation of item with orthodoxy scale.
[†] Mean scores (1 = highest priority; 10 = lowest priority).

been an integral part of the Christian church since New Testament days. True, a rare conservative may express strong reservations about charity: one Assemblies of God minister complained that "in my forty years of ministry, most we helped were bums or leeches, who felt the church was for helping them even if they had no reason for going to church, but for money for more of the same." But on the whole, helping the poor directly is one of the few priorities shared by orthodox and modernist pastors. Similarly, counseling has become a major feature in modern American church life, although subject to some criticism from both right and left for occupying resources better spent on doctrinal instruction, evangelism, or social reform (Wells 1993; Bellah et al. 1985).

More divisive is "working for Christian moral standards in America," which attracts many of the orthodox but is rejected by modernists who, as we have seen, are not particularly enthusiastic about moral traditionalism. The reverse pattern holds for the social and political priorities. Although these functions are given fairly low ratings by the clergy as a whole, the global figures hide the large gap between modernists and the orthodox. Generally, local activity to achieve social change and assistance to self-help programs are most favorably regarded by all groups, but in every instance modernists put social and political reform much higher on the church's priority list than do the orthodox. When it comes to national social reform campaigns, though, even the modernists have some strong reservations. Indeed, this fact points out an intriguing aspect of the ratings: modernists are more divided on the primary tasks of the church than are the orthodox; they give none of the functions uniformly high ratings.

A summary of pastors' views of church priorities by denomination, religious movement, and eschatology produces results consistent with the findings for orthodoxy. Nevertheless, there are some interesting departures that suggest the continuing influence of historic denominational emphases, the theological movements with which pastors identify, or their eschatological perspective. On all three evangelistic tasks, for example, the Assemblies of God, the Southern Baptists, and the Reformed churches are even more enthusiastic than would be predicted even by their strong theological orthodoxy, while Presbyterians, Methodists, and Covenant clergy are less "evangelistic." Within each denomination, those affiliating with the most conservative internal movement are also more supportive than their orthodoxy scores would suggest, while the most liberal faction shows far less "zeal for missions." On charity and counseling, the Assemblies, Methodist, and Covenant ministers score higher than expected, and the Southern Baptists and Disciples lower. When it comes to social and political activism, the Assemblies and Southern Baptists give these items lower priority than one might predict, while ministers in liberal movements in every denomination are much more enthusiastic.

Morality building presents the most complex picture. Although orthodoxy plays an important role, so do other religious factors. Methodists are much more likely to give this task priority, as are those identifying with the most conservative factions within their churches and, especially, those with a strong premillennial eschatology. Conversely, those placing themselves in liberal movements generally downgrade this function. Thus, although orthodoxy has a powerful influence, denomination, religious movement affiliation, and eschatology also have an impact on priorities. Interestingly, ministers see their congregations agreeing with them on priorities, but the orthodox ministers rate evangelism higher than they think their congregations do, while modernists rank social and political action higher than they think their congregations would.

To summarize these preferences and calculate scores for later exploration, we used factor analysis to identify the structure of clerical attitudes toward church functions. The most economical and pleasing solution produced three factors, one each for evangelism, political, and charity and counseling priorities. The morality item did not fit cleanly with any factor, although it loaded modestly on the evangelism factor. Because of its theoretical importance and for purposes of presentation and analysis in the following, we have kept it separate.

## THE IMPACT OF ACTIVISM ON THE CHURCH

Ministers' sentiments about social and political action are also influenced by perceptions of how such activities affect the church. Evangelism, if successful, is institution building, bringing in new members, finances, and other resources. Social and

political activism, on the other hand, poses risks: diversion of institutional resources, conflict within the congregation, loss of members, and a host of other woes
(perhaps even a Federal Election Commission or Internal Revenue Service investigation) that threaten organizational health. As one dissident Disciples conservative
argued, "To confuse religion with Christianity, politics for theology, social action
for evangelism empties the Mainline churches."

We also asked ministers in several denominations slightly different questions
about whether political activism hurts churches. As Table 4.5 shows, once again
theological conservatives tend to perceive dangers: a solid majority of the most orthodox agree that political activism hurts churches, while an overwhelming majority of modernists disagree. A look at the same responses by theological movement
and eschatology shows even sharper divisions: fundamentalists and strong premillennialists are even more likely to see danger to churches from political involvement, while liberals and those scoring low on conservative eschatology are convinced that activism does not create problems for the church (data not shown).

As a final assessment of ministers' views, we asked whether their denomination should "devote more energy and resources to vital social and political issues."
As the final section of Table 4.5 shows, once again modernist clergy lean toward an
(even more) active political role for their denomination. Interestingly, however, the
pattern differs from the usual one, in that the most orthodox are not the least likely
to approve activism; that role falls to the moderately orthodox. The complexity of
attitudes results in part from some clear denominational differences: many generally orthodox Southern Baptists agree that their denomination should be more active (40 percent), compared with Covenant pastors (26 percent), Methodists (32
percent), Presbyterians (36 percent), and Disciples (43 percent). Even so, within

Table 4.5
Pastors' Views on Denominational and Church Activism (Percent)

|  | All | Most Orthodox 1 | 2 | 3 | Most Modernist 4 | r=* |
|---|---|---|---|---|---|---|
| Political activism is bad for churches |  |  |  |  |  |  |
| Agree | 44 | 55 | 53 | 42 | 21 | .40 |
| Not sure | 20 | 25 | 25 | 19 | 11 |  |
| Disagree | 36 | 20 | 22 | 39 | 69 |  |
|  | 100% | 100% | 100% | 100% | 100% |  |
| Need more denominational activism on vital social and political issues |  |  |  |  |  |  |
| Agree | 35 | 28 | 20 | 35 | 53 | −.27 |
| Not sure | 15 | 17 | 19 | 13 | 11 |  |
| Disagree | 50 | 55 | 61 | 52 | 36 |  |
|  | 100% | 100% | 100% | 100% | 100% |  |

*Pearson correlation between responses and full orthodoxy scale.

each denomination, the most modernist clergy were always most enthusiastic about more political action, but divisions are widest among Mainline pastors, where modernists urge more involvement and the orthodox resist.

At least some of the orthodox skepticism may not be about activism itself but rather the "liberal" version practiced by national church agencies, a fact noted by more than a few Methodist, Presbyterian, and Disciples conservatives. An indirect test of this hypothesis is made possible by comparing data from the 1988 and 1992 Southern Baptist surveys. In 1988 the SBC resembled Mainline denominations: modernists preferred more activism than did the orthodox. By 1992, however, as victorious conservatives tightened their grip on SBC social agencies, moving them into alliance with the Christian Right, the situation reversed: 61 percent of the most orthodox Baptist ministers favored more activism, but only 18 percent of the most modernist did. This pattern repeated itself in 1996. Clearly, orthodox theology does not preclude some kind of denominational "political witness."

Like issues of social theology, church priorities create internal divisions, which are reflected in ministers' assessments of national church agencies, the many special interest caucuses that exist in all denominations, and the various interdenominational organizations such as the National Council of Churches and the National Association of Evangelicals, which speak for many of these churches in Washington, D.C. In every denomination but one, statistical analysis of ministers' evaluations of denominational institutions reveals two dimensions: the first based on evangelism and the other on social action. As we might expect, orthodox and individualist clergy give high marks to agencies focused on evangelism, feel closer to special interest groups devoted to "the old-time religion," and laud the National Association of Evangelicals (even if their denomination is part of the liberal National Council), while modernist and communitarian ministers applaud the denominational social agencies and the various liberal caucuses that support their work. They also feel close to the National Council of Churches, the chief national vehicle for liberal church activism. (The one exception to all these generalizations is the Assemblies of God, where there is no disagreement on social action because the clergy is so focused on evangelism.)

Useful illustrations of these internal patterns can be found in the Southern Baptist Convention and the United Methodist Church, the nation's two largest Protestant communions. Despite the SBC's general theological conservatism, there are still distinct differences in evaluation of denominational agencies. Well over 90 percent of the most orthodox Baptists give high marks to the Foreign Mission Board, compared with about half of the most modernist, while the Baptist Joint Committee, the SBC's (former) Washington representative on church-state issues, was approved by only 31 percent of the orthodox but by 90 percent of modernists. The Methodist situation is even clearer: three-quarters of the most orthodox feel close to "Good News," the evangelical caucus, compared with only one-tenth of the most modernist, while ratings for the Methodist Federation for Social Action are almost reversed, with three-fifths of the most modernist approving but only one-fifth of the most orthodox. Clearly the theology and social theology of clergy affect not only their own activity but their support for denominational and interdenominational social and political work as well.

Thus, we find that the theological orientations of clergy are reflected in their conceptions of the most important roles for the church. Generally, the most orthodox clergy emphasize evangelism, helping those in need, and fostering traditional moral standards in their communities. Liberal clergy are more divided on the functions of the church, sharing no clear consensus on "first things." Nevertheless, modernist clergy are much more inclined to see a part for the church in social and political reform activity and may, indeed, envision a personal role for themselves as instruments of such reform.

## CONCLUSIONS

Theology obviously has an enormous impact on social theology and church priorities as seen by clergy. What other factors influence these perspectives? To discover this, we ran several multiple regressions designed to explain the origins of each set of attitudes. This procedure determines the independent impact of each variable, holding constant the influence of other factors. We looked first at the origins of our individualism/communitarianism and civic gospel measures, both important influences on ministerial politics. As Table 4.6 illustrates, individualism and adherence to the civic gospel are both influenced most strongly by theological variables. Orthodoxy has the greatest impact: orthodox clergy are individualists and proponents of the civic gospel, while modernists are communitarian and reject the civic gospel. Our other theological measures also have substantial impact, with religious movement identification having more influence on individualism, and premillennialism on the civic gospel.

In both instances, a pastor's denomination adds little to the explanation. Once all other factors are accounted for, Assemblies and Christian Reformed ministers are slightly more communitarian than their theology would predict, while Methodists and Presbyterians are slightly more individualist. Similarly, Assemblies and Evangelical Covenant pastors are slightly cooler toward the civic gospel than expected, while Baptist, Christian Reformed, Methodist, and Disciples pastors are somewhat more favorable. Demographic traits have even less independent impact, although usually in the predicted direction. Southerners, older ministers, males, and those with less education are slightly higher on both individualism and the civic gospel. In substantive terms, however, a minister's theology matters most: the three theological measures alone explain 51 percent of the variance in individualism and 55 percent of that for the civic gospel (compared with 53 and 57 percent, respectively, in the full models in Table 4.6).

Do the same variables—with the addition of individualism and the civic gospel—help us understand church priorities? As Table 4.7 shows, these factors have

Table 4.6
Explaining Social Theologies: Regression Analysis

|  | Individualism | Civic Gospel |
|---|---|---|
|  | b | b |
| Religious variables |  |  |
| Christian orthodoxy | .50** | .50** |
| Conservative eschatology | .13** | .18** |
| Fundamentalist movement ID | .19** | .15** |
| Denominational effects |  |  |
| AG | −.06* | −.04* |
| SBC | .02 | .09** |
| ECC | −.02 | −.03 |
| CRC | −.09** | .03* |
| RCA | † | † |
| UMC | .06** | .05* |
| PRES | .04* | .00 |
| DOC | .00 | .06** |
| Demography |  |  |
| Born in South | .04* | .03* |
| Age | .06** | .04* |
| Gender (male) | .04** | .03* |
| Liberal education | −.06** | −.06** |
| Adjusted $R^2$ | .53 | .57 |

$^*p<.05; ^{**}p<.001.$
† Suppressed reference category.

somewhat varying impacts on ministers' assessments of missions, political and social action, and working for higher moral standards in America. Preferences for evangelism are predicted by orthodoxy, by identification with a fundamentalist movement, and by individualism. On balance Southern Baptists, not surprisingly, are somewhat more committed to missions than other variables would predict, while Methodists and Presbyterians are less so. Southerners and males are also slightly more committed to mission activities. Almost a mirror image appears on political and social priorities. Orthodoxy, premillennial theology, and fundamentalist identification are negative influences on political priorities, while those at the other end of these scales are more likely to put a premium on political witness, as are Methodists and Presbyterians. When all else is accounted for, older clergy, women, and those with a liberal education score higher on this scale as well.

The morality item produces a somewhat different pattern, one that confirms many conclusions reached earlier about the critical role of moral traditionalism in the contemporary Christian Right movement. Although theology retains some influence, it is social theology, especially the civic gospel, that best predicts emphasis

Table 4.7
Explaining Church Priorities: Regression Analysis

|  | Missions | Politics | Morality |
|---|---|---|---|
| Religious variables |  |  |  |
| Christian orthodoxy | .30** | −.21** | .08* |
| Premillennial eschatology | .08** | −.05* | .06* |
| Religious movement ID | .17** | −.17** | .03 |
| Social theology |  |  |  |
| Individualism | .15** | −.14** | .10** |
| Civic gospel | .04 | −.07* | .20** |
| Denomination |  |  |  |
| Assemblies of God | .03 | .02 | .00 |
| Southern Baptist | .06* | −.03 | −.07* |
| Evangelical Covenant | † | † | † |
| United Methodist | −.07** | .10** | .09** |
| Presbyterian | −.05* | .12** | −.08** |
| Disciples of Christ | .03 | .05 | −.10** |
| Demographic variables |  |  |  |
| South | .05* | .01 | .01 |
| Age | −.02 | .11** | .16** |
| Male | .07** | −.04* | .01 |
| Liberal education | −.01 | .08* | −.03 |
| Adjusted $R^2$ | .38 | .30 | .26 |

*$p<.05$; **$p<.001$.
†Suppressed reference category.

on building and defending national moral standards. Denomination bears some connection to responses, with Southern Baptists less committed to this task than one might expect—perhaps reflecting their traditional separationism—but with pastors in all three Mainline churches in the table considerably less likely to emphasize morality building than their other traits and beliefs would predict. Consistent with earlier studies, older clergy are also, on balance, more likely to stress morality.

Thus, we have shown that the modern versions of the historic alternative Protestant social theologies are important influences over clergy thinking about their social and political role. As a Reformed Church minister took pains to remind us, "Politics and theology go hand in hand." As we shall see, although theology plays a major role, these social theologies and priorities also help shape the clergy's public agenda, their political attitudes and attachments, and their conception and execution of the proper role of clergy in the political process. It is to the political agenda of ministers that we turn next.

# 5
# The Issue Agendas
# of Protestant Clergy

Over the course of American history, clergy have addressed an enormous range of political issues. Nevertheless, the growth of the two-party system among American Protestants led to what might be characterized as "partial issue agendas," in which the private or Evangelical party focused on one set of issues, and the public or Mainline party addressed quite different concerns. Thus, the two contestants have often resembled the proverbial battleships in the night, passing without any real engagement. And yet, this situation may be changing as orthodox Protestants mobilize for political battle and modernists extend their concerns to issues previously ignored—or, perhaps, arm for counterattack. With changes in agendas on both sides, the argument goes, confrontation and religious combat are inevitable, triggering a culture war (Hunter 1991).

In this chapter we address the contemporary issue agendas of orthodox and modernist pastors, the *moral reform* and *social justice* agendas, respectively. We first review some of the ways these agendas may be changing, according to close observers of Protestant churches. Then we turn to the data and discover that traditional preoccupations of both private and public parties remain largely intact, albeit with a few common concerns and some modifications to traditional ones. We then analyze the theological sources of each agenda, considering the impact of theology, denomination, eschatology, and religious movement. Finally, we present the results of a broader multivariate analysis which help us understand the factors that influence commitment to these historic religious agendas.

## A BROADENING OF AGENDAS?

Many analysts have argued that the social justice and moral reform agendas are partial ones, each advanced by one wing of Protestantism and ignored by the other. Ac-

78

cording to this perspective, modernists speak on social justice and remain silent on moral reform, while the orthodox reverse the pattern. Although the two-agendas thesis is supported by the literature on clerical politics of the 1960s and 1970s, one suspects that the situation had changed by the 1990s. Observers point to several possible modifications: (1) that orthodox Protestants have largely given up the classic moral reform agenda, in an accommodation with the culture, and are instead focusing on a new but narrower set of moral concerns; (2) that the Christian Right has shifted conservative Protestant concerns to a broader range of issues, including economic and foreign policy issues; (3) that liberal Protestant clergy today have a more truncated "real" agenda than formal resolutions from church bodies might suggest; and (4) that Christian Right assertiveness has intensified Mainline concern with moral issues, in a natural reaction against Evangelical "intolerance." We will consider each argument briefly.

First, a few observers argue that the old moral reform agenda no longer characterizes either the rhetoric or the activity of Evangelical clergy. In 1987 Benton Johnson replicated his pathbreaking 1962 study of Oregon fundamentalist clergy and found that few preached on alcohol and drug abuse, gambling, divorce, or the other moral issues that had preoccupied them twenty-five years earlier. Rather, he argued, they now focused almost entirely on education and sexuality issues, a much more truncated agenda. Liberal clergy, however, had changed very little in their assessment of the vital issues confronting society. Thus, Johnson saw the moral reform agenda shrinking but the social justice agenda remaining intact (reported in Marty 1997).

A very different contention is that the Christian Right has actually broadened the orthodox agenda but with issues other than moral ones. Jerry Falwell, Pat Robertson, Ralph Reed, and many others have tried to teach their followers that limited government, low taxes, fiscal conservatism, free enterprise, and a vigorous defense and foreign policy stance are all Christian political concerns (Himmelstein 1990; Reed 1996). Scholars have generally counted this effort a failure (Wilcox 1996), arguing that economic issues and foreign policy do not stir Evangelical Protestants as much as abortion, sex education, or gay rights. Activist Lynn Buzzard has contended, however, that "from the evangelical side . . . that moral sweep has also become broader to include within its gambit questions that were previously deemed only political in nature" (1989, 141).

Whatever the changes in the moral reform agenda, others may have occurred in the social justice agenda. Even if modernist clergy were outspoken on a broad agenda in the 1960s, a more conservative national mood and resistance from conservative laity may have limited the breadth of their concerns three decades later. Friendly and critical observers alike doubt that the sweeping agenda of Mainline headquarters and the National Council of Churches is really shared by parish clergy. The annual meetings of Mainline Protestant churches typically pass resolutions on almost any political issue capturing national attention (and many that don't), but local pastors often ignore their denominations' social action agencies, showing little interest in most issues. While some parts of the social justice agenda may be addressed by local clergy, much is probably neglected. Thus, although the social justice agenda may appear quite comprehensive at first glance, among parish clergy in the 1990s it may be more limited.

Finally, if many Mainline clergy neglect social justice issues, they are even more likely to ignore moral issues, despite official church positions. For example, Mainline denominations invariably endorse pro-choice policies, but local pastors may not address abortion. And although these same church bodies support civil rights for gays and lesbians, many clergy avoid participation in local gay rights debates. However, pressure from the Christian Right may ultimately lead to counter-mobilization on these issues. Indeed, the newspapers of the 1990s abound with reports of new national clergy alliances formed to combat political encroachments of conservative Christians, whether in school board elections, gay rights referenda, or textbook controversies. Thus, for several reasons, the real agenda of contemporary Protestant clergy is not altogether clear.

## NATIONAL PROBLEMS

What issues do, in fact, concern Protestant clergy? One way of answering this question is to ask about their perceptions of major national problems. Over the years, social scientists have found that citizens' views of the most important problems facing the country are quite fluid and change with events, the preoccupations of elites, and coverage by the media (Smith 1980). And although there are natural variations in the problems Americans see as most pressing, there is usually some consensus among different groups at any time. Scholars have noted that definition of important problems may have an impact on citizens' political decisions, ranging from choice of candidate to direct involvement in the political process (Iyengar and Kinder 1987).

Clergy, however, may well have more stable perceptions of national needs than most citizens, given their highly constrained belief systems shaped by their theological orientation and social theologies. As Shanto Iyengar (1991) has shown, how the media frames issues in an individualist or structural mode influences the way citizens react to a problem. In analogous fashion, Evangelical and Mainline ministers might be alert to different national problems, reacting on the basis of the beliefs most salient to them (Zaller 1992). Given the individualist social theology of orthodox clergy, they should perceive spiritual and moral problems as salient, perhaps with the addition of public order concerns (cf. Jelen 1993). On the other side, modernist and communitarian clergy should see more structural policy concerns, such as economic justice, social welfare, and, perhaps, issues of war and peace. Protestant clergy live in the same political world, but do they see the same political world?

To investigate this question, we asked ministers in six denominations to name "the two or three biggest problems facing the U.S. today." We classified their first

Table 5.1
Most Important National Problem by Denomination and Orthodoxy
(Percent Naming Each Type)

| | AG | SBC | ECC | UMC | PRES | DOC |
|---|---|---|---|---|---|---|
| Problem type | | | | | | |
| Spiritual and moral | 47 | 36 | 51 | 24 | 19 | 18 |
| Public order | 29 | 15 | 12 | 31 | 17 | 17 |
| Abortion | 12 | 14 | 9 | 5 | 3 | 1 |
| Political process | 1 | 2 | 4 | 1 | 5 | 5 |
| Environmental | 0 | 1 | 0 | 4 | 4 | 3 |
| Defense, foreign policy | 1 | 3 | 1 | 7 | 12 | 12 |
| Economic/social welfare | 10 | 29 | 23 | 28 | 40 | 44 |
| | 100% | 100% | 100% | 100% | 100% | 100% |

| | Most Orthodox 1 | 2 | 3 | Most Modernist 4 |
|---|---|---|---|---|
| Problem type | | | | |
| Spiritual and moral | 47 | 40 | 23 | 14 |
| Public order | 21 | 19 | 23 | 18 |
| Abortion | 15 | 9 | 2 | 1 |
| Political process | 2 | 3 | 3 | 5 |
| Environmental | 0 | 1 | 2 | 5 |
| Defense, foreign policy | 1 | 2 | 8 | 14 |
| Economic/social welfare | 14 | 26 | 39 | 43 |
| | 100% | 100% | 100% | 100% |

responses and report the results in Table 5.1. Ministers perceive very different issues confronting the country, depending on their denominational affiliation. Assemblies of God pastors are strongly convinced that the major problems are spiritual and moral, such as loss of faith or proliferation of pornography, followed by public order questions, especially crime, while a significant minority puts abortion at the top of the list. Only a handful think of economic and social welfare issues as most important. Southern Baptists and Evangelical Covenant ministers are also very concerned with spiritual and moral issues, but also show somewhat more interest in economics and somewhat less in public order issues. Methodists put even greater stress on economics but also on public order questions (they list both crime and civil rights problems). The Presbyterians and Disciples of Christ, on the other hand, have a plurality of clergy concerned with economic matters, as well as the only significant number listing military and foreign policy. In stark contrast with Evangelicals, few Mainline ministers name spiritual and moral problems, and virtually none mention abortion.

Not surprisingly, as the second part of Table 5.1 shows, ministers' perceptions are deeply influenced by theology. Orthodox clergy see spiritual and moral problems, with substantial attention to public order and abortion. Modernist clergy are much more preoccupied with economic and social welfare issues, but they add various other concerns, such as foreign policy or the environment. Thus, each group of clergy produces an assessment fundamentally in accord with their perception of the basic problems of human existence. For the orthodox, it is alienation from God, sinful behavior in individual lives, and the adverse consequences resulting from these conditions. All comport with individualist social theology and the new civic gospel. For modernists, with their communitarian outlook, problems are essentially those of human community and the need to build a just society, pointing naturally to issues of human welfare, international peace, and, increasingly, the natural environment.


## THE ISSUE AGENDA OF PROTESTANT CLERGY: CUE-GIVING PRIORITIES

Do these perceptions of national problems influence the "active agendas" of the clergy? Do ministers address policy issues growing out of their sense of national priorities and needs? For a more specific picture of how ministers allocate their energies among issues, we asked how frequently they addressed twenty issues: "very often," "often," "seldom," or "never." To avoid biasing results by including issues only from the agenda of particular denominations or theological groups, a defect of some early studies, our checklist was drawn from among those emphasized by either Mainline or Christian Right lobbyists during the 1980s.

For presentation purposes in Table 5.2, we have assigned the issues to the moral reform and social justice agendas. Not only does this division comport with the historic concerns of the "private" and "public" parties, but it replicates the work of other researchers: very similar categories have been used by Hofrenning (1995) to describe religious lobbying agendas in Washington, and by Beatty and Walter (1989) in analyzing clergy cue-giving. Besides its historical and comparative merit, these categories have empirical warrant as well, deriving from a factor analysis (see later discussion). As we shall show, clergy of different denominations and competing theological camps have clear preferences for one or the other agenda.

First, pastoral agendas vary distinctly by denomination. Pastors from the Evangelical tradition devote a good bit more attention to the moral reform agenda. Although family issues are a central theme of Christian Right rhetoric and are almost universally addressed by conservative pastors, they are also favorites of Mainline clergy. As Hofrenning notes, concern with these issues has become pervasive in the American religious community (1995, 81). Alcohol and drug abuse also draw greatest attention from the Assemblies and Southern Baptists but are not ignored by Mainline churches, either. From this point in the table, however, the attention of Mainline clergy declines. Abortion, not surprisingly, receives almost universal interest from the Assemblies and solid involvement by other Evangelicals, but among Mainline pastors only about half the RCA and UMC clergy speak on abortion, and this drops to one-third of the Presbyterians and Disciples. The same pattern reappears on pornography, which has agitated both conservative clergy and many feminists (Downs 1989) but apparently not the liberal Protestant clergy.

Another "hot-button" issue of the 1990s, gay rights, receives somewhat less attention than other elements of "pelvic politics," involving two-thirds of the Assemblies clergy but only minorities in the other Evangelical churches. Despite (or perhaps because of) the gay issues agitating Mainline churches, few ministers there report personal activity. On the other hand, some moral issues fail to mobilize most Evangelicals. School prayer evokes majority interest only among the Assemblies, although a plurality of Southern Baptists also report fairly frequent involvement. Education follows about the same pattern. Interest in Israel and Middle East policy is fairly even in all denominations, except for the Assemblies' special interest, presumably reflecting their dispensationalism. Gambling laws and the death penalty

Table 5.2
Issue Agendas of Protestant Clergy by Denomination
(Addressed "Very Often" or "Often," Percent)

|  | AG | SBC | ECC | CRC | RCA | UMC | PRES | DOC |
|---|---|---|---|---|---|---|---|---|
| Moral reform agenda |  |  |  |  |  |  |  |  |
| Family issues | 91 | 92 | 85 | 79 | 74 | 82 | 82 | 83 |
| Alcohol and drug abuse | 91 | 86 | 68 | 76 | 74 | 84 | 73 | 78 |
| Abortion | 89 | 72 | 60 | 81 | 52 | 53 | 36 | 29 |
| Pornography | 89 | 74 | 54 | 59 | 43 | 50 | 30 | 34 |
| Gay rights, homosexuality | 67 | 46 | 39 | 17 | 20 | 34 | 19 | 19 |
| School prayer | 60 | 49 | 33 | 09 | 20 | 35 | 18 | 22 |
| Education issues | 57 | 48 | 31 | 73 | 25 | 37 | 40 | 39 |
| Israel, Middle East policy | 53 | 28 | 24 | 15 | 22 | 25 | 27 | 25 |
| Gambling laws | 44 | 56 | 31 | 21 | 22 | 45 | 15 | 19 |
| Death penalty | 38 | 36 | 15 | 16 | 21 | 34 | 22 | 26 |
| *Mean for "moral issues"* | *67* | *58* | *44* | *43* | *36* | *48* | *36* | *37* |
| Social justice agenda |  |  |  |  |  |  |  |  |
| Hunger and poverty | 61 | 70 | 70 | 82 | 80 | 89 | 87 | 90 |
| Civil rights | 33 | 35 | 45 | 50 | 53 | 66 | 65 | 70 |
| Environment | 25 | 26 | 34 | 51 | 54 | 67 | 61 | 64 |
| Defense spending, military | 17 | 23 | 13 | 26 | 40 | 44 | 50 | 55 |
| Economics, jobs | 28 | 27 | 39 | 35 | 34 | 56 | 54 | 55 |
| ERA, women's issues | 21 | 22 | 28 | 22 | 34 | 44 | 42 | 50 |
| South Africa and apartheid | 12 | 09 | 12 | 34 | 39 | 41 | 40 | 42 |
| Budget deficits | 26 | 22 | 26 | 16 | 21 | 35 | 33 | 38 |
| Relations with USSR | 22 | 15 | 22 | 13 | 23 | 32 | 34 | 36 |
| Latin America | 11 | 07 | 08 | 15 | 21 | 25 | 29 | 26 |
| *Mean for "social justice issues"* | *25* | *25* | *29* | *33* | *38* | *49* | *49* | *52* |

are of special interest to the Assemblies and Baptists, both with historic interests in personal morality.

Although the issue agendas seem to be shaped by theology (see later discussion), there are distinct reminders of historic denominational traditions or preoccupations. Methodists are far more involved in moral issues than we might expect, given their theology, no doubt reflecting historic Methodist preoccupation with both individual "sanctification" and "social holiness." Something similar may be said of Southern Baptist concerns with alcohol, gambling, and other moral issues. And Christian Reformed clergy seldom speak on school prayer—the denomination officially encourages members to patronize Christian schools—but are intensely interested in education policy and, presumably, its impact on parochial institutions.

Nevertheless, when we calculate the mean number of issues that ministers addressed "often" or "very often," most of the special denominational preferences disappear and something closer to the usual monotonic relationship between denomination and political variables reappears. Assemblies pastors addressed 67 percent of moral reform issues frequently, with this proportion declining somewhat for other Evangelical pastors: Southern Baptists (58 percent), ECC (44 percent), and CRC (43 percent). Indeed, ECC and CRC ministers are actually surpassed by the Methodists (48 percent), but clergy from the other three Mainline churches address moral issues at only about one-half the rate of the Assemblies. As we shall see, lack of activity is not always due to the absence of strong personal feelings on these issues.

The social justice agenda presents a mirror image of the moral reform agenda. Here Mainline pastors excel. Hunger and poverty are the most popular, but these also receive much attention from Evangelicals. No doubt the orthodox version emphasizes Christian charity and individual responsibility for helping the needy, while modernists may well stress structural impediments to food and justice for the poor, but these issues do present some degree of commonality between the two Protestant parties. Beyond this point in the table, however, most Evangelicals ignore the social justice agenda, whether on civil rights, the environment, military spending, employment, or women's issues. Indeed, with the important exception of the environment, other social justice issues are addressed frequently by only about half the Mainline clergy, even though many of these issues were topics of great religious agitation in Washington, D.C., during the period of our survey, such as the struggle against apartheid, cutting the defense budget, achieving better relations with the former USSR, and changing American policy toward Central and South America.

On the social justice agenda, too, we find continuing denominational interests: the Disciples' high score on civil rights; Methodist interest in the environment; and the two Reformed Churches' strong concern for South Africa, reflecting common Calvinist affiliations with religious groups on both sides of the apartheid struggle. Such evidence suggests that more than Christian orthodoxy may be at work in producing these agendas. Nevertheless, we find the expected pattern of overall activity on social justice issues: the average activity score rises from a low of 25 percent among the Assemblies pastors to a high of 52 percent among the Disciples.

Comparing the averages for the moral reform and social justice agendas produces some interesting insights: first, the "highs" for most Evangelical denominations on the moral reform agenda tend to exceed those for the Mainline churches on the social justice agenda; second, this tendency is offset somewhat by the tendency for Mainline "lows" on moral issues to be higher than the comparable "lows" among Evangelicals on social justice questions. Both results probably reflect the presence of strong conservative minorities in the "liberal" Mainline denominations, whereas the Evangelical churches have only a handful of liberal clergy. Another list of issues might have produced somewhat different averages. Still, it is instructive that on several major items of the conservative agenda, clergy from the two largest Evangelical churches are quite vocal, while Mainline churches seldom produce a majority of activists on any social justice issue, with the exception of consensus questions such as hunger, which involve most conservative pastors as well.

As the pattern of denominational activity suggests, theological orthodoxy also provides a remarkably clear guide to political agendas. Table 5.3 reports the percentages of ministers in the four orthodoxy categories who address various issues with some frequency. For almost all items on both agendas, orthodoxy shows the expected connection to agenda. On all but three of the moral agenda issues—gay rights, Middle East policy, and the death penalty—involvement drops monotonically as we move from the most orthodox to the most modernist clergy. On those three issues, the pattern is slightly different, with one or both of the intermediate categories falling below the level of the most modernist ministers. These issues represent the few cases where activist orthodox ministers and activist modernists actually confront each other on opposite sides of the same issues; even here, however, it is an uneven battle, with the orthodox outnumbering the modernists. Overall, the difference on the typical moral issue between orthodox and modernist clergy is quite wide: among the most orthodox, 63 percent of the clergy address the "average" moral issue, while only 35 percent of the most modernist do.

The social justice agenda reveals the opposite pattern from the moral reform agenda, with attention rising as we move from the most orthodox category toward the most modernist clergy. Note that on most social justice issues, the most orthodox and orthodox are usually quite similar in their very modest attention, while the proportions jump considerably in the modernist category, and then once again in the most modernist group. The same pattern appears in the mean scores for the social justice agenda, with low activity in the two orthodox categories, rising substantially among the modernist, and again among the most modernist. We see, then, the considerable asymmetry in attention: very few theologically conservative clergy focus much on the issues that most concern their modernist colleagues—except for the issues of hunger and poverty. Thus, the evidence is clear: the orthodox and modernists still have very different political agendas.

Has the frequency with which clergy address issues changed over time (Marty 1997)? We can trace agenda changes in one denomination, the Southern Baptist Convention. In 1984, 1988, 1992, and 1996, we asked about the same battery of issues presented in the preceding two tables. As we might expect, there was considerable continuity in the concerns of Baptist clergy, with the moral agenda dominating the discourse of most pastors, except for a "moderate" minority attuned to social justice concerns. Still, some changes did reflect the natural flux of the national political agenda and, perhaps, consciousness-raising by the Christian Right. Economic issues rose to attention in 1992, while concern with Latin American and defense policies fell, reflecting the economic policy debates during the 1992 campaign and the demise of the Sandinista and Soviet regimes. More important, however, was the significant rise in concern over most moral questions, especially abortion, pornography, gay rights, school prayer, and education—all of which peaked in 1992 and remained at a high plateau in 1996. As we would expect, these increases were marked among the most orthodox. Modernists, on the other hand, were more concerned

Table 5.3
Issue Agendas of Protestant Clergy by Orthodoxy
(Addressed "Very Often" or "Often," Percent)

|  | Most Orthodox | | | Most Modernist |
| --- | --- | --- | --- | --- |
|  | 1 | 2 | 3 | 4 |
| **Moral reform agenda** | | | | |
| Family issues | 89 | 84 | 81 | 79 |
| Alcohol and drug abuse issues | 87 | 79 | 73 | 73 |
| Abortion | 85 | 71 | 43 | 28 |
| Pornography | 84 | 63 | 39 | 21 |
| Gay rights, homosexuality | 57 | 30 | 14 | 23 |
| Education issues | 56 | 47 | 36 | 31 |
| School prayer | 54 | 28 | 18 | 17 |
| Gambling laws | 47 | 32 | 24 | 20 |
| Israel, Middle East policy | 40 | 21 | 20 | 28 |
| Death penalty | 35 | 20 | 17 | 30 |
| *Mean for "moral issues"* | *63* | *47* | *36* | *35* |
| **Social justice agenda** | | | | |
| Hunger and poverty | 65 | 76 | 85 | 93 |
| Civil rights | 31 | 44 | 61 | 78 |
| Environment | 27 | 40 | 59 | 73 |
| Defense spending, military | 18 | 19 | 40 | 63 |
| ERA, women's issues | 19 | 21 | 36 | 61 |
| Economics, jobs | 29 | 34 | 46 | 60 |
| South Africa and apartheid | 12 | 21 | 34 | 52 |
| Relations with USSR | 19 | 16 | 26 | 41 |
| Budget deficits | 23 | 22 | 26 | 38 |
| Latin America | 9 | 10 | 19 | 37 |
| *Mean for "social justice issues"* | *25* | *29* | *43* | *59* |

with the economy and the environment but became less vocal on moral questions. Thus, the data from the SBC demonstrate that Christian Right efforts to encourage clerical agenda setting probably bore fruit (data not shown).

The structure of clerical agendas is apparent not only from their reports about the issues they address but also from the rationales provided for involvement. The moral reform agenda is not just a statistical production; it also represents those issues that orthodox pastors regard as legitimate targets of activity:

The key is whether it is a moral issue or not. (Assemblies of God)

Social issues are appropriate subjects for sermons, but political issues have no place in the pulpit. (Southern Baptist)

With 180 babies being aborted every hour, alcoholism, drug abuse, divorce, homosexuality, and crime increasing, the pastors and the churches must take a stand on these issues. (Southern Baptist)

I believe in speaking out strongly on political issues that are moral issues against God's teaching such as gay rights and abortion, but not to speak on governmental issues. (Southern Baptist)

I deal very practically with these moral issues in sermons, including a series on what I termed "America's Deadly Sins." (Christian Reformed)

I make a distinction between political and moral items even though some moral items are also political. I would approve a sermon on an issue like abortion, which I consider moral (i.e., Christian ethics and understanding apply). I would strongly disapprove of a sermon on the arms race, South Africa, though illustrations might come from these areas. The pulpit is for the exposition of the Bible, not other agendas. (conservative Presbyterian)

If a question is social but clearly addressed in the Bible, I will preach on it. My preaching must be first and foremost an exposition of Scripture with application to today. I will not, however, preach a sermon oriented topically on a political/social issue which is not clear in the Bible. I believe that homosexuality and abortion are clearly against God's word. Political issues such as contra support should be left to Congress. (conservative Presbyterian)

So many political and social actions have moral overtones. These I get involved in. Issues like abortion, homosexuality, gambling, . . . liquor sales, paramutual betting, bingo, and so on. When we have a clear word from God and go against that word as individuals or as a nation, we all suffer the consequences. (Southern Baptist)

Thus, as Robert Wuthnow (1983) observed over a decade ago, the politicization of conservative Protestantism has come in part from the growing perception that moral issues have entered the realm of political contest. Not all political issues, in the eyes of these pastors, necessarily have moral components. Unlike their conservative counterparts, however, modernist clergy have a strong tendency to reject any distinction between moral and political issues. When we incorporated this distinction in a battery of questions for pastors in the Assemblies, Covenant, and Methodist churches, orthodox clergy accepted the difference between "moral" and "political" without dissent, but liberal clergy did not. "I find it hard to make a clear distinction between moral and political," one Methodist pastor objected, speaking for many Mainline colleagues, for whom all issues have essential religious and moral elements. One moderate Southern Baptist offered an explanation for this distinction among conservative clergy, noting that some pastors argue "that is a political issue, not a moral one when they favor non-involvement or the opposing position." He rejected that distinction, concluding that "the Lordship of Christ makes all political issues moral issues" (Parham 1996, 3).

## RELIGIOUS VARIABLES AND ISSUE AGENDAS

Theological perspectives obviously influence agendas. What is the relative importance of orthodoxy, denomination, religious movement, and eschatology in determining the clerical agenda? We have some earlier evidence on these issues and a growing debate over the current situation. Beatty and Walter (1989) claimed that in producing clerical agendas, at least, denomination is more powerful than theology. Others, such as Wuthnow (1988), have made a competing argument, emphasizing the fading impact of denomination and the growing role of theologically based moral communities in choosing the issues to be addressed by contemporary Christians. Whether eschatology and theological movement affiliations have an effect is less clear, although they should not rival the influence of orthodoxy or denomination, except on a few issues.

To sort out these claims and summarize our findings, we conducted a multiple classification analysis (MCA) of all the agenda items, with the religious measures as independent variables. MCA allows us to look at the effect that each independent variable has on an agenda item, while holding the others constant; it also permits us to identify the particular groups that contribute power to the analysis. Thus, for example, we can gauge the overall impact of denomination on clerical attention to abortion, while holding constant the effects of orthodoxy, eschatology, and religious movement—and also spot whether Methodists behave differently than their theological traits might predict. The beta coefficients from these analyses are reported in Table 5.4, as well as the proportion of the variance in each item that is explained by all four religious variables.

Theological orthodoxy emerges as the best predictor of ministerial focus, but denomination comes in a close second. Religious movement attachments almost always provide additional explanatory power, and eschatology is also helpful at points. Interestingly, denomination often prevails on the moral reform agenda, exhibiting the largest coefficients on education, family issues, gay rights, gambling, and the death penalty. Orthodoxy is a close second, influencing abortion, pornography, and school prayer, and tying with denomination on alcohol and drugs. The social justice agenda, on the other hand, clearly reflects orthodoxy, which exhibits the largest coefficient on all issues except relations with the USSR, where it is tied with denomination, and budget issues, where it barely misses being the most powerful.

As anticipated, eschatology and religious movement have considerable influence, often just where expected. Conservative eschatology influences Middle East policy, where it is the best predictor, and several moral questions, especially school

Table 5.4
Influences on Issue Agendas of Protestant Clergy

|  | Orthodoxy | Denomination | Movement | Eschatology |  |
| --- | --- | --- | --- | --- | --- |
|  |  |  |  |  | $r^2 =$ |
| **Moral reform agenda** |  |  |  |  |  |
| Abortion | **.37** | .18 | .09 | .05 | *.29* |
| Pornography | **.36** | .11 | .14 | .06 | *.30* |
| School prayer | **.21** | .20 | .07 | .16 | *.22* |
| Education issues | .19 | **.28** | ns | .04 | *.12* |
| Alcohol and drug abuse issues | **.16** | **.16** | .05 | ns | *.07* |
| Family issues | .13 | **.16** | ns | ns | *.05* |
| Gay rights, homosexuality | .13 | **.20** | .08 | .12 | *.16* |
| Gambling laws | .12 | **.27** | .12 | .05 | *.15* |
| Death penalty | .09 | **.16** | .11 | .09 | *.11* |
| Israel, Middle East policy | .06 | .15 | .08 | **.17** | *.10* |
| **Social justice agenda** |  |  |  |  |  |
| ERA, women's issues | **.30** | .08 | .15 | .05 | *.16* |
| Latin America | **.26** | .12 | .16 | .06 | *.15* |
| Civil rights | **.25** | .09 | .16 | .06 | *.17* |
| South Africa and apartheid | **.25** | .23 | .14 | ns | *.20* |
| Defense spending, military | **.24** | .16 | .16 | .05 | *.20* |
| Environment | **.20** | .17 | .09 | .09 | *.17* |
| Relations with USSR | **.18** | **.18** | .11 | .04 | *.11* |
| Economics, jobs | **.17** | .15 | .11 | ns | *.10* |
| Hunger and poverty | **.15** | .13 | .09 | .06 | *.11* |
| Budget deficits | .12 | **.13** | .06 | ns | *.05* |

*Entries are beta coefficients from a multiple classification analysis (MCA) and show the relative influence of theological orthodoxy, denomination, religious movement, and conservative eschatology on the frequency with which ministers address each topic. The most influential variable is indicated by **bold italics** for each issue.
ns = $p > .05$.

prayer, gay rights, and the death penalty. These findings support the contention that dispensationalism buttresses a radical moral critique of degenerate American culture. Only on alcohol and family issues does eschatology not add substantially to our predictions (these issues, of course, are widely addressed by all types of clergy). Religious movement has even more impact than eschatology, especially on the social justice agenda and on less frequently addressed issues, such as the Equal Rights Amendment (ERA), United States policy in Latin America, civil rights, and defense spending.

Indeed, inspection of the MCA category scores reveals many cases of influence by specific denominational attachments, movement identifications, or eschatology (data not shown). Special denominational concerns pop out clearly, as AG, SBC and UMC ministers address moral issues more frequently than would be predicted by theological leanings or movement identifications, a tendency that is especially apparent on alcohol, pornography, and gambling, as well as on school prayer and capital punishment. On the other hand, ECC and CRC ministers are often both less moralistic than might be expected and less active than theology would indicate on alcohol issues and gambling, as are the clergy of another ethnic church, the Mainline RCA. Similarly, the Methodists (especially), the Presbyterians, and the Disciples are more involved with hunger, defense, and the environment than we might expect. Once again, the Assemblies' interest in Middle East policy shows up, even with eschatology controlled, and the Reformed denominations' special concern with South Africa also appears clearly.

Similarly, religious movement affiliation is also a frequent aid in predicting involvement. Most often, liberals are active beyond the level predicted by other influences, especially on hunger and poverty, civil rights, the ERA and women's issues, the environment, Latin America, the economy, the Middle East, peace with the USSR, and apartheid in South Africa. Thus, self-identified religious liberals clearly carry the internal denominational responsibilities for action on the National Council of Churches' lobbying list. On the other side of the scale, fundamentalists also exceed expectations on many issues: alcohol and drugs, gay rights, abortion, pornography, gambling, school prayer, and family issues. On a few of these moral issues, such as pornography and gambling, liberals are much less active than one might predict, even given their theology. Again the pattern tends toward asymmetry: only on rare items, such as Israel and capital punishment, are both fundamentalists and liberals more involved.

Finally, the effects of conservative eschatology are usually due to the behavior of the strong dispensationalists, who are fascinated by Israel and Middle East issues, while those low on this same scale are less likely to be attentive. Elsewhere, the dispensationalists also show stronger concern with the moral reform agenda, especially on gay rights, abortion, pornography, gambling, capital punishment, and school prayer. Each is a reminder of the decline of Christian moral values in society. Interestingly, when all other variables are accounted for, dispensationalists usually show some concern for issues ignored by other orthodox clergy, such as Latin American policy, the USSR, defense spending, and South Africa, perhaps reflecting their special preoccupation with "reading the signs of the [end] times."

Thus, ministerial agendas are shaped theologically by the complex interplay of theological orthodoxy, denominational affiliation, religious movement, and conservative eschatology. While the orthodox-modernist divide shows some evidence of subsuming the other dimensions, each measure still helps us understand how Protestant ministers are led to be involved in moral and social justice issues. As the adjusted $R^2$ figures suggest, theological variables alone do quite well in explaining the variation in activity on issues, ranging from 30 percent on pornography to around 20 percent for most issues, and falling to only 5 percent on family issues and budget concerns. To see whether we can add to our explanatory power, we now turn to a fuller analysis of the range of variables that contribute to ministerial activism on the two agendas.

## THE MORAL REFORM AND SOCIAL JUSTICE AGENDAS: A MULTIVARIATE ANALYSIS

At this juncture we need to step back a bit from specific issues and focus on the larger constellations of ministerial concern. To this point we have discovered that the theological variables identified in chapter 3 have a strong relationship to pastors' agendas. Of course, social theologies may also contribute to the way ministers address these issues, and their sense of church priorities might play a role. Finally, as Iyengar and Kinder have pointed out, personal traits "can contribute directly and powerfully to the priorities Americans assign to national problems" (1987, 51). In this vein, we anticipate that ministers' demographic and personal characteristics might have such an impact: gender, age, education, and perhaps region. Women, for example, might have a distinctive pattern of concerns, with special attention to gender-related issues, such as abortion or the ERA. Similarly, older clergy might reflect more conservative worries about morality. Distinctive types of education or educational concentrations may produce special interests, captured on one of the agendas. On the other hand, these variables might have no independent effect, exerting influence through the theological or social theological perspective of the clergy.

To examine the overall impact of these influences, we produced scores for each minister on the moral reform and social justice agendas by using a principal components factor analysis with a varimax rotation (an oblique rotation produces very similar results, as the factors are only mildly intercorrelated, $r = .22$). The analysis reveals three components: the social justice agenda factor (accounting for 32 percent of the variance); the moral reform agenda (17 percent); and a residual factor with the three universally popular items of hunger, alcohol, and family issues

(6 percent of the variance). Because the variables on this minor factor also load on the major agendas (hunger on the social justice factor, alcohol and family issues on the moral agenda), we removed it from further examination. Two items on the moral reform factor, capital punishment and Middle East policy, also had sizable loadings on the social justice factor, indicating considerable modernist interest on these questions.

A quick look at the bivariate relationships (data not shown) between each of the independent variables and ministers' scores on the two agendas shows fairly strong correlations: in addition to the expected correlations with theological and denominational variables, the moral reform agenda is strongly correlated with individualism, missions and moral priorities, and the civic gospel. The relationships are somewhat weaker with the demographic variables, although working-class and rural origins, southern birth, age, and male gender are all mildly associated with moral reform. All the educational variables, on the other hand, are much stronger and work in the anticipated direction: the longer the education and the more prestigious the institution, the lower the adherence to the moral reform agenda. As expected, the correlations of these variables with the social justice factor presents a mirror image, running in exactly the opposite direction and at about the same magnitude.

To render a final accounting for ministerial agendas, we incorporated these variables in a multiple regression analysis of the moral reform and social justice agendas. The analysis is based on six denominations, as clergy from the Christian Reformed Church and the Reformed Church in America were not asked some of the demographic questions. As the denominational variables are dummy variables (1 if member, 0 if not), one must be eliminated from each equation. The coefficient for each of the other denominations then indicates the impact of that membership compared with the baseline of the reference category. We have suppressed the Assemblies of God from the moral reform agenda equation and the Disciples from the social justice agenda equation. Because the Assemblies were most attached to the moral reform agenda and the Disciples to the social justice agenda, they are reasonable choices. Table 5.5 reports the beta weights (b) from the multiple regression, with all the independent variables entered simultaneously.

The results are a reminder of the powerful impact of theological variables on ministerial behavior. Christian orthodoxy is by far the most powerful: the orthodox adopt the moral agenda, modernists the social justice agenda. Conservative eschatology promotes the moral reform agenda as well but has no influence on the social justice dimension, while religious movement influences only the social justice agenda. Some denomination effects remain, even when other variables are accounted for, especially on the moral reform agenda. All denominations except the UMC are significantly less likely than the Assemblies to be engaged on the moral agenda, once other influences are controlled. Denomination has less independent influence on the social justice dimension, but Southern Baptists and Evangelical Covenant clergy are even less active than might be predicted on the basis of other factors, and Methodists are a little more involved than might be expected. Thus,

Table 5.5
Influences on Ministers' Agenda: A Regression Analysis

| | Moral Reform | Social Justice |
|---|---|---|
| | b | b |
| Religious variables | | |
| Christian orthodoxy | .41** | −.33** |
| Conservative eschatology | .14** | .03 |
| Fundamentalist movement ID | .03 | −.05* |
| Denominational effects | | |
| AG | † | .01 |
| SBC | −.08* | −.13* |
| ECC | −.11** | −.11* |
| UMC | .00 | .05* |
| PRES | −.11* | .01 |
| DOC | −.10* | † |
| Social theology and church priorities | | |
| Individualism | .11** | −.09** |
| Civic gospel | .15** | −.02 |
| Missions priorities | .00 | −.08** |
| Political priorities | .06* | .19** |
| Moral priorities | .03 | −.05* |
| Charitable priorities | .07** | −.03 |
| Demography | | |
| Working class | .03 | .00 |
| Rural origins | .02 | .01 |
| Born in South | .00 | −.02 |
| Age | .09** | .09** |
| Gender (male) | .03 | −.01 |
| Education | | |
| Quality of seminary | .00 | .02 |
| Quality of college | −.12* | .06 |
| Seminary education | .03 | .02 |
| Secular education | −.04* | .03 |
| Liberal major | −.01 | .01 |
| Adjusted $R^2$ | .41 | .39 |

$**p<.001; *p<.05.$
$†$ Suppressed reference category.

there are some denominational differences beyond those that can be explained by the theological beliefs and demographic factors that have shaped their ministerial corps.

The social theology and church priorities held by clergy are themselves strongly influenced by theology, of course. But even when that relationship is taken into account, social theology has an independent impact. Individualists prefer the moral agenda, communitarians the social justice issues. And the new civic gospel is a fairly strong predictor of the moral reform agenda but has little impact on the social justice agenda. Political priorities influence the social justice dimension, as expected, but surprisingly, they also influence the moral agenda once all other variables are controlled, albeit to a more modest degree. A preference for charitable functions helps predict the moral reform agenda, while moral priorities have a negative impact once again on the social justice agenda.

Once ideational variables are accounted for, demography counts for very little. Working-class background, rural origins, southern upbringing—all drop out of the equations. Older ministers are more committed to activity on both agendas. Gender drops out: when theological and other variables are controlled, male and female ministers do not differ significantly in their agenda activity. Among the educational variables, only two retain statistical significance in the regression, both on the moral reform agenda. Those who attended less selective or prestigious colleges are substantially more likely to emphasize the moral reform agenda, while those with less extensive secular training are also slightly more active on moral issues. All the other education variables drop out, despite strong bivariate relationships to agenda activity, suggesting once more that socioeconomic factors operate primarily through their influence on the theological perspectives clergy develop as a result of childhood social environment and educational track to the ministry.


CONCLUSIONS

We have found the historic political agendas of the Evangelical and Mainline Protestant traditions largely intact, although the specific issues addressed have shifted somewhat over time, in natural movement with the course of events. The moral reform and social justice agendas are products of the fundamental theologies of ministers. The most powerful influence is clearly attachment to historic Christian orthodoxy, but conservative eschatology and membership in competing religious movements also have considerable effect, especially on particular issues. In the same vein, the agenda of each denomination is partly determined by the theological composition of its clergy, but each has some distinctive concerns—especially on individual issues, reflecting its historic traditions. In fact, denomination probably retains more influence on agendas than on most other political characteristics of the clergy. And although social theology and ministers' priorities for the church are largely the product of the theological orientations that produce agenda preferences, they often provide independent impetus for activity on different sets of issues: individualists and civic gospel proponents focus on moral questions, communitarians on social justice issues. And while each agenda is associated with different background traits, it is the religious values that count. In the next chapter we consider the ways that theological perspectives influence the positions that ministers take on critical political issues on both moral and social justice agendas.

# 6
# Shepherds Divided: Issues and Ideology among Protestant Clergy

An early discovery of the empirical studies of political behavior in the 1950s was that the average American did not fit the textbook model of the democratic citizen—an interested, well-informed, and active participant in the political process. Instead, these studies revealed an electorate that cared little about election outcomes, was poorly informed, and did not seem to connect opinions on one issue with those on others (Campbell et al. 1960; Converse 1964). At about the same time, other scholars found that this portrait of the mass public did not resemble those of political activists and elites, who were more engaged, were better informed, and connected their opinions on diverse issues into relatively coherent worldviews (McClosky, Hoffman, and O'Hara 1960).

This brief review suggests that pastors, as a religious elite, should have a constrained set of political attitudes, flowing from their highly organized theological perspectives. In this chapter we address the ideological orientations of Protestant clergy. First we look at their political attitudes on contemporary issues, drawn from both the moral reform and social justice agendas, finding that most orthodox clergy take conservative stances, while modernists are much more liberal. Then we examine in more detail the impact of orthodoxy, denomination, eschatology, and religious movement on particular issues. Next we consider the question of ideological structure: Is ministerial ideology one-dimensional, or is it more complex? We also discover that some ministers have adopted new ideological perspectives during their careers and discuss the reasons. Finally, we revisit an old concern of students of pastoral politics: the relationship between the minister's views and those of the people in the pews, discovering that not much has changed in this respect over the past thirty years.

## ISSUES ON THE MORAL REFORM AND SOCIAL JUSTICE AGENDAS

If the past is any guide, we anticipate a strong relationship between orthodoxy and political stands, both across and within denominations. The classic studies found that ministers who hold orthodox theological views generally express conservative political beliefs, while modernists hold more liberal political positions (Hadden 1969; Quinley 1974). We have no reason to expect different results, but issues have changed and, some have argued, political alignments have altered in the three decades since these groundbreaking works on ministerial politics.

To ascertain the clergy's political views, we asked our ministers a variety of questions related to specific political issues of the day, as well as a number of questions related to general statements of political belief. The questions were designed to tap their political attitudes across a variety of political issue domains—social and cultural issues, foreign policy, economic liberalism, and civil liberties. In Table 6.1 we report our findings on clerical opinion, organized by the issue agendas discussed in chapter 5 and arrayed by our orthodoxy scale. Correlations between the full orthodoxy index and attitudes on each issue are shown, indicating the strength of association between political views and theological orientation.

Perhaps the most dramatic difference among Protestant clergy is the evident gap between the conservative or traditionalist views held by orthodox clergy on moral reform issues and the considerably more liberal views of modernist ministers. Not surprisingly, the orthodox clergy almost universally favor tighter controls over pornography, more emphasis on traditional family structures in government policy, and ending the use of lotteries to raise state revenues, but these positions are also widely, though not universally, held by the less orthodox. As Harold Quinley pointed out in the 1970s, even modernist clergy retain some moralistic tendencies, although often defended by alternative rationales (1974, 87–90). For example, feminist arguments about the sexist impact of pornography and liberal concerns about the regressive nature of "taxation by lottery" probably influence modernists more than ancient concerns about personal morality.

On most other moral issues, however, orthodox and modernist clergy disagree more directly and dramatically. The orthodox favor a pro-life amendment to the Constitution, the teaching of creationism along with evolution in public schools, the death penalty, restrictions on gays, tuition tax credits for Christian schools, a school prayer amendment to the Constitution, and emphasis on enforcement and punishment, rather than on education, in the war on drugs. The most orthodox also oppose sex education in the public schools, but here they are deserted by a majority of the moderately orthodox. On all these questions, a majority of the moderately and strongly modernist clergy take a more liberal or libertarian position. A small coterie of the orthodox (mostly dispensationalists) oppose a Palestinian state, but majorities of all groups agree that such an entity might be the price of peace in the Middle East.

The distribution of responses in the first section of Table 6.1 suggests that conservatism on the moral issue agenda is generally confined to the two orthodox categories, and especially to the most orthodox. On the central Christian Right agenda issues of abortion, gay rights, education-related policies, and criminal justice issues, the core of support is confined to the orthodox clergy, and, on some of these issues, to the most orthodox. Only on questions such as pornography, lotteries, and family-friendly policies does there seem to be much ground for alliances across theological boundaries. There have been some striking examples of clerical cooperation in these areas in the 1990s (for the gambling case, see Zipperer 1994), but as we saw

Table 6.1
Political Attitudes of Protestant Clergy (Percent)

|  | Most Orthodox | | Most Modernist | | |
|---|---|---|---|---|---|
|  | 1 | 2 | 3 | 4 | r= |
| Moral reform agenda |  |  |  |  |  |
| Communities need more power over pornography | 99 | 97 | 84 | 65 | .52 |
| Government policy should stress traditional families | 95 | 94 | 83 | 61 | .46 |
| Favor abortion amendment to Constitution | 91 | 77 | 35 | 7 | .75 |
| Creationism should be taught if evolution is | 88 | 74 | 42 | 20 | .60 |
| Favor the death penalty | 88 | 73 | 45 | 22 | .60 |
| Oppose use of lotteries by states | 87 | 84 | 74 | 74 | .17 |
| Oppose gay rights legislation | 74 | 46 | 18 | 8 | .61 |
| Favor tuition tax credits for Christian schools | 72 | 61 | 41 | 14 | .51 |
| Favor a constitutional amendment on school prayer | 68 | 43 | 20 | 8 | .62 |
| Oppose sex education in the public schools | 57 | 23 | 7 | 1 | .57 |
| Drug policy should stress enforcement, not treatment | 56 | 44 | 27 | 23 | .30 |
| Oppose Palestinian state in Mideast | 35 | 14 | 5 | 3 | .45 |
| Social justice agenda |  |  |  |  |  |
| Cut defense spending | 40 | 56 | 81 | 95 | .52 |
| Government should do more in social welfare | 30 | 55 | 81 | 95 | .39 |
| Take aggressive action to protect environment | 47 | 65 | 85 | 94 | .40 |
| Implement strategic arms limitation pacts | 49 | 60 | 87 | 93 | .41 |
| The federal government should foster day care | 40 | 58 | 76 | 88 | .37 |
| U.S. should cut off aid to the contras in Nicaragua | 20 | 37 | 69 | 88 | .59 |
| Favor affirmative action policies for minorities | 35 | 57 | 74 | 86 | .42 |
| Favor government-sponsored national health care | 43 | 56 | 76 | 85 | .37 |
| Don't turn government services over to business | 10 | 31 | 60 | 79 | .52 |
| Favor the Equal Rights Amendment | 11 | 21 | 50 | 78 | .62 |
| Favor sanctions against apartheid in South Africa | 26 | 48 | 64 | 76 | .39 |
| U.S. should not support nondemocratic regimes | 39 | 40 | 55 | 71 | .26 |

in the last chapter, liberal clergy are not moved to speak out by the moral agenda issues they share with conservative colleagues.

Not surprisingly, the direction of support reverses as we move to the social justice agenda. Modernist clergy are most likely to favor cuts in defense spending, arms limitation agreements, expansion of social welfare, environmental protection, federally sponsored day care, affirmative action to help minorities, a federal health care plan, and the ERA. They also reject privatization of more government functions. In foreign affairs, in addition to espousing dovish defense policies, they also oppose aid to the contras in Nicaragua, favor economic sanctions against the former apartheid regime in South Africa, and emphasize that the United States should not consort with nondemocratic regimes, even if they were friendly to American policy. Unlike the situation on the moral reform agenda, however, where modernists have little use for traditionalist positions, the social justice agenda has some resonance for the orthodox (as demonstrated by the smaller correlations). On most issues, the moderately orthodox clergy actually show majority support for liberal policies, especially on the environment, military ("peace") issues, and most social welfare questions. Even among the most orthodox, a substantial liberal minority appears on a good many items, such as arms limitation, protecting the environment, and social welfare issues, especially health and day care.

Of course, there may be practical implications of the fact that theological perspective is more closely tied to the moral reform agenda than to the social justice agenda. As Table 6.1 shows, on many moral reform issues, fewer than one-quarter of the most modernist express a conservative position, while more than three-quarters of the most orthodox do. But on many social justice issues, a substantial proportion of the most orthodox pastors (frequently one-third to nearly one-half) are in political agreement with the bulk of the most modernist clergy. The same tendency is evident if we organize the data by denomination; many ministers in the Assemblies of God, Southern Baptist Convention, Evangelical Covenant, and Christian Reformed churches are somewhat liberal on social welfare programs, strategic arms limitations, and the environment. On social welfare issues, this modest liberalism probably reflects ministers' perception of the needs of working-class and lower-middle-class congregations; on others, such as environmentalism, it may simply express the contemporary public mood.

That greater polarization exists over the moral reform agenda than over social justice issues suggests that Christian Right hopes for a systematic political conservatism incorporating traditionalist social policy, laissez-faire economics, and international militancy may be difficult to attain across the entire range of Evangelical denominations and among all the orthodox. The social justice agenda, incorporating economic and foreign policy, simply does not divide clergy to the same extent that the moral reform agenda does. Many orthodox clergy are quite supportive of many social justice policies. As a result, while the Christian Right may be able to mobilize theologically orthodox pastors for conservative forays on moral reform, they will find less response to conservatism on some of the social justice agenda. On such issues there is—at least in theory—some possibility of broader liberal coalitions, but only if conservative clergy become convinced that these issues deserve attention and activity. As we have already seen in chapter 5, however, most of these questions attract very little interest from the more orthodox clergy. Indeed, only a minority of the modernists speak out on many of these issues, despite their liberal attitudes.

As both the percentages and the correlation coefficients in Table 6.1 remind us, among clergy political attitudes are closely related to theological perspective. Orthodoxy is strongly connected with conservatism on abortion ($r=.75$), school prayer and the ERA (both .62), gay rights (.61), creationism and the death penalty (both .60), aid to the contras (.59), and sex education (.57). These issues are often most directly connected to religious values. The somewhat weaker correlations on most foreign affairs, civil rights, and social welfare policies suggest that other factors beyond orthodoxy influence ministers' attitudes. Still, there is no doubt that theological perspective is a pervasive influence on political views. And, as expected, orthodoxy is still conducive to ideological conservatism, while modernism consorts with more liberal political viewpoints.

Of course, we suspect that in addition to orthodoxy and denominational location, religious movement affiliation and eschatology affect ministers' attitudes as well, with the size of that impact varying from issue to issue. Indeed, these factors may help us identify those clergy most responsive to either the moral issue or social justice agendas. To investigate this possibility, we entered all the issue variables into a series of multiple classification analyses (MCA), with the religious measures as independent predictors, similar to the operation in Table 5.4 in the previous chapter. Here the results can be summarized more easily. Although all four religious measures usually bear a significant independent relationship to attitudes on each issue, orthodoxy is the most powerful predictor, showing the strongest relationship on all but two of the issues listed in Table 6.2. As one might expect, orthodoxy has the most powerful effects on attitudes on abortion (beta $=.53$), prayer in schools (.42), gay rights and creationism (both .41), sex education (.39), and pornography (.36). The coefficients for the remaining moral agenda issues range from .35 for family policy to .18 for lotteries. Given some conservative support for the social justice agenda, it is not surprising that the relationships with orthodoxy are not as strong, but orthodoxy is still the best predictor for the ERA (.40), aid to the contras (.37), privatization of government programs (.34), sanctions against apartheid and federally sponsored day care (both .31), and, finally, cuts in defense spending (.30). Smaller relationships are found for other social justice issues, ranging from .25 for affirmative action programs to .18 for opposing close United States ties with friendly but nondemocratic regimes.

After Christian orthodoxy, movement affiliation has the largest impact on issue preferences. In fact, the relationships between movement attachments and issues are consistently strong across both agendas, with most in the range of .12 to .26. Specific denominational effects are usually much smaller but, with few exceptions, consistently significant. Denomination is actually the best predictor on tuition tax credits and the environment. On the former, Southern Baptists and Christian Reformed pastors take positions that are not well predicted by theological orthodoxy or movement attachments. The Baptists are more hostile to tuition tax credits than their doctrinal conservatism would predict, reflecting their historical "separationism," while CRC emphasis on Christian education makes pastors friendlier to such devices than other variables suggest they should be. On the environment, SBC pastors are distinctly more liberal, and Covenant ministers more conservative, than might

Table 6.2
Political Attitudes and Ideology of Protestant Clergy: Influence of Orthodoxy, Religious Movement, Denomination, and Eschatology

| | Orthodoxy | Movement | Denomination | Eschatology | |
|---|---|---|---|---|---|
| | | | | | $R^2 =$ |
| **Moral reform agenda** | | | | | |
| Abortion | **.53**[*] | .21 | .10 | .07 | .60 |
| Prayer in schools | **.42** | .18 | .14 | .21 | .43 |
| Gay rights | **.41** | .18 | .11 | .06 | .42 |
| Creationism | **.41** | .18 | .04 | .15 | .40 |
| Sex education in schools | **.39** | .18 | .14 | .05 | .39 |
| Pornography laws | **.36** | .19 | ns | .07 | .27 |
| Family policy | **.35** | .15 | ns | ns | .22 |
| Death penalty | **.34** | .25 | .11 | .06 | .40 |
| Tuition tax credits | .31 | .15 | **.32** | .11 | .37 |
| Mideast policy | **.25** | .12 | .17 | .08 | .27 |
| Drug policy | **.21** | .10 | .08 | .05 | .11 |
| Lottery laws | **.18** | .13 | .12 | .05 | .05 |
| **Social justice agenda** | | | | | |
| Equal rights amendment | **.40** | .26 | .10 | .04 | .41 |
| Support contras | **.37** | .20 | .11 | .09 | .38 |
| Private enterprise | **.34** | .24 | .05 | .06 | .31 |
| South Africa apartheid | **.31** | .19 | .13 | .06 | .18 |
| Day care aid | **.31** | .12 | ns | .09 | .17 |
| Military spending | **.30** | .15 | .12 | .12 | .31 |
| Affirmative action | **.25** | .17 | .17 | .09 | .22 |
| Social welfare programs | **.24** | .22 | .14 | .05 | .18 |
| National health care | **.24** | .21 | .07 | .09 | .17 |
| Salt III agreements | **.24** | .12 | .14 | .05 | .20 |
| Environmental protection | .21 | .09 | **.24** | .12 | .24 |
| Oppose dictators | **.18** | .12 | .11 | .10 | .10 |

[*] Coefficients are betas from a multiple classification analysis, representing the independent influence of each variable when all others are accounted for in the analysis. The beta coefficient of the religious variable with most influence on an issue is in **bold italics**; ns = coefficient not statistically significant: $p > .05$.

be predicted. A number of other notable denominational effects also show up. Presbyterians are more liberal than expected on several issues, such as school prayer, arms limitation, and support for the Palestinians in the Middle East, while the Christian Reformed and Reformed Church in America pastors are more liberal on civil rights issues than would be anticipated. Similarly, Methodist clergy exceed expectations on a number of social welfare issues, invariably on the "liberal" side. All these tendencies reflect historic concerns of these denominations or recent programmatic emphases.

Although many scholars have argued that dispensationalism is a declining force in Evangelical Protestantism, eschatology remains a significant predictor on almost every issue, but its impact is usually small. Strong dispensationalists are invariably on the conservative edge and the least premillennial category on the liberal side, even when other religious variables are accounted for. The largest effects are in three areas: education, environment, and foreign policy. The coefficients on education questions are largest: prayer in school (beta = .21), creationism (.12), and tuition tax credits (.11), while the relationship with the environment is solid (.12). Similarly, eschatology has a modest relationship with defense spending (.12), support for friendly nondemocratic regimes (.10), aid to the contras (.09), and Mideast policy (.08). Even smaller, but still significant, relationships appear with most other economic and social policy issues, with strong dispensationalists invariably the most conservative.

In sum, the four religious measures predict clergy attitudes on political and social issues quite well, explaining between 25 and 60 percent of the variance on most issues. As expected, theological orthodoxy is clearly the primary shaper of political attitudes, with religious movement affiliation a powerful additional aid. Distinct denominational factors have receded into the background, but a few such historic preoccupations still appear to influence results. Clerical attitudes are influenced by eschatology, although it is a slightly less potent factor than denomination.

These findings clarify considerably the potential for Christian Right and "Christian Left" politics: the Christian Right's best constituency is among orthodox ministers, dispensationalists, and fundamentalists, while the Christian Left finds the best response not just among theological modernists but with self-conscious "liberals," who reject any otherworldly eschatology.

## IDEOLOGICAL STRUCTURES

What is the larger structure of ministerial ideology? Social scientists have long argued about whether citizens connect specific attitudes to larger ideological frameworks. Scholars discovered long ago that ideological thinking, or "high attitudinal constraint," was characteristic of few in the mass public but much more prevalent among political activists and institutional elites. The complexity or dimensionality

of such ideologies is still a subject of contention, however. Some analysts have discovered that elites organize issues in a single liberal to conservative dimension,
which incorporates positions on social welfare, economic management, moral issues, and even foreign policy. Others find two or more dimensions distinctly unrelated to each other, such as social welfare attitudes on the one hand and cultural or
moral views on the other (cf. Shafer and Claggett 1995; Maddox and Lilie 1984;
Ladd and Hadley 1975; Green and Guth 1991b). Although the results are often contingent upon the particular elite studied and the range of questions asked, the degree
to which elites structure individual issues has important consequences for their activity and impact. If ministerial opinion is one-dimensional, religious conflict may
take the form of culture wars; if, however, pastoral opinion has two or more cross-
cutting dimensions, "pluralist politics" may be dominant, as religious alliances
shift from issue to issue, and clergy who are opponents on one issue find themselves
allied on others.

There are many reasons to expect that clergy would approach politics in a rather
systematic fashion and that their political beliefs would be more fully structured
than those of the average voter. First, people with advanced education, like most
clergy, engage in more ideological thinking than those with fewer years of schooling. Second, ministers often think that "because of their positions in society, clergymen have a special obligation to stay politically informed" (Quinley 1974, 64).
Such attentiveness, coupled with the likely possession of strong analytical skills,
enables clergy to package the political information they receive. Finally, since
clergy have a highly structured religious belief system that is central to their thinking and through which they process information, political beliefs may be well structured simply by their conjunction with their theological orientations. More specifically, ministers' theological beliefs claim primacy over other attitudes; as a result,
these beliefs are likely to be the primary conduit by which ministers process information, develop attitudes, and instigate involvement.

The data presented thus far are generally consistent with Wuthnow's (1988) argument that American religion is becoming organized along a single liberal-
conservative dimension. Although we saw in the last chapter that denomination still
influences ministers' agendas, that influence is much less powerful on attitudes
about issues. The growing ideological polarization within and across denominations means that those in different communions who fall within the same ideological
camps have more in common than they do with denominational colleagues on the
other side of the ideological divide. But other analysts see two or three dimensions
to religious elite ideology, albeit intercorrelated ones (Olson and Carroll 1992, 769;
McKinney and Olson n.d.). Should we expect two dimensions of political ideology,
perhaps reflecting each of our two agendas? Or will clerical worldviews reveal a
more constrained, one-dimensional structure? Evidence on political elites, the mass
public, and religious elites points in uncertain directions. We followed two strategies in attempting to assess the overall structure of ministerial opinion. First, we

used a traditional, straightforward measurement approach, asking ministers to place themselves on an ideological continuum. Second, we used factor analysis to determine the underlying dimensions of ministerial ideology. As it turns out, both techniques produce very similar results.

First, we asked ministers to place themselves on a seven-point ideological scale, ranging from "extremely conservative" at one end to "extremely liberal" on the other. Self-identification has long been used successfully in tapping the ideology of political activists and elites. Of course, such a scale assumes a single dimension and precludes finding two or more, but the very ease with which the overwhelming majority of clergy chose a response suggests their comfort with a one-dimensional measure. The top part of Table 6.3 reports the results, collapsing the two most conservative and liberal options for ease of presentation. As the correlation of .73 shows, the clergy's choices bear a powerful relationship to orthodoxy, with the most orthodox being overwhelmingly strong conservatives, although many modernist

Table 6.3
Ideologies of Protestant Clergy (Percent)

| | Most Orthodox 1 | 2 | 3 | Most Modernist 4 | r= |
|---|---|---|---|---|---|
| **Ideological self-identification** | | | | | |
| Most conservative | 58 | 22 | 3 | 0 | |
| Somewhat conservative | 32 | 45 | 22 | 5 | |
| Moderate | 7 | 24 | 37 | 21 | |
| Somewhat liberal | 2 | 10 | 31 | 45 | |
| Most liberal | 0 | 1 | 0 | 28 | |
| | 100% | 100% | 100% | 100% | .73 |
| **Summary of issue ideology** | | | | | |
| Most conservative | 55 | 14 | 3 | 0 | |
| Somewhat conservative | 29 | 33 | 8 | 2 | |
| Moderate | 13 | 30 | 25 | 7 | |
| Somewhat liberal | 3 | 18 | 37 | 24 | |
| Most liberal | 0 | 5 | 28 | 68 | |
| | 100% | 100% | 100% | 100% | .78 |
| **Summary of ideological change** | | | | | |
| Much more conservative | 8 | 5 | 4 | 1 | |
| Somewhat more conservative | 35 | 34 | 32 | 31 | |
| No change | 46 | 33 | 26 | 23 | |
| Somewhat more liberal | 11 | 25 | 31 | 36 | |
| Much more liberal | 0 | 3 | 7 | 9 | |
| | 100% | 100% | 100% | 100% | .26 |

clergy prefer a "moderate" or "somewhat liberal" label to a more extreme category choice. Thus, our expectation that ministerial theology should structure political ideology certainly seems to be confirmed.

As a second approach, we analyzed the issues in Table 6.1, using a factor analysis with a varimax rotation, a procedure likely to reveal multiple dimensions, if they exist. The results strongly suggest that ministerial attitudes are structured primarily by a powerful liberal-conservative dimension. The analysis produced one large factor, with an eigenvalue of 6.49, accounting for 47 percent of the variance. The analysis did produce a smaller factor with an eigenvalue of 1.14, accounting for 8 percent of the variance, but no variable loaded primarily on the second factor, and it admits of no easy interpretation. The variables loading most strongly on the main factor were, in order: abortion (.78), the ERA (.78), the death penalty (.76), gay rights (.76), aid to the contras (.74), school prayer (.71), Mideast policy (.66), affirmative action (.66), sanctions against South Africa (.63), military spending (.62), tuition tax credits, strategic arms limits, and social welfare programs (all .61), and environmental protection (.58). Thus, moral and foreign policy orientations are the most powerful determinants of the structure of ministerial ideology, but even the more consensual economic and social welfare issues are clearly subsumed in this dimension. Interestingly, the variables loading most highly on the first principal component are also the best predictors of ideological self-identification in a regression analysis (data not shown).

We then reran the procedure, using principal components analysis to produce a component accounting for as much of the variance in all the variables as possible. We used ministers' scores on this unrotated principal component as a measure of *issue ideology,* which includes items asked in at least five denominational surveys. Would incorporation of other issues have made a significant difference in our findings? Probably not. This issue ideology score quite strongly correlates with other items contained in three or four surveys: support for the Strategic Defense Initiative ($r = .75$), privatization of government programs (.67), creationism (.62), federally sponsored day care (.58), national health care (.53), and strict regulation of pornography (.49). Indeed, experimentation with inclusion of questions asked in at least three surveys, using mean substitution in the principal components analysis, produces essentially the same dimension, with correlations of at least .98 with the issue ideology score. Thus, inclusion of other issues seems unlikely to modify our conclusions. In the middle section of Table 6.3 we report a summary of issue ideology, dividing clergy into quintiles for purposes of illustration, and using our orthodoxy categories. Not surprisingly, issue ideology also correlates very strongly with orthodoxy ($r = .78$).

Both ideological measures array our denominations in the expected order. Using the seven-point self-identification scale, Assemblies clergy hold down the conservative end of the spectrum with a mean score of 5.48, followed closely by Southern Baptists (5.39) and, at some greater distances, by Covenant (4.64), CRC (4.31), and Reformed Church (4.14) ministers. Methodists, on balance, fall just on the liberal side of the center point (3.98), while Presbyterians (3.60) and Disciples (3.47) fall farther to the left. A look at the standard deviations shows that the Assemblies pastors are the most unified politically, followed by the CRC ministers, while the Covenant and especially the Methodists show the greatest internal differences on ideological self-identification. The patterns for issue ideology are similar but, because of the wider range of scores, reveal somewhat more variation within and between denominations. On this measure, Presbyterians actually edge out Disciples as the most liberal group, and both denominations exhibit larger internal differences than is evident from the self-identification measure.

All in all, the two strategies produce very similar measures of ideology. The correlation between issue ideology and self-identified ideology is a powerful .81, strongly suggesting that while the measures are not identical, they tap the same underlying ideological continuum (cf. Beatty and Walter 1989, 133). Indeed, the issue items correlate almost as strongly with self-identified ideology as with the ideological factor score they collectively produce. And both measures bear roughly the same relationship to our religious measures. In an MCA, Christian orthodoxy predicts issue ideology a little better than self-identified ideology (betas = .47 and .42, respectively), while religious movement affiliation does better for self-identified ideology than for issue ideology (betas = .32 and .22). Denomination and eschatology have almost identical impacts on each (.16 and .14 for denomination; .11 and .09 for eschatology). Further analysis using multiple regression suggests that ideology is almost entirely the result of these theological factors, which collectively account for the overwhelming amount of variance in both ideological measures (68 percent for self-identification; 72 percent for issue ideology); only social theology and education measures add much to our ability to predict either score. Thus, both measures suggest that a powerful, single ideological dimension characterizes the political worldview of these clergy, one determined by theological perspective. Using a combination of our ideological measures in the following analysis will allow us to capture that dimension.

Although these findings fit well with contemporary descriptions of the restructuring of American religion (Wuthnow 1988) and the rise of "culture wars" (Hunter 1991) between religious liberals and conservatives, they are at variance with the findings of scholars who see elite ideology in two-dimensional terms, arguing that personal morality and social justice issues form distinct orientations (McKinney and Olson n.d.). How can we account for these differences? Part of the disagreement stems from the different elite populations studied, on the one hand, and the inevitable differences in questions asked, on the other. Such differences cannot be resolved without further surveys. Another explanation is that elite ideology may be in process, changing from a simple to a more complex formulation, or, alternatively, being reduced from complexity to simplicity. Thus, with different questions, different elite populations, and different time frames, it is not surprising that surveys produce varying assessments of ideological structure among religious elites.

Our best hunch, however, is that clerical ideology is becoming simpler, as attitudes on social justice and moral issues are assimilated into a single dimension. We cannot address the possibility of temporal change for all the clergy, but we do have data from Southern Baptists spanning the years from 1980 to 1992. If attitudinal restructuring is occurring, we should see it among Southern Baptists, a superb test case for religious realignment (Ammerman 1990). Not only has a vigorous orthodox movement seized control of the SBC, but Southern Baptists have been subject to much attention from the Christian Right, which hopes to move them away from traditional church-state separationism and, often, political passivity, to more conservative involvement. If these polarizing developments have reshaped the political cognition of SBC clergy, it should be by simplifying ideological perspectives. And that is what we find. Following Philip Converse's (1964) seminal analysis of ideological constraint, we looked at the correlations among issue items present in all the SBC surveys from 1980 to 1992. Over that period, we find that various issue items from different policy domains have increasingly stronger correlations. Although space precludes presenting a full matrix of intercorrelations for each year, a few illustrations may suffice. In 1980, for example, the correlation between preferences for privatization of government services and attitudes on social welfare was .38, rising to .43 in 1984, .49 in 1988, and .52 in 1992. Similar increases occurred for other variables such as gay rights, defense spending, abortion, gun control, the ERA, tuition tax credits, environmental policy, and affirmative action. Baptist clergy have increasingly made connections between seemingly disparate areas of public policy, producing a consistent conservatism or liberalism across the full range of moral reform and social justice questions.

As a more systematic test of the growth of ideological constraint, we entered all common variables from the four surveys (1980, 1984, 1988, 1992) into a principal components analysis for each year. When this is done, the proportion of variance explained by the first component rises over time, indicating growing ideological consistency, especially among certain clergy. First, in each year younger ministers show more evidence of one-dimensional ideological thinking, although with the passage of time even older clergy have been educated in "what goes with what." Much, though not all, of the apparent influence of youth reflects rising education levels. Separate analyses for each year among ministers with no seminary training reveal four components, with the first rarely accounting for more than 25 percent of the variance. Among those with postseminary training, only one principal component appears, accounting for almost half the variance. Similar results obtain when secular education is analyzed. Thus, at least among Southern Baptists, Christian Right mobilization efforts, other national political forces, and increases in education have produced a simpler ideological structure, one that exhibits greater consistency across issues.

These findings have enormous implications for clerical politics, suggesting the ideological basis for pastoral activism, especially on the Christian Right. If other political science studies of activists and elites are any guide, the growing attitudinal constraint among young, well-educated orthodox pastors will contribute to stronger partisanship and greater political activity, leading to more efforts to instruct the people in the pews. Clergy with highly constrained belief systems are also more available for outside mobilization. Indeed, the Southern Baptist case suggests that, as the dominant religious force in their regional homeland, they have played an important role in the much-noted ideological transformation of southern politics in the last generation.

## IDEOLOGICAL CHANGE AMONG CLERGY

The fundamental transformations in the nature of religious politics seen by such analysts as Wuthnow (1988) and Roof and McKinney (1987) should be evident in the ideological adjustments that ministers make over the course of their adult lives. We asked ministers from all our denominations, except the Christian Reformed Church and the Reformed Church in America, to recall their ideological self-identification at age twenty-one. Then we compared this position with their current ideology to determine the extent of change. For purposes of presentation at the bottom of Table 6.3, we have included changes of three or more points on the seven-point scale as "much more" conservative or liberal, and smaller movements as "somewhat more" liberal or conservative. We anticipated that most ideological changes would be toward conformity to dominant religious patterns in each theological group and denomination.

Ideological change varies considerably by orthodoxy level. As Table 6.3 shows, almost half of the most orthodox clergy report no change, a proportion that drops steadily across the table to fewer than one-quarter of the most modernist pastors. As expected, most of the orthodox "movers" have become more conservative, with only a handful moving in a liberal direction, while the pattern is almost a mirror image among modernists, except for their greater tendency to report a small conservative change. An inspection of the data reveals that this is most often a move from "extremely" or "very" liberal at age twenty-one to "somewhat" liberal today.

Not surprisingly, ideological change also varies across denominations. On the whole, Evangelical ministers exhibit the least change. Over half (51 percent) of the Assemblies clergy report no movement whatever, while Southern Baptists (40 percent) and Covenant clergy (31 percent) are somewhat more prone to change. For Assemblies and SBC ministers, any ideological changes are in a markedly conservative direction. Among the Assemblies, for example, 81 percent reporting liberal preferences at age twenty-one became more conservative, while 97 percent of those with a conservative placement at that age stood fast. Increased conservatism among Southern Baptists was smaller in magnitude but still pronounced. Nearly 60 percent of Southern Baptists who were liberals at age twenty-one became conservatives, while 90 percent of the conservatives remained conservative. Moreover, those who abandoned early conservatism did not move nearly as far as did their liberal counterparts. Of the 13 percent of Southern Baptists who abandoned conservatism, most became moderates, not liberals (data not shown). As another indication of the pre-dominant political culture within the Assemblies and the SBC, most who were polit-ically moderate at age twenty-one moved toward a conservative stance. These pat-terns appear, if less strikingly, among Evangelical Covenant clergy.

Mainline clergy are even less stable ideologically than Evangelicals. Only 28 percent of Methodists and Disciples and 24 percent of Presbyterians report no movement. Moreover, both Disciples and Presbyterians move in a distinctively lib-eral direction. While 60 percent of the early Presbyterian liberals remained that way, only 35 percent of early conservatives stood firm. Moreover, among Presbyterian "changers," liberals shift slightly toward moderation, while conservatives more often jump across the spectrum to full-blooded liberalism. A similar pattern appears among Disciples: 68 percent of liberals at age twenty-one stood fast, compared with only 34 percent of conservatives. Once again, liberal Disciples who modify their ideology become moderates, but conservatives often join the liberal ranks (data not shown). Moderate Presbyterians and Disciples who changed also report moving distinctly to the left.

Ideological movement among Methodists, on the other hand, reveals a political ferment different from other denominations, being of approximately equal magni-tude in both liberal and conservative directions. Only 59 percent of the Methodist clergy who were liberal at age twenty-one stayed that way, and only 57 percent of Methodist conservatives held to their early convictions. Moreover, those clergy who were political moderates in their early political lives marched in almost equal columns in conservative and liberal directions (data not shown).

What influences these results? Quite evidently, these tendencies are strongly tied to the changing theological understandings that result, as we have seen, from the effects of professional socialization. Not surprisingly, ideological change is strongly correlated ($r = .56$) with our measure of theological change (see chapter 3). Ministers becoming more liberal theologically move to the left politically, and vice versa. The patterns of movement also suggest that ideological changes are tied to particular denominational cultures. Those who enter the ministry in a predomi-nantly orthodox or modernist denomination move in the direction of the dominant ethos. Whether this represents selective recruitment, in which those who are predis-posed to change gravitate to compatible environments, or indicates the power of de-nominational climates to socialize even those who start with a different perspective, the tendency itself is clear.

Some preliminary work suggests that the denominational environment influ-ences ministerial change primarily through the process of different kinds of educa-tion. When we analyzed ideological movement with only denominational affilia-tion and theological change as predictors, both proved about equally important: ministers who moved theologically reported ideological movement, regardless of their denomination, and Evangelical ministers reported ideological movement to the right, while Mainline clergy recounted migration to the political left, indepen-dent of theological changes. Further analysis shows that these "denominational effects" are primarily an artifact of the different educational experiences of clergy in each tradition. Mainline ministers move left politically in part because of theological liberalization that is the result of their more extended studies in more prestigious educational institutions and in liberal arts majors, but that same experience also influences ministerial ideology directly. In other words, clergy who attend selective colleges and prestigious seminaries and who study the liberal arts become more liberal politically via two paths: indirectly through theological liberalization and more directly as the dominant political liberalism of American academia influences their perspectives. Once educational factors are accounted for, experience within a particular denomination retains only very modest effects (cf. Wuthnow 1988).

## CLERGY AND LAITY: THE "GATHERING STORM" REVISITED

How do the political views of ministers compare with those of their congregations? We have many reasons to suspect that they may differ. Studies of nonreligious elites, such as political party leaders, show that they often adopt more extreme positions than those held by their followers (Bibby 1987, 111–113). Moreover, the classic studies of clergy revealed that Protestant ministers often expressed far more liberal attitudes than did their parishioners (Hadden 1969; Quinley 1974). In fact, it was this clergy-laity gap that prompted Hadden to warn of the "gathering storm in the churches" and James Adams (1970) to christen liberal Protestant leaders as "generals without armies." Other scholars, however, have argued that liberal Protestant leaders are more representative of their constituencies than these images would suggest (Hertzke 1988; Hofrenning 1995), and a few scholars have claimed that many politically conservative Evangelical clergy are now far out of line with their moderate parishioners (Campolo 1995).

What is the significance of this ideological gap between pastors and those sitting in the pews? In the short run, of course, ideological proximity influences the minister's ability to mobilize the congregation for political action. In the longer term, other effects may be evident: the liberal attitudes of the Mainline clergy, for example, may have at least a modest liberalizing effect on their congregations. Or parishioners might have a moderating influence on their ministers, although probably more on *behavior* than on attitudes (Hadden 1969, 86–89). Other ramifications are also possible. It may well be, for example, that parishioners who disagree with the political and social ideologies expressed by their minister become less involved in church activities, cut back their financial support, or even leave the congregation (Hadden 1969, 30–33).

An ideological gap between clergy and laity may also affect the long-term fortunes of a denomination. For most contemporary Americans, religion is becoming a free, individual choice (Warner 1993). Churches and denominations are increasingly forced into the religious marketplace, competing for adherents (Finke and Stark 1992). It is no secret that Mainline denominations have been declining in membership, while conservative churches have been growing. Might not such growth and decline be related to the magnitude of political differences between the clergy and parishioners? Although most scholars have concluded that the political liberalism of Mainline churches is not a direct cause of their decline, much membership switching among Protestant bodies is related to attitudes on moral issues and thus, at least indirectly, to political differences (Roof and McKinney 1987, 218–222; Green and Guth 1993).

Does the clergy-laity gap still exist? If so, where? To answer these questions we followed two different strategies. First, in four denominations (the SBC, ECC, CRC, and RCA), we asked respondents to place themselves on a five-point scale from "I'm much more conservative than my congregation" to "I'm much more liberal than my congregation." In the other four denominations (as well as the ECC), we asked ministers to assess their congregations' views on the same political issues we asked the clergy about. We then calculated the differences and summed them to produce a net score for the ideological "gap" between clergy and laity. As the Evangelical Covenant clergy were asked both types of questions, we used their scores as a rough guide to partitioning the specific issue summary scores into categories comparable to those used for the SBC, CRC, and RCA. As very few clergy reported that they were "much more conservative" than their congregations, on either the five-point scale or the measure drawn from the individual policy items, those respondents are merged with the "somewhat more conservative" pastors in Table 6.4.

The tale of clergy-congregational differences is an old story to students of ministerial politics. Evangelical clergy report a fairly high degree of consensus with their parishioners, although a substantial minority in both the Assemblies (39 per-

Table 6.4
Political Differences with Congregation by Denomination and Orthodoxy (Percent)

| | AG | SBC | ECC | CRC | RCA | UMC | PRES | DOC |
|---|---|---|---|---|---|---|---|---|
| Pastor is: | | | | | | | | |
| More conservative | 39 | 29 | 16 | 8 | 8 | 14 | 3 | 3 |
| About the same | 45 | 59 | 42 | 41 | 39 | 15 | 10 | 13 |
| More liberal | 13 | 13 | 34 | 45 | 42 | 22 | 28 | 29 |
| Much more liberal | 3 | 2 | 8 | 7 | 12 | 50 | 59 | 55 |
| | 100% | 100% | 100% | 100% | 100% | 100% | 100% | 100% |

| | Most Orthodox 1 | 2 | 3 | Most Modernist 4 |
|---|---|---|---|---|
| Pastor is: | | | | |
| More conservative | 34 | 14 | 4 | 1 |
| About the same | 54 | 44 | 22 | 5 |
| More liberal | 12 | 33 | 45 | 28 |
| Much more liberal | 1 | 9 | 29 | 66 |
| | 100% | 100% | 100% | 100% |

cent) and Southern Baptists (26 percent) say they are more conservative than their people. (But keep in mind that this is generally a modest difference.) The numbers in this category decline as we move toward the Mainline churches, although a distinct group of UMC clergy find themselves in an unusual mismatch of being more conservative than their congregations. Among most Mainline clergy, however, the generalization is clear: ministers are either somewhat more liberal or much more liberal than the people in the pews. Indeed, among the UMC, PCUSA, and Disciples clergy, half or more perceive themselves as rather far to the left of their parishioners (cf. Ice 1995, 135).

Thus, the situation described by Hadden and Quinley a generation ago still obtains: liberal Mainline clergy confront laity with a distinctly more conservative coloration than their own. There may be an analogous confrontation developing among the theologically orthodox, where some conservatives report political attitudes to the right of their congregations', but this tendency is much less pronounced. The bottom of Table 6.4 shows that the relationship of ministerial and congregational ideology is, as expected, structured by theology. One-third of the most orthodox clergy find themselves to the right of their congregations, while virtually all of the most modernist are to the political left of theirs, with two-thirds "much more liberal" than their people. The moderately orthodox resemble their congregations or vary slightly in either direction, while the moderate modernists are mostly the same or somewhat more liberal. Once again, we see the powerful impact of theology.

Do these differences result from uniform ideological divisions, or do certain issues contribute disproportionately to the political distance between pastor and people? Are the same issues likely to divide minister and congregation in different religious settings? Or, perhaps, do orthodox ministers and congregations split over different questions than their modernist counterparts? Although we have specific data for only five denominations, we can demonstrate where the largest gaps are.

A cursory glance at the first column in Table 6.5 shows that clergy generally are more liberal than the laity. The largest gaps between ministers as a group and their congregations are (in order) on sanctuary for refugees, gun control, defense issues, school prayer, national health care, affirmative action, the environment, and privatization of government programs. On these issues, even orthodox clergy are usually more liberal than their parishioners. Smaller differences appear on a host of other issues, but only on regulation of pornography do ministers in the whole sample actually see themselves as more conservative than their people—and then only by a very small margin.

These global figures hide massive disparities among theological groups, however. As the rest of Table 6.5 shows, the most modernist clergy perceive larger and more consistent differences with their congregations than does either group of orthodox ministers. The largest gaps for modernist clergy, in order, are on the death penalty, gay rights, defense spending, school prayer, affirmative action, Star Wars, and several other social and cultural issues, but the differences extend to virtually every other issue. The orthodox clergy, for their part, differ more modestly from

Table 6.5
Differences in Political Attitudes of Protestant Clergy and Congregations
as Perceived by the Pastor

| | All | Most Orthodox 1 | 2 | 3 | Most Modernist 4 | |
|---|---|---|---|---|---|---|
| | | | | | | eta= |
| Refugees | −1.01* | −.15 | −.50 | −.95 | −1.24 | .29 |
| Gun control | −1.08 | −.60 | −.71 | −1.00 | −1.24 | .17 |
| Star Wars | −.97 | .06 | −.46 | −.84 | −1.25 | .31 |
| Defense spending | −.77 | −.10 | −.55 | −.99 | −1.37 | .44 |
| School prayer | −.77 | −.11 | −.55 | −1.03 | −1.35 | .43 |
| Health program | −.75 | .07 | −.44 | −.70 | −.90 | .24 |
| Affirmative action | −.75 | −.11 | −.66 | −.94 | −1.26 | .42 |
| Gay rights | −.73 | −.01 | −.43 | −1.02 | −1.37 | .49 |
| Environment | −.73 | −.20 | −.64 | −.98 | −1.11 | .37 |
| Privatization | −.71 | .13 | −.21 | −.57 | −.98 | .30 |
| Sex education | −.63 | .08 | −.34 | − .64 | −.75 | .24 |
| Contras | −.57 | .14 | −.27 | −.69 | −1.15 | .46 |
| Dictators | −.55 | −.04 | −.25 | −.49 | −.69 | .18 |
| Death penalty | −.52 | .27 | −.13 | −.72 | −1.38 | .52 |
| Apartheid | −.48 | .10 | −.24 | −.61 | −.93 | .39 |
| Mideast | −.47 | −.06 | −.51 | −.65 | −.69 | .31 |
| Day care policy | −.45 | .15 | −.19 | −.42 | −.57 | .22 |
| ERA | −.40 | .27 | −.06 | −.59 | −1.12 | .50 |
| Creationism | −.38 | .28 | .12 | −.30 | −.59 | .29 |
| Arms control | −.36 | .05 | −.29 | −.51 | −.61 | .33 |
| Abortion | −.35 | .28 | .05 | −.55 | −1.08 | .50 |
| Drug policy | −.17 | .09 | −.14 | −.49 | −.64 | .32 |
| Tuition tax credits | −.12 | .21 | .10 | −.22 | −.51 | .32 |
| Family policy | −.03 | .10 | .04 | −.13 | −.45 | .31 |
| Pornography | .03 | .11 | .18 | −.01 | −.37 | .25 |

* Entries are the mean differences between clergy attitudes and the attitudes they perceive to be held by their congregations, based on issue items with five-point scales. All questions are coded so that greater ministerial liberalism is indicated by negative scores, greater conservatism by a positive score.

their congregations, sometimes in a liberal direction (as on gun control, refugees, and the environment) but more often in a conservative one (especially on abortion, creationism, the death penalty, and the ERA). Note, however, that the gaps in the first column are very small. As the eta coefficients show, the pastor-congregation differences are most closely related to pastoral theology on the death penalty, the ERA, abortion, and gay rights. Not surprisingly, the two intermediate theological categories fall between the most orthodox and most modernist, although it is critical to note that even among the moderately orthodox, the minister is usually more liberal than the congregation, while among the moderately modernist, the differences become uniformly liberal in direction and larger in magnitude. Thus, almost any pastoral deviation from historic orthodoxy marks significant ideological distance between pulpit and pew.

## CONCLUSIONS

Thus, we have found some very old and some new ideological formations among our Protestant clergy. As Hadden and Quinley discovered a generation ago, there is a powerful tendency for orthodox clergy to take conservative positions on a wide range of political issues, especially moral and cultural issues, while modernist clergy are even more uniformly liberal on those same issues. And although some scholars have found at least two dimensions of ministerial ideology, our data suggest a higher degree of ideological constraint, with all but a few issues attaching themselves to a single liberal-conservative dimension. When clergy deviate from the stances characterizing their theological group, it is most often the orthodox, who sometimes take liberal stands on social welfare, environmental, and a few other issues—usually, however, issues to which they devote little attention.

Not only is theology in all its guises a powerful shaper of ministerial ideology, but there is considerable evidence for systematic ideological change among clergy. Although each denomination does attract prospective clergy who lean in the direction of the dominant internal forces, these clergy are further influenced by the process of professional socialization. Denominations affect clerical ideology in different ways: Evangelical churches bend clergy toward the right, while ministers socialized in Mainline denominations move predominantly to the left. And, in centrist churches such as the United Methodists, movement goes in both directions. There is also some tantalizing evidence that ministerial ideology has become more structured along liberal-conservative lines in recent years. Just as the great debate between LBJ and Barry Goldwater in 1964 fostered more ideological sophistication in the American electorate (Nie, Verba, and Petrocik 1976), increasing education among ministers—especially in Evangelical denominations—and efforts by Christian Right leaders (and their critics) to politicize the clergy may well have produced a simpler ideological structure among many clergy, as our review of Southern Baptist developments suggests.

One aspect of clerical politics has not changed since the era studied by Hadden and Quinley: there is still a yawning gap between ministers' views and those of their parishioners. Whether couched in terms of ministers' own assessment of the general direction of that ideological gap, or in specific judgments of where they and their parishioners stand on major national issues, clergy see themselves as politically different. But much of that difference is concentrated on the left; conservative clergy feel a basic compatibility with their congregations. Thus, reports of a new "gathering storm" in Evangelical churches between conservative activist pastors and moderate laity are probably premature. Indeed, our data suggest (see chapter 8) that some moderately conservative clergy in Evangelical churches find themselves under pressure from even more conservative laity.

Our findings do show, however, an increasingly firm ideological basis for a "two-party system" in American Protestantism, using that term in its literal political sense, as well as in Martin Marty's religious one. Evangelical clergy generally represent the political right in ideological terms, while Mainline pastors provide the religious shock troops for the political left. Ministers are not all political activists, of course. But as important institutional elites, respected public figures, and spiritual guides for many Americans, they hold ideological perspectives that are potentially important. But has the ideological potential for a "two-party system" been converted into political reality? That is the story of the next chapter.

# 7

# The Real "Two-Party System": Partisanship and Voting Behavior among Protestant Clergy

*I have remarked that the American clergy in general . . . are all in favor of civil freedom; but they do not favor any particular political system. They keep aloof from parties and from public affairs. . . .*

*I perceived that these ministers of the Gospel eschewed all parties, with the anxiety attendant upon personal interest.*

Alexis de Tocqueville, *Democracy in America* (1945), 2:314, 320

Fifty years of political science research has consistently found that partisanship is one of the most potent factors in explaining political attitudes and behaviors in the United States. Partisanship is an individual's self-conscious identification with a political party. Most Americans feel some degree of attachment to a political party, and, intuitively, it makes sense that voters will support candidates of the party they identify with. Indeed, many other criteria for political choices are embodied in partisanship, connecting the individual's values and interests to politics in a direct and efficient fashion. Partisanship is particularly important in the United States because of the dominance of the two-party system: individuals routinely face the necessity of choosing between two candidates, neither of which may be completely satisfactory.

Nevertheless, there is much scholarly disagreement about the meaning and sources of partisanship. Three alternatives have been suggested. First, there is affectual partisanship, or attachment to the party's symbols, history, leaders, and basic values, which are largely inherited from the individual's family and community, and reflect the historical experience of particular ethnic groups, regions, or social classes—or all of these. Affectual partisanship serves both as a cue for voting behavior and as a perceptual screen through which political information of all kinds is interpreted. Despite being rooted in family and community, party identification in this affectual sense can change or develop as a result of an individual's life experience or important political events. A second source of partisanship is past behavior, the sum of the individual's past political experience. Individuals develop habits in their political choices, as in other choices they are regularly called upon to make, and stick with these "standing decisions" as long as they prove satisfying. This we might call "conative partisanship." Beliefs and values are a third source of partisanship. Simply put, individuals choose to identify with the party that reflects their ideological stance or position on issues. A few people have elaborate political philosophies that direct them toward one party, while others have a simpler sum of likes and dislikes drawn from their experience with politics. We might refer to these aspects as "cognitive" or "ideological" partisanship.

Affectual partisanship is especially important, for most citizens participate only sporadically and have few well-developed political beliefs. But for politically active and well-educated individuals, conative and cognitive partisanship are at least as important, if not more so, than partisan affections. Indeed, one distinguishing mark of political and social elites is a direct connection between political behavior and political beliefs, mediated and expressed through partisan identification. Among such elites, partisanship is both a potent description of their location in politics and a powerful predictor of that behavior. And yet, as we noted in chapter 1, little attention has been given to the forces shaping partisanship among clergy or, for that matter, among other professional elites.

In this chapter, then, we will investigate the partisanship of Protestant clergy. First we report the substantial differences in party identification among ministers from our eight denominations and four theological categories. Then we trace the routes of partisan change among clergy, tying this transformation to ideological perspectives and attitudes on issues. Next we look at ministers' vote choices in presidential elections, long the centerpiece of American party conflict. Finally, we review involvement by clergy in the 1988 and 1992 Democratic and Republican presidential campaigns.

## PARTY IDENTIFICATION AMONG PROTESTANT CLERGY

How do ministers align with our national parties? We asked ministers to characterize themselves, using a mail questionnaire variant of the standard National Election Studies (NES) seven-point party identification scale. As Table 7.1 shows, there are systematic differences in party attachment. A solid majority of Assemblies pastors are Republican; most of the rest are independents who lean toward the GOP. Southern Baptists and Evangelical Covenant pastors include a plurality of Republicans, but almost as many are independents leaning toward the GOP. Among Christian Reformed clergy, independent leaners actually outnumber explicit Republicans. The CRC's Mainline sister, the Reformed Church in America, has about the same number of Republicans, but many fewer Republican leaners, more Democrats, and more independents leaning toward the Democrats. Methodist diversity appears once again, with almost identical numbers of strong Republicans and strong Democrats, weak Republicans and weak Democrats, and independents leaning each way! Democrats become a plurality among Presbyterians and Disciples, reinforced by a large contingent of independent leaners. Indeed, Republicans and their independent allies constitute only a third of the clergy in these denominations.

Despite these distinct partisan patterns, many clergy shun strong party ties and prefer an independent or, more often, an independent-leaning classification. Indeed, if all "independents" are grouped together, they constitute a plurality in several denominations. While this may show that ministers are like other Americans, less partisan than several decades ago (Miller and Shanks 1996, 126–128), there may be special reasons for this proclivity. Clergy may avoid strong party attachments because they need to be accessible to all members of their congregations; strong partisanship might interfere with pastoral functions (cf. Parham 1996). That many "true" independents (those who claim to lean toward neither party) have never changed that stance suggests that some have adopted just such a strategy. Other pastors produce theological rationales for independence. For example, a Southern Baptist eschewed "Republican" and "Democratic" in favor of another label: "I prefer to think of myself as Biblical." The number of independent leaners, on the other hand, may reflect ideological and partisan change among clergy since youth. These categories do, in fact, have a disproportionate number of "movers," and thus may

Table 7.1
Clergy's Partisanship by Denomination and Orthodoxy (Percent)

| | AG | SBC | ECC | CRC | RCA | UMC | PRES | DOC |
|---|---|---|---|---|---|---|---|---|
| Strong Republican | 37 | 25 | 21 | 15 | 14 | 16 | 9 | 7 |
| Weak Republican | 21 | 12 | 17 | 16 | 15 | 8 | 9 | 7 |
| Lean Republican | 31 | 31 | 28 | 36 | 22 | 20 | 15 | 16 |
| Pure Independent | 6 | 10 | 10 | 10 | 13 | 10 | 8 | 10 |
| Lean Democratic | 1 | 8 | 15 | 15 | 19 | 19 | 20 | 20 |
| Weak Democrat | 2 | 8 | 4 | 5 | 7 | 9 | 14 | 14 |
| Strong Democrat | 2 | 6 | 6 | 3 | 10 | 18 | 25 | 26 |
| | 100% | 100% | 100% | 100% | 100% | 100% | 100% | 100% |

| | Most Orthodox 1 | 2 | 3 | Most Modernist 4 |
|---|---|---|---|---|
| Strong Republican | 35 | 19 | 8 | 4 |
| Weak Republican | 15 | 20 | 12 | 5 |
| Lean Republican | 34 | 32 | 22 | 8 |
| Pure Independent | 7 | 11 | 13 | 8 |
| Lean Democratic | 3 | 10 | 25 | 25 |
| Weak Democrat | 3 | 5 | 10 | 16 |
| Strong Democrat | 3 | 4 | 11 | 35 |
| | 100% | 100% | 100% | 100% |

be way stations to a stronger attachment. This is especially true among Southern Baptists, where many Republican leaners are former Democrats, and in the PCUSA and Disciples, where many Democratic leaners were reared as Republicans.

Whatever its source, this avoidance of direct partisan identification may not be as significant as it first appears. Not all independents are indifferent to partisanship. Keith et al. (1992) claim that, unlike true independents, partisan leaners in the electorate are really "closet Democrats and Republicans." And although this argument is controversial among political scientists, we found such a pattern among political activists in an earlier study (Green and Guth 1986). The same tendency occurs among clergy, particularly on the Republican side. Republican-leaning independents voted more frequently for George Bush in 1988 than did "weak" Republicans, actually matching "strong" Republicans, but Democratic leaners varied more by denomination, sometimes voting like strong Democrats but often acting like true independents, with a closer division of the vote.

Not surprisingly, theological orthodoxy is strongly linked to party identification ($r = .57$). As the bottom of Table 7.1 shows, the most orthodox clergy are overwhelmingly Republican or leaning that way (84 percent), while among the most modernist only 17 percent have any attraction toward the GOP. The intermediate theological categories prefer the independent label, with 53 percent of the moderately orthodox and 60 percent of the moderately modernist claiming some form of independence, though a majority of the former lean toward the GOP and a plurality of the latter lean toward the Democrats. Similar patterns appear for theological movement and eschatology: fundamentalists and dispensationalists are most Republican, while liberals and nonpremillennialists are most Democratic (data not shown).

Thus, we confirm the association of theological orientations and partisanship discovered by earlier studies. Of course, as we have seen, theological variables have an enormous impact on many aspects of the ministerial worldview, which may in turn have their own effects on partisanship. In addition, many denominations have traditional connections to the party system, based on region, ethnicity, social class, and other factors—many of which may still influence the distribution of party loyalties.

## THE IDEOLOGICAL TRANSFORMATION OF CLERICAL PARTISANSHIP

The strong contemporary coincidence of theological and partisan lines across these diverse denominations may result from a variety of forces. To set a baseline for an analysis of partisan change, we turn to the ethnocultural historians, who argue that American partisan alignments have always been shaped by competing religious, ethnic, and cultural groups (Kleppner 1970). An alternative perspective is provided by analysts who stress the role of social class, especially since the New Deal of the

1930s, in shaping both religious and partisan divisions (Niebuhr 1929; Petrocik 1981).

Drawing on such perspectives and the information presented in our denominational profiles, we can "retrodict" the traditional partisan hue of clergy. In some cases, such as the Evangelical Covenant and the two Reformed churches, ethnic preferences clearly favored the GOP at the turn of the twentieth century. Similarly, the northern Presbyterians and Methodists were also historically Republican, a tendency buttressed by middle-class economic status. Other denominations (or segments thereof) had strong Democratic tendencies. This is especially true of Southern Baptists, a linchpin of the solid Democratic South, reflecting both Civil War loyalties and working-class interests (cf. Guth 1985–86). Similarly, substantial numbers of southern clergy in the Assemblies of God, United Methodist Church, the Disciples of Christ, and the PCUSA's southern antecedent were also likely to be Democrats. And among working-class churches everywhere, but especially in the Assemblies, the Disciples, and the Methodists, one might expect Democratic clergy as well.

Although we have little survey data on clerical partisanship for earlier periods, we can partially reconstruct historic patterns from ministers' reports on their partisanship at age twenty-one (cf. Andersen 1976). If we look at those over fifty-six years old in 1988 (those whose first voting opportunity was no later than 1952), we see the partisan configuration of each denomination during the New Deal–Fair Deal era. This procedure confirms the historical portrait provided by the ethnocultural historians but with some exceptions. The biggest surprise comes from the Assemblies of God, where 63 percent in this age cohort report an early Republican preference, despite their upbringing in a working-class denomination. Of course, clergy in such churches may have a different perspective than laity (cf. Johnson 1966, 1967). As a knowledgeable observer of the Assemblies told us, "Assemblies clergy have *always* been natural Republicans, even if their congregations were not" (Richardson 1996). Southern Baptists fit expectations much better, being solidly Democratic, with fewer than a third of senior clergy reporting youthful Republican leanings. As expected, the "ethnic" churches were overwhelmingly Republican, especially the RCA (71 percent), the CRC (67 percent), and the Evangelical Covenant (58 percent). The oldest Methodist and Presbyterian cohorts report strong GOP contingents (52 and 49 percent, respectively), but the Disciples, with their border state and southern representation, mustered only 38 percent. Thus, it appears that ethnocultural, regional, and social class patterns in partisanship clearly persisted as late as midcentury.

With the "restructuring of American religion" (Wuthnow 1988), however, theology forged a much stronger link with partisanship among clergy, superseding ethnocultural and class divisions. Many traditionally Democratic and orthodox ministers gravitated toward the Republicans, while modernists left the GOP for a Democratic alignment. (Indeed, the correlation between current party identification and that at age twenty-one is remarkably similar for all denominations, ranging from .54 for the Reformed pastors to .47 for the Assemblies. While this suggests a certain amount of stability, some clergy are obviously moving.) That the realignment is theological (and hence ideological) is suggested by the higher correlation between theology and current partisanship (.57) than that for early theology and early party identification (.22). To investigate the causes of partisan movement, then, we calculated a party change score by tallying how far and in which direction ministers moved on our seven-point partisan scale since age twenty-one. While there are some risks in relying on ministers' recollections, we think they are minimal in a well-educated, politically interested elite. If they err, ministers are more prone to understate than overstate changes. For purposes of presentation in Table 7.2, we classified those shifting three or more points as "strong" movers, those moving one or two points as "weak" movers.

Majorities in almost every denomination reported at least some partisan shift (Table 7.2). There has been a considerable migration toward the GOP among the Assemblies, already quite Republican, and among SBC clergy, historically Democratic. Indeed, almost half the Baptists report moving toward the Republicans. The Evangelical Covenant clergy recall some movement in each direction, with a slight Republican advantage, while among CRC pastors the change goes in both directions in almost equal proportions. On the Mainline side, among the RCA ministers net changes favor the Democrats, toning down the historically dominant Republican hue of that Dutch denomination. Changes among Methodists are almost perfectly offsetting, while among Presbyterians and Disciples Democratic gains solidly exceed those of the Republicans. And as the bottom of Table 7.2 shows, partisan change varies with theology—the orthodox have been drawn toward the GOP and modernists toward the Democrats, both in the sample as a whole and, as further analysis shows, in each denomination.

We cannot untangle here the exact route of ministers' theological and political pilgrimages, but the pattern varies by denomination. Many Southern Baptists, for example, have always been orthodox and ideologically conservative but have recently switched party allegiances, abandoning the Democrats for the GOP. Indeed, fully half the current Republicans among Southern Baptists are former Democrats and independents. Slightly smaller proportions of southern Republicans in the other denominations are also "converts." Other clergy, especially Mainliners, have adopted a new partisanship as their theology evolved. For example, the Presbyterians and Disciples who are more fundamentalist or more liberal than they were at age twenty-one also have swung toward the Republicans or Democrats, respectively. In each of these Mainline cases, about a third of the current Democratic and Republican partisans are "new," although new Democrats outnumber GOP converts two to one. This is a lower proportion of converts than among Southern Baptists, but it is significant nevertheless. Thus, there are systematic partisan changes both within denominations and among competing theological groups.

Of course, conversion is only one source of change in the partisan composition of denominational clergy. Another is the partisan bias of new clergy. If new age co-

Table 7.2
Clergy's Partisan Change by Denomination and Orthodoxy (Percent)

| | AG | SBC | ECC | CRC | RCA | UMC | PRES | DOC |
|---|---|---|---|---|---|---|---|---|
| Strongly Republican | 18 | 21 | 10 | 7 | 6 | 8 | 6 | 6 |
| Weakly Republican | 21 | 27 | 23 | 19 | 17 | 20 | 20 | 19 |
| No change | 55 | 42 | 42 | 46 | 39 | 44 | 40 | 44 |
| Somewhat Democratic | 6 | 7 | 21 | 23 | 29 | 19 | 20 | 18 |
| Strongly Democratic | 9 | 2 | 5 | 6 | 9 | 9 | 14 | 12 |
| | 100% | 100% | 100% | 100% | 100% | 100% | 100% | 100% |

| | Most Orthodox | | | Most Modernist |
|---|---|---|---|---|
| | 1 | 2 | 3 | 4 |
| Strongly Republican | 17 | 11 | 7 | 4 |
| Somewhat Republican | 23 | 24 | 20 | 15 |
| No change | 49 | 45 | 39 | 42 |
| Somewhat Democratic | 10 | 17 | 25 | 22 |
| Strongly Democratic | 1 | 3 | 9 | 18 |
| | 100% | 100% | 100% | 100% |

horts are distinctly different than older ones, the partisan composition will shift over time. And that has clearly happened, as younger clergy reflect their denomination's current partisan coloration, shaped by its dominant theology and ideology, while older clergy retain more of the historic partisan alignments. Among Southern Baptists, for example, clergy under thirty-five years of age are the most Republican (mean = 2.89 on seven-point scale), while those aged fifty-six years or over are least Republican (mean = 3.44), reflecting their origins in the solid Democratic South. And as our studies of SBC clergy since 1980 demonstrate, each new age cohort starts with more ministers who have always been Republicans, in contrast to older GOP adherents, many of them converts (Guth 1985–86). In contrast, the oldest RCA cohort is the least Democratic (mean = 3.08), while the youngest straddles the midpoint of the scale (mean = 4.00), suggesting that younger ministers have brought stronger Democratic tendencies with them into the ministry. The oldest Methodist, Presbyterian, and Disciples clergy are least Democratic, while the youngest cohorts are more solidly in that party's camp. Thus, whatever partisan diversity remains in most denominations is partly an artifact of the confrontation of those reared under the "old political order" and newer age cohorts, whose partisanship reflects the contemporary theological and ideological tenor of their denominations.

## PARTISANSHIP AND PARTISAN CHANGE: MULTIVARIATE ANALYSIS

In many ways, our data reveal the culmination of trends already evident in studies by Johnson, Hadden, and Quinley in the 1960s, in which Evangelical denomination and doctrinal orthodoxy bear strongly on both partisanship and partisan change. Of course, these same religious variables produce distinctive social theologies, views on the church's role in politics, and political attitudes. In addition, we suspect that historic ethnocultural and demographic traits may have at least a residual influence. For a systematic review, we report the results of two operations in Table 7.3. First, we list the bivariate correlation *(r)* between both Republican identification and movement in a Republican direction, and a variety of theological, political, and de-

Table 7.3
Influences on Ministers' Party Identification and Partisan Change

| | Party Identification | | Party Change | |
|---|---|---|---|---|
| | r | b | r | b |
| Theological variables | | | | |
| Christian orthodoxy | .57**† | .02 | .52** | .02 |
| Fundamentalist movement | .52** | .01 | .46** | .01 |
| Conservative eschatology | .33** | .08** | .35** | .05* |
| Denomination | | | | |
| Assemblies | .26** | .02 | .24** | .00 |
| Southern Baptist | .09** | −.09** | .16** | .04* |
| Evangelical Covenant | .09** | −.02 | .06** | .03 |
| Christian Reformed | .08** | −.01 | .03* | .04 |
| Reformed Church | .01 | −.02 | −.06** | .05* |
| United Methodist | −.09** | −.01 | −.07** | .00 |
| Presbyterian USA | −.20** | −.00 | −.18** | .01 |
| Disciples of Christ | −.21** | ‡ | −.18** | ‡ |
| Individualist social theology | .53** | .07** | .50** | .07** |
| Civic gospel | .59** | .12** | .55** | .11** |
| Political ideology | | | | |
| Issue conservatism | .66** | .35** | .60** | .30** |
| Self-identified conservatism | .67** | .34** | .61** | .29** |
| Social and demographic variables | | | | |
| Education | −.23** | .07** | −.23** | −.06** |
| Age | −.01 | −.00 | .01 | .02 |
| Southern residence | −.03* | −.07** | .07** | .01 |
| Female | −.13** | .01 | −.11** | −.01 |
| $R^2$ | | .54 | | .44 |

* Coefficient significant at $p<.05$; ** $p<.001$.
† Positive coefficients indicate positive relationships with Republicanism and movement toward the Republican party; negative coefficients indicate negative relationships with Democratic identification and movement toward the Democratic party.
‡ Suppressed reference category for regression.

mographic factors, summarizing potential influences over partisanship. Then, to sort out the influence of each, we report the beta weights (b) from multiple regressions using these same variables to predict party identification and partisan change.

At the bivariate level, partisanship is strongly associated with many attitudes and personal traits. Republican identification is positively correlated with Christian orthodoxy, fundamentalist affiliation, and, to a lesser extent, conservative eschatology. And denominational identity still makes a difference. Compared with the rest of the sample, Assemblies clergy are more Republican, as are Southern Baptist, Evangelical Covenant, and Christian Reformed pastors; Methodist and, especially, Presbyterians and Disciples are significantly more Democratic. Social theology is tied to party affiliation: individualists and civic gospel adherents are strongly Republican, while communitarians and those rejecting the civic gospel identify Democratic.

Political ideology, however, has the strongest correlation with partisanship, whether measured by self-identification or by ministers' positions on contemporary political issues (see chapter 6). This strongly suggests that among clergy, as among political activists and, perhaps, the mass public, the American party system has become ideological, with the GOP attracting conservatives and the Democratic party attracting liberals (cf. Levine, Carmines, and Huckfeldt 1997). In contrast to strong correlations of partisanship with ideational variables, both theological and ideological, most demographic factors have limited influence. Higher education is modestly associated with Democratic identity, but age has no relationship either way. Southerners are still slightly more Democratic, but women clergy are distinctly more Democratic than men, reflecting the "gender gap" that has become a commonplace in describing partisanship in America.

The multiple regression confirms the tentative conclusions derived from the bivariate analysis: ministerial partisanship is largely ideological. The two ideological measures have the greatest impact, far surpassing all other variables. And although ideological identity and issue ideology are strongly correlated, both make distinct contributions. In other words, partisanship is influenced both by a minister's self-classification and by views on political issues. On the other hand, orthodoxy and religious movement disappear from the equation, but conservative eschatology makes a distinctive contribution not otherwise accounted for. Social theology retains a significant impact, with individualism and civic gospel sentiments aiding the GOP. Thus, we can safely conclude that theology influences partisanship indirectly: orthodoxy produces individualism, civic gospel notions, and conservatism, which in turn produce Republican preferences.

The coefficients' magnitude shows that ideology has overwhelmed any denominational influences. And, in fact, the denominational dummies all drop out, excepting Southern Baptists, who show a residual Democratic tendency. Even this effect seems destined for extinction, however, as it vanishes if the analysis is confined to Baptists under age forty-five, thereby eliminating the remnant of older "yellow-dog" southern Democrats. Traditional social and demographic influences over partisanship are reduced in power, as well. The correlation of higher education with Democratic partisanship reverses signs in the multivariate analysis as education becomes an influence for Republicanism once its theologically and ideologically liberalizing effects have been accounted for directly. Southern residence remains a modest predictor of greater Democratic affiliation, but women are no longer distinct, once their greater political liberalism is included in the equation.

We should also note one variable that is not in the equation: social class. We have no direct data on current income, but clergy salaries are closely tied to their congregations' size. This proxy variable reveals no influence, however, in either bivariate or multivariate analysis. We also have data on parental occupation for six denominations. In each the pattern is identical: pastors from farm and blue-collar homes lean Republican, while scions of business and professional families are most Democratic, just the reverse of the usual class alignment in American partisanship. Further examination suggests two explanations. First, those from wealthier backgrounds have attended more selective colleges and more prestigious seminaries, and have studied liberal arts subjects, resulting in theological and ideological liberalization. Second, for clergy unmoved in a liberal direction by educational experience, the greater theological, social, and moral traditionalism of blue-collar families finds better expression in the contemporary GOP. Nevertheless, even this modest bivariate relationship ($r = .11$) between social class and partisanship does not survive the multivariate analysis. Thus, religious polarization has eroded the old partisan alignments of specific denominations—once rooted in ethnicity, region, and class—and has created new, ideological alignments. In other words, ministers of similar ideological bent take on the same party identity, whatever their denomination, region, or social class. All in all, the model explains a very healthy 54 percent of the variance in partisanship.

If contemporary party alignments among clergy are predominantly ideological, partisan change should reflect the same influences; indeed, the results are consistent with that expectation. At the bivariate level, orthodox theology and social theology, and especially conservative ideology, are strong correlates of pilgrimage toward the GOP. The denominational dummies confirm the tabular results in Table 7.2: a Republican trend has been strongest among Assemblies, Southern Baptists, and Evangelical Covenant pastors, while ministers in the RCA, UMC, PCUSA, and Disciples of Christ have gravitated toward the Democrats. Higher education also is associated with pro-Democratic movement, but southern residence produces a drift toward the GOP, reflecting the much-noted regional transformation. Finally, women not only are more Democratic than men, as we saw earlier, but also are more likely to report a pro-Democratic shift as adults.

The picture presented by the multiple regression is quite clear: movement toward the GOP is predicted above all by conservative self-identification and issue positions, then by adherence to the civic gospel and social individualism, and by conservative eschatology. Once more, orthodoxy and theological movement identification drop out once the social theologies and ideological variables are entered.

Other variables have some modest effect: not surprisingly, Southern Baptists have moved toward the GOP, even when all else is accounted for, as have (more surprisingly) RCA pastors, but once again, most denominational locations have no independent effect. Among demographic factors, only higher education produces some movement toward the Democrats. Here again, partisan realignment among clergy has been predominantly ideological, with theological differences at the root. Our regression model predicting partisan change is quite successful, accounting for a very respectable 44 percent of the variance.

The ideological origins of partisan change are confirmed and elaborated by further analysis, using a slightly different set of variables. For six denominations, we have an ideological change measure comparable to that for partisan shifts (see chapter 5). If we include this measure in the regression, we find that it replaces self-identified ideology as the second most powerful predictor of partisan change in the sample as a whole, and for four of the six denominations. For the Covenant, Methodist, Presbyterian, and Disciples samples, both current issue attitudes and previous ideological movement have strong influence on partisan movement. This result suggests that some ministers have adopted a party label in line with stable ideological perspectives, while others have made choices that reflect changing views. Among Assemblies ministers, however, ideological change is a much more important predictor of partisan change, given the uniform conservatism and Republicanism of most of this group. In contrast, for Southern Baptists, current ideology overwhelms ideological change. Southern Baptists have always been predominantly conservative; the appropriate party selection has just changed.

## DEMOCRATIC AND REPUBLICAN PARTY IMAGES IN 1988

Thus, the traditional partisanship of clergy based on ethnic, regional, and social class characteristics of their denominations has given way to an ideological alignment, rooted in differing theologies, social theologies, and political attitudes. As social elites, however, clergy might be expected to have fairly sophisticated and differentiated perceptions of the two major political parties. In this section we look at the "party images" held by clergy around the time of the 1988 presidential election to get a richer picture of clerical partisanship.

One way citizens judge the two major political parties involves what political scientists have called "party image." As Flanigan and Zingale note in their standard treatment of partisanship, "Even though party images are strongly colored by long-standing party loyalties," they represent a set of variable attitudes which can have considerable effect on vote choice (1994, 176). Although each party had distinct images among the general public in the late 1980s, we would expect more specialized assessments to be present among clergy. And these images should be strongly linked to the moral reform and social justice agendas discussed in chapter 5, providing clear guidance to ministers on the performance that might be expected from each party on vital issues.

In the Wheaton study of religious activists, we asked clergy how they would evaluate the Republican and Democratic parties on ten kinds of issues, using a five-point scale ranging from 1 ("Democrats much better") to 5 ("Republicans much better"). As Table 7.4 shows, ministers as a group gave the GOP the nod over the Democrats on national defense, maintaining economic growth, protecting "family values," upholding moral standards, and maintaining social order, but they gave the Democrats high scores for representing minorities, helping the poor, protecting the environment, supporting free speech, and giving people more say in government. Thus, ministers did differentiate between the parties' performance on a wide variety of issues—and in ways that are consistent with public images of the parties at the time of our surveys (Flanigan and Zingale 1994, 176–178).

There are also consistent differences in evaluation by opposing theological camps. On all issues favoring the GOP, the orthodox give the party much higher ratings than modernists do, although on several even the latter give Republicans the edge. The exceptions are protecting family values and upholding morality, on which the most modernist clergy rate the Democrats better, creating a very wide gap indeed between the most modernist and most orthodox groups. Conversely, on three "Democratic issues" (representing minorities, helping the poor, and protecting the environment), even the most orthodox give that party a better rating, while modernists provide a very warm endorsement. On issues of free speech and giving people more say in government, the orthodox and modernists divide, but with an overall edge to the Democrats. Thus, orthodox clergy see Republicans as defenders of the

Table 7.4
Clergy's Partisan Images by Orthodoxy, Wheaton Religious Activist Clergy

|  | All | Most Orthodox 1 | 2 | 3 | Most Modernist 4 |
|---|---|---|---|---|---|
| GOP better |  |  |  |  |  |
| National defense | 63* | 80 | 78 | 54 | 17 |
| Economic growth | 63 | 71 | 69 | 61 | 40 |
| Family values | 54 | 83 | 78 | 44 | −25 |
| Public order | 51 | 66 | 58 | 49 | 14 |
| Promote morality | 47 | 69 | 64 | 36 | −4 |
| Give people more say | −7 | 28 | 6 | −25 | −62 |
| Protect free speech | −9 | 35 | −1 | −23 | −68 |
| Protect environment | −40 | −8 | −31 | −55 | −78 |
| Help the poor | −53 | −20 | −49 | −65 | −89 |
| Help minorities | −56 | −26 | −51 | −66 | −91 |
| Democrats better |  |  |  |  |  |

* The entries represent the difference between the proportion of ministers saying that the Republicans did better in handling each issue and the proportion saying the Democrats did better. Those seeing no difference between the parties are not scored. Positive entries are issues with a GOP advantage and negative entries represent a Democratic advantage.

moral reform agenda, embracing policies to protect the nation's security, public order, and social morality, while modernists see Democrats embodying the social justice agenda of caring for the outcast, the poor, and the environment. And proponents of each agenda recognize the opposing party's areas of strength.

## PARTY VOTING IN 1988 AND 1992

These party images certainly were cultivated by both Republicans and Democrats during the 1988 presidential campaign. Vice President George Bush burnished the GOP's strong images on defense and economic growth, while appealing to the electorate's concern with national values and public order (remember the Willie Horton episode). Bush's competitors in the GOP primaries, such as Senator Robert Dole or Congressman Jack Kemp, cast themselves as more effective proponents of Republican virtues, or put particular emphasis on one part of the party's image, as in Pat Robertson's appeal to traditional social values. In the other party, candidates focused on different Democratic virtues: Jesse Jackson sought to mobilize minorities and those concerned for the poor and disenfranchised, Senator Al Gore of Tennessee stressed environmental questions, while Governor Michael Dukakis extolled the Massachusetts "Economic Miracle," trying to steal a Republican issue, but also underlined his longtime commitment to free speech, bragging about his "card-carrying" membership in the American Civil Liberties Union.

Of course, the 1988 presidential election presents an especially interesting case for clerical choice for other reasons. First, two ordained ministers were running for the presidential nominations of their parties: religious broadcaster Pat Robertson was seeking the Republican endorsement, while civil rights leader Jesse Jackson had renewed his quest to win the Democratic nod. Both were Baptists but from different traditions. Robertson was ordained a Southern Baptist minister but had become a national spokesman for "spirit-filled" Christianity, more popular among Pentecostals and charismatics than with historically anticharismatic Southern Baptists. Jackson, of course, came out of the Black Baptist tradition and, like Robertson, depended on both the efforts of clergy and the support of churches (Hertzke 1993). Indeed, no fuller personifications of the moral reform and social justice agendas could be found than these two ministerial politicians.

The candidacies of Robertson and Jackson not only appealed to religious activists but also prompted their opponents to make their own religious appeals and attempt to line up other religious activists. George Bush's campaign, for example, sought to neutralize "Robertson churches," and other Republicans made undisguised appeals to religious leaders and laity. In the general election, Bush and the Republicans made many clear overtures to conservative clergy and laity, while at least some efforts were mounted to mobilize liberal religious leaders for the Democratic ticket, although Dukakis had a distinctly "secular" image and had a strong constituency of secular Democratic activists (Green, Guth, and Fraser 1991).

How did clergy respond to the 1988 presidential election choices? To find out, we asked ministers about the party nominations and their choices between George Bush and Michael Dukakis in the general election. Table 7.5 reports their answers. First, note the high voting rate among ministers. About two-thirds in each denomination voted in the primaries or participated in the caucuses, with no difference between the supposedly "otherworldly" Assemblies and Southern Baptists and the "this-worldly" Mainliners, although the Reformed clergy's participation rate is depressed by their location in the early caucus states of Iowa and Michigan.

Ministers' choice of primary reflected their partisan leanings. Virtually all Assemblies pastors and most Southern Baptists voted in the GOP contests, despite the

Table 7.5
Clergy's Presidential Choices by Denomination (Percent)

|  | AG | SBC | CRC | RCA | UMC | PRES | DOC |
|---|---|---|---|---|---|---|---|
| **Voting** | | | | | | | |
| Voted in primary | 69 | 64 | 48 | 50 | 69 | 67 | 73 |
| Voted in November | 99 | 99 | 98 | 98 | 98 | 99 | 99 |
| **Primary choice** | | | | | | | |
| Republican primary | 98 | 70 | 73 | 59 | 49 | 27 | 29 |
| Democratic primary | 2 | 30 | 27 | 41 | 51 | 73 | 71 |
|  | 100% | 100% | 100% | 100% | 100% | 100% | 100% |
| **GOP primary vote** | | | | | | | |
| George Bush | 64 | 64 | 64 | 67 | 67 | 67 | 65 |
| Pat Robertson | 27 | 11 | 5 | 7 | 16 | 5 | 11 |
| Jack Kemp | 4 | 12 | 11 | 4 | 3 | 4 | 3 |
| Robert Dole | 5 | 13 | 20 | 22 | 13 | 22 | 19 |
| Others | 0 | 0 | 1 | 0 | 1 | 2 | 2 |
|  | 100% | 100% | 100% | 100% | 100% | 100% | 100% |
| **Democratic primary vote** | | | | | | | |
| Jesse Jackson | 29 | 13 | 54 | 44 | 33 | 40 | 41 |
| Michael Dukakis | 29 | 20 | 29 | 33 | 40 | 38 | 34 |
| Dick Gephardt | 29 | 8 | 2 | 1 | 5 | 2 | 5 |
| Albert Gore | 14 | 50 | 0 | 0 | 11 | 10 | 7 |
| Paul Simon | 0 | 6 | 13 | 16 | 9 | 9 | 10 |
| Others | 0 | 3 | 0 | 3 | 2 | 1 | 3 |
|  | 100% | 100% | 100% | 100% | 100% | 100% | 100% |
| **Vote in general election*** | | | | | | | |
| George Bush | 98 | 82 | 73 | 58 | 50 | 34 | 34 |
| Michael Dukakis | 1 | 17 | 25 | 41 | 50 | 65 | 65 |

*Totals for Bush and Dukakis do not always add to 100 for each denomination because of votes for third-party candidates.

hopes of the inventors of Super Tuesday to attract traditional southern Democrats back to the party. Most Christian Reformed and Reformed Church pastors also voted in the Republican primaries, Methodists revealed their political division by marching in two equal-sized columns to Republican and Democratic polls, and over two-thirds of the Presbyterians and Disciples cast Democratic ballots. Once in the voting booth, Republicans from all denominations behaved quite similarly, but Democratic clergy took different paths. In the GOP contest, Bush won a uniform two-thirds among Republicans in all churches, but the distant runners-up varied. Robertson got one-quarter of the vote from fellow spirit-filled Christians in the Assemblies of God, a crucial target of his campaign, but failed badly among his fellow Southern Baptist ministers, in part because he was "spirit-filled" (cf. Shie 1991, 189). His failure to attract more support among these critical religious elites was the death knell for his hopes in the South. Surprisingly, Robertson also ran second among Methodist Republicans, but elsewhere Bob Dole was the alternative to Bush. Jack Kemp had appeal only to Baptists—and not much there.

Compared with the Republicans, Democratic ministers had diverse preferences, but there were some clear denominational favorites. The faithful remnant of Southern Baptist Democrats wanted one of their own, Tennessee senator Al Gore, but Democratic Methodists liked eventual nominee Michael Dukakis. Other Democratic clergy, however, preferred a fellow minister: the Reverend Jackson won a majority among the few Christian Reformed Democrats and a plurality of Reformed Church, Presbyterian, and Disciples Democrats, finishing second among Methodists and third among Baptists. Jackson's popularity illustrates the strikingly liberal preferences of many Mainline clergy, although the extent of that support may have surprised his followers. More than a few Presbyterian and Disciples pastors wrote on the survey form, "I'm probably the only minister in my denomination who voted for Jesse!"

Although the pattern is somewhat complex, the influence of theology and ideology extends even to intraparty choices. Among Republicans, Pat Robertson's supporters were most orthodox and ideologically conservative, followed by voters for Jack Kemp, George Bush, and Robert Dole, in that order. Although Democratic clergy, as we have seen, are much more modernist than Republicans, theology and ideology were still important: those preferring Richard Gephardt and Al Gore were more orthodox and conservative than those choosing Paul Simon or Michael Dukakis, who in turn were more orthodox and conservative than Jackson voters, the most theologically modernist and ideologically liberal (data not shown). The same general pattern applies to the impact of specific issues. Whether on abortion, gay rights, the death penalty, sex education in the schools, defense spending, or the environment, Robertson voters were the most conservative Republican clergy, followed by Kemp and the Bush voters, and finally Dole supporters. Among Democratic primary voters, a similar relationship existed between more conservative support for Gore, moving through more liberal support for Dukakis, and with Jackson voters holding down the left end on most issues.

Virtually all the pastors reported voting in November, bettering even the typically high turnout rates of college-educated professionals, even though not all Assemblies or Southern Baptist clergy have college degrees. Obviously, there is very little participatory advantage of modernist clergy when voting is involved. The November choices were considerably simpler than those required by the presidential primaries, eliciting starkly differing responses by denomination. Assemblies pastors voted almost unanimously for Bush, joined by four-fifths of Southern Baptists and 70 percent of the CRC. In the Mainline churches, RCA pastors gave Bush 58 percent of the vote, and Methodists again split down the middle. But Presbyterians and Disciples gave Dukakis overwhelming majorities, voting in the opposite direction from those in their pews (cf. Greer 1991). As expected, theology was strongly correlated with the vote: 94 percent of the most orthodox voted for Bush, while only 17 percent of the most modernist did.

Once again we employ a multivariate analysis to sort out influences over presidential voting choices. Because presidential choice is dichotomous, ordinary multiple regression is not appropriate. We used logistic regression to test the impact of the same variables used in Table 7.3, with the addition of party identification. As we might have anticipated from the voting literature, party identification overwhelms all other influences, producing 89 percent accuracy in predicting vote choice (data not shown). Political ideology and the civic gospel together add 2 percent, bringing the success rate up to 91 percent, a very respectable showing. No other variable adds any explanatory power. Thus, insofar as theological perspectives, denominational locations, social and demographic factors—and even ideology—influence electoral choices, they operate primarily through party identification. In many ways, our findings are reminiscent of the "funnel of causality" discovered by the early Michigan voting theorists: many factors operate to produce party identification, which in turn dominates vote choice (Campbell et al. 1960). Like more recent scholars, however, we find that ideology is not only the key component of partisanship among religious elites; it also adds some explanatory punch on its own to voting decisions.

## A NOTE ON AGENDA AND ISSUES

Perhaps it is not surprising that partisanship and ideology are such powerful predictors of the way clergy vote. Indeed, we found it almost impossible to find additional variables that increase our already near-perfect predictions of 1988 presidential voting. But we are also interested in what elections communicate to the victorious party (and to the losers as well). What do the elites, activists, and voters on the winning side expect of the successful candidates? Efforts by the newly elected to claim a policy mandate, and the attempts of interest groups, journalists, and scholars to explain the election's meaning, often entail an analysis of the special concerns of parts of the victorious electoral coalition and, thus, specific issues that influenced the vote.

For these reasons, we can look at the 1988 presidential vote from another angle. What agenda items and what issues influenced ministers' choices? Using logistic regression once again, we first incorporated the moral reform and social justice agenda scales from chapter 5 in an analysis predicting presidential vote. Not surprisingly, ministers high on the moral reform agenda had a strong tendency to vote for Republican Bush ($R = .33$), while high scores on the social justice agenda moved clergy toward Democrat Dukakis ($R = .39$). If we use the original agenda items, we find an even more specific set of influences: agenda concerns that produced the strongest Republican tendencies (controlling for all other agenda items) were concern with pornography ($R = .14$), abortion (.12), and education issues (.07). On the other side, the agenda concerns most strongly predicting a Democratic vote were more broadly dispersed: Reagan's policy in Latin America (.08), apartheid in South Africa (.07), civil rights (.06), hunger and poverty (.06), and the environment and jobs (both .05). Of course, these merely represent the areas of concern felt by clergy. Still, the analysis correctly predicts almost 83 percent of the vote.

When we turn to the specific issues encapsulated in our issue ideology score, we gain some additional insight. Support for Reagan's Latin American and defense policies, and backing for constitutional amendments prohibiting abortion and allowing school prayer, were strong predictors of a vote for Bush, while endorsing more generous social welfare policies, women's rights, abolition of the death penalty, and sanctions against apartheid in South Africa moved clergy strongly toward Dukakis. A comparable analysis using a somewhat wider range of issues in the Wheaton religious activist study produces very similar results, adding only opposition to gay rights and support for creationism as positive influences on the vote for Bush. Thus, while general ideological measures are powerful predictors of partisanship and, indirectly, of voting decisions, some issues are clearly more important ideological elements than others, at least in the context of particular election campaigns.

Table 7.6 summarizes the overall differences in policy views between Bush and Dukakis voters in 1988 on the moral reform and social justice agendas. The correlations (*r*) indicate the size of the difference between the two groups of clergy on each issue. As the data show, Republican and Democratic voters are deeply split over the death penalty, abortion, gun control, school prayer, creationism, gay rights, and sex education in the schools. Gaps are more modest on tuition tax credits, pornography, family policy, drug policy, and lotteries. Only on a few issues do a majority of Dukakis supporters take "conservative" positions, and on all these issues, Bush voters are more conservative still. On the social justice agenda, of course, the situation is a mirror image, with the Dukakis voters taking staunch liberal positions on virtually every issue and Bush partisans taking more conservative ones. Note, however, that on quite a few questions a large proportion of Bush voters, often a majority, nevertheless take a liberal position. Despite this finding, there is clearly an attitudinal basis for the real two-party system among clergy, if not clear evidence of a "culture war."

The resilience of these partisan, ideological, and theological cleavages is con-

Table 7.6
Political Attitudes and Presidential Vote in 1988: Bush and Dukakis Voters
among Protestant Clergy (Percent)

| | Bush | Dukakis | |
|---|---|---|---|
| | | | r= |
| Moral reform agenda | | | |
| Favor the death penalty | 79 | 36 | −.60 |
| Favor abortion amendment to Constitution | 77 | 33 | −.48 |
| Oppose gun control | 58 | 16 | −.48 |
| Favor a constitutional amendment on school prayer | 58 | 18 | −.47 |
| Creationism should be taught if evolution is | 71 | 30 | −.45 |
| Oppose gay rights legislation | 57 | 20 | −.42 |
| Oppose sex education in the public schools | 49 | 12 | −.42 |
| Oppose Palestinian state in Mideast | 49 | 17 | −.36 |
| Favor tuition tax credits for Christian schools | 63 | 32 | −.33 |
| Communities need more power over pornography | 97 | 86 | −.25 |
| Government policy should stress traditional families | 95 | 81 | −.25 |
| Drug policy should stress enforcement, not treatment | 51 | 35 | −.20 |
| Oppose use of lotteries by states | 85 | 80 | −.07 |
| Social justice agenda | | | |
| U.S. should not implement Star Wars defense | 25 | 86 | .64 |
| Oppose privatization of governmental services | 20 | 80 | .58 |
| U.S. should cut off aid to the contras in Nicaragua | 28 | 87 | .48 |
| Favor the Equal Rights Amendment | 18 | 57 | .44 |
| Favor sanctions against apartheid in South Africa | 36 | 88 | .43 |
| Favor government-sponsored national health care | 50 | 86 | .41 |
| The federal government should foster day care | 57 | 89 | .40 |
| Cut U.S. defense spending | 49 | 82 | .39 |
| Implement strategic arms limitation pacts | 60 | 91 | .37 |
| Government should do more in social welfare | 56 | 83 | .33 |
| U.S. should not support nondemocratic regimes | 40 | 67 | .29 |
| Favor affirmative action policies for minorities | 48 | 75 | .21 |
| Take aggressive action to protect environment | 63 | 78 | .17 |

firmed by ministers' votes in 1992. Of course, the electoral configuration in 1992 was quite unlike that in 1988, with a weakened President Bush challenged by a Democratic ticket of two Southern Baptists, Bill Clinton and Al Gore, a strong third-party candidate in Ross Perot, and a focus on economics produced by a stubborn recession. Nevertheless, our 1992 surveys of the SBC, Covenant, and CRC clergy show continuity rather than change in electoral patterns. Party identification shifted hardly at all from 1988 among Southern Baptist and Christian Reformed clergy (we had no data from 1988 in the Covenant sample). And Bush won 78 percent of the

SBC vote in the three-way race (down only 3 percent from 1988), 66 percent from the Evangelical Covenant clergy, and 79 percent of the Christian Reformed pastors, actually a slight increase from 1988. The agenda items associated with the vote in 1992 shifted somewhat, including the economy and jobs, and the deficit (both major campaign issues), along with holdovers from 1988, such as civil rights, gay rights, abortion, and the environment. Nevertheless, despite the changing political agenda, a logistic regression analysis of the vote in these three Evangelical churches shows that party identification, ideology, and adherence to the civic gospel were even more powerful predictors in 1992 than they were in 1988. No doubt, then, the predominantly Democratic, liberal, and modernist ministers in the UMC, PCUSA, and Disciples of Christ voted overwhelmingly for the Democratic ticket.

## PRESIDENTIAL CAMPAIGN INVOLVEMENT

A final aspect of clerical partisanship is behavioral: working for party candidates, a commitment that goes far beyond mere identification or voting. Remarkably, scholars have paid very little attention to ministers' participation in some of the most common forms of partisan activism, preferring to focus on social movement activities, such as protest marches and civil disobedience, or on church-related actions, such as forming social action groups or preaching on issues. We, too, address such activities in the next two chapters, but at this point we look at a neglected aspect of ministerial partisanship: supporting presidential candidates.

In 1988 we asked ministers in five denominations whether they had been active in the presidential campaign in any way. We have similar data from 1992 on Evangelical Covenant and Southern Baptist clergy. As Christian Right organizational activity has sought to mobilize conservative Christian voters, we can discover whether ministers have been activated and, perhaps, have assisted in activating their parishioners. We can also determine, for the first time, whether Mainline modernists are involved in conventional electoral actions in large numbers or instead prefer to work within their congregations or, at times, through more unconventional techniques.

We measured campaign involvement quite directly. After ascertaining a preference for their party's nominee, we asked ministers two questions: "Many people also work for a candidate by wearing campaign buttons, putting a sign in the yard, attending speeches and rallies, etc. Beyond voting, did you *actively support* a candidate during the primaries and caucuses? If YES, which candidate? How actively? Very, Somewhat, Slightly." We asked the same questions about the general election, after eliciting a preference between George Bush and his Democratic opponents, Michael Dukakis in 1988 and Bill Clinton in 1992. The results for 1988 are reported in Table 7.7, with all levels of activity combined into "active."

First, note that the proportion of ministers reporting campaign activity beyond voting varies considerably by denomination in both primaries and the general election, with the latter predictably drawing more interest. In the primaries, Disciples

Table 7.7
Clergy's Partisan Activism by Denomination, 1988

|  |  | All | AG | SBC | UMC | PRES | DOC |
|---|---|---|---|---|---|---|---|
| Percent active in |  |  |  |  |  |  |  |
| *Primary* |  |  | 14 | 17 | 11 | 22 | 26 |
| Most orthodox | 1 | *16* | 14 | 20 | 10 | 11 | 30 |
|  | 2 | *13* | 11 | 14 | 7 | 19 | 22 |
|  | 3 | *16* | — | 13 | 10 | 19 | 17 |
| Most modernist | 4 | *23* | — | 6 | 11 | 26 | 29 |
| *General election* |  |  | 17 | 37 | 11 | 36 | 41 |
| Most orthodox | 1 | *27* | 17 | 44 | 16 | 33 | 46 |
|  | 2 | *23* | 17 | 33 | 7 | 28 | 38 |
|  | 3 | *25* | — | 19 | 9 | 35 | 34 |
| Most modernist | 4 | *35* | — | 31 | 15 | 40 | 44 |
| Beneficiary of activism in general election |  |  |  |  |  |  |  |
| George Bush |  |  | 99 | 86 | 49 | 26 | 31 |
| Michael Dukakis |  |  | 1 | 14 | 51 | 74 | 69 |
|  |  |  | 100% | 100% | 100% | 100% | 100% |

and Presbyterians have a slight edge, although a considerable number of Southern Baptist and somewhat fewer Assemblies pastors also report activity. Surprisingly, perhaps, in view of their reputation for social activism, United Methodist ministers are the least involved. Indeed, Assemblies and Methodist ministers are barely more visible in the general election (and those involved are the same people), but the activist core more than doubles among Southern Baptists and also swells among Presbyterians and Disciples. Theologically, modernists have a slight edge across denominations: in the primaries, 16 percent of the most orthodox were active, compared with 23 percent of the most modernist; in the general election, 27 percent of the most orthodox were active, but 35 percent of the most modernist were.

Still, a careful look at denominational figures suggests one reason for theological differences. Among the primarily orthodox Evangelical churches, the Assemblies of God ministers are quite inactive, but the SBC pastors match the involvement of the predominantly modernist Presbyterians and approach that of the overwhelmingly modernist Disciples. In the SBC, moreover, the orthodox are the *most active:* 44 percent of the most orthodox Baptists report general election involvement. In all the Mainline churches, there is a curvilinear pattern on such activism: the most modernist are relatively active, but so are the most orthodox. Of course, the practical import of this pattern varies. Among the inactive Methodists, the modest level of involvement is fairly well balanced numerically, given the even theological division among UMC clergy. Because of the clear numerical advantage of modernists in the

PCUSA, their advantage in activism rates produces an abundance of liberal Democratic activity. And although the remnant of orthodox Disciples more than matches the activism rate of their modernist colleagues, they are swamped in actual numbers.

Ministers' decisions to enter electoral politics may thus depend in part on denominational context. Among the overwhelmingly conservative Southern Baptists, a decision to work for the Republican candidate is "appropriate," while in the liberal environment of Mainline churches, modernist and Democratic ministers feel more comfortable getting involved. And there must be constraints that preclude widespread activism among Assemblies and Methodist clergy. Perhaps the persistence of "otherworldly" and apolitical expectations among the former prevents strong commitment to candidates, even when one as close theologically as Pat Robertson makes direct, overt, and religious appeals to clergy (cf. Poloma 1989, 155–157). The Methodist case is also somewhat puzzling, given the UMC's historic reputation for social activism. Methodists' noninvolvement in presidential politics may reflect extreme personal caution, given the precarious theological, ideological, and partisan balance we find among the UMC clergy (and, to a considerable extent, among Methodist laity as well). This caution may well have been reinforced by warnings from UMC headquarters in 1988 against church involvement in the presidential campaign (Plowman 1988). Or, perhaps, the reluctance to get involved may come from the UMC's itinerant system, in which clergy move regularly every few years. Pastors may never feel secure enough with their parishioners or familiar enough with their communities to set down partisan political roots. Unfortunately for this thesis, the data show only a slight tendency for Methodist clergy with longer tenures to be more active. In any event, we find denominational location more important in explaining presidential campaign activism than in analyzing many other aspects of ministerial politics.

By this point, the beneficiaries of pastoral assistance should come as no surprise. During the primaries, clerical activists were distributed among the candidates in much the same fashion as ministerial voters. Bush was the favorite of Republican activists in all denominations, even among the Assemblies and Southern Baptists, where Robertson failed to make the inroads he hoped for among the clergy. Among Democrats, Jesse Jackson and Michael Dukakis drew almost equal numbers (data not shown). In the fall, Bush was the favorite of virtually all the Assembly activists, the overwhelming majority of Southern Baptists, and half the Methodists, while Dukakis secured an even higher proportion of work than votes from the Presbyterians and Disciples. And the correlation of activists' orthodoxy with their choice of campaigns was impressive ($r = .73$).

Did these activism patterns change in 1992? We can comment only on Evangelical Covenant ministers and Southern Baptists, the two denominations asked the activism questions in that year. Still, we find some interesting and important facts. First, the very modest degree of involvement by Covenant clergy shows that in some Evangelical denominations partisan politics is still not a habit for pastors. Although we have no longitudinal data on Covenant ministers, we suspect on the basis of interviews that results for earlier elections would not differ significantly. Second, and more politically portentous, is the striking increase in Southern Baptist involvement in the 1992 primaries and, especially, the general election. Baptist ministers reported extraordinary activity beyond voting in 1992: fully 27 percent reported participation during the primaries and 59 percent in the general election. This activity was concentrated among, though not confined to, the most orthodox, fundamentalist, and dispensationalist clergy. Clearly, then, for Southern Baptists the 1988 contest was simply a "warm-up" for more extensive electoral campaigning in 1992 and, if preliminary results from our 1996 SBC survey are any indication, for the foreseeable future. In fact, looking at other routine kinds of political activities, we also find steady increases among Baptists over the presidential election years from 1980 to 1992 (Guth 1996).

## CONCLUSIONS

Thus, we find that ministerial partisanship, electoral choice, and campaign activism have coalesced into a clear two-party system, with orthodox Republican clergy and more modernist Democrats confronting each other across an ideological divide. Most of the traditional denominational, regional, and class distinctions that may have once shaped the alignments of Protestant clergy have been overwhelmed by the impact of these basic ideological forces, resulting in a true "restructuring" of political partisanship among religious elites (cf. Wuthnow 1988).

By and large, Protestant clergy have chosen partisan affiliations consistent with their theological and ideological perspectives. Orthodox clergy with conservative ideological views have become part of the Republican constellation of forces, while modernist, liberal clergy have aligned with the Democrats. Although various factors lead some clergy to reject full psychological identification with a party, they nevertheless act like strong partisans. As a result of these developments, traditional influences over partisanship—such as ethnicity, region, and social class—have diminished in importance.

Not only do their partisan attachments suggest considerable psychological engagement in the electoral process, but many ministers' involvement in presidential election activism suggests that clergy have become important elements in the activist coalitions of the two parties, although it is clear that some of the orthodox have reservations about involvement and that even some liberal clergy, such as those in the UMC, may refrain from activism for various reasons. Of course, presidential elections are infrequent events, and only one opportunity for ministerial activity. Nor are they necessarily the best indicator of overall clerical engagement. In the next two chapters, then, we begin our look at the larger picture of ministerial involvement, investigating first the general attitudes about political activity that ministers bring to their decision making and then the overall involvement level of clergy and the factors that influence that involvement.

# 8
# Public Witness: Clergy Attitudes toward Political Activism

*I don't think as a general rule that pastors should speak for or against particular candidates.*

*I think it is appropriate for clergy to find out where candidates stand on moral issues and inform their congregations.*

*I strongly disapprove of a pastor endorsing a candidate from the pulpit. However, I strongly support a pastor who, on his or her own time, is politically active.*

*I have begun to believe that the only answer to effect change from a political standpoint is for Christians and conservatives to form a new party.*

Clerical attitudes toward the appropriate forms of political involvement vary tremendously. Some ministers shy away from the very idea of participation in any form, while others become "complete" activists. We have already observed many of the factors underlying broad orientations toward religion's role in the political process and, in the last chapter, discovered that many clergy have strong partisan attachments. Ministers constantly make decisions about the acceptable channels of political involvement: some think a broad variety of activities are appropriate, others approve a much more limited range of actions. Some ministers endorse only activity outside the church, while others find appropriate opportunities within the traditional pastoral role.

The classic studies of ministerial politics sought to determine ministers' attitudes toward various political activities, but they did not go very far in systematically explaining those attitudes. And there has been little effort to integrate these studies into the political science literature on political participation. This rich literature has identified many personal attitudes and traits that encourage political involvement, including high political interest, feelings of political efficacy, partisan commitment, and issue intensity, among others (Verba, Schlozman, and Brady 1995). Certainly, we would expect these findings to apply to ministers as much as to other citizens. But this literature has ignored what the earlier pastoral studies implied—that occupational roles and the expectations associated with them have a major bearing on political participation as well. Such special political opportunities and the norms surrounding them are present in many occupations, whether union shop steward, county extension agent, or college professor.

In this chapter we look at both personal attitudes that encourage participation of the kind which clergy share with other citizens, and those concerning the appropriateness of political expression by professional clergy. Our purpose is to determine whether either orthodox or modernist ministers have a consistent advantage in personal attitudes about politics, or in the way they see their professional role. We will then provide a multivariate analysis of ministers' professional role orientations toward "direct action" and "political cue-giving." Finally, we turn to ministers' perceptions of the support they expect to receive from their most significant "role" partners: their congregations. All this analysis is designed to evaluate what we might call the clergy's political potential: attitudes that either facilitate or constrain activism.

## PSYCHOLOGICAL AND ATTITUDINAL RESOURCES

What personal orientations enhance or inhibit pastoral political involvement? In their studies of the general public, political scientists have long noted the importance that interest in politics, a sense of political efficacy, and other personal attitudes have in predisposing citizens to political activity. And the literature on pastoral politics has strongly implied that positive sentiments about politics are not equally distributed among clergy. Hadden and Quinley both argued (often without evidence) that orthodox "otherworldly" clergy were less interested in politics, had less desire to be involved, felt less able to affect political outcomes, and saw less to be accomplished through politics than modernist "this-worldly" clergy. Nevertheless, this situation may have changed in the last two decades. Both Quinley's discovery of the disillusionment of modernist clergy with political action by the mid-1970s (1974, 3–4) and Robert Wuthnow's account of the political mobilization of conservative Protestants (1988, chap. 9) suggest that we should find fewer differences today.

### Political Interest

We begin with the crucial question of political interest. As Verba, Schlozman, and Brady recently noted, "Citizens who are interested in politics—who follow politics, who care about what happens, who are concerned with who wins and loses— are more politically active" (1995, 345). Although interest is only one measure of psychological engagement (van Deth 1990), the link between interest and activism is so powerful that some studies take it for granted. And yet historically, Protestant clergy may have differed in their concern with this-worldly politics, as some modernists made political activity a theological imperative, while orthodox ministers, and especially dispensationalists, disparaged political life.

Are the orthodox still less interested than their modernist colleagues? As Table 8.1 reveals, the relationship today is slightly curvilinear: the least orthodox clergy still claim a narrow lead, but the most orthodox clergy come in close behind, barely ahead of the two moderate categories. All groups of clergy reported much higher levels of political interest than did the American public at the time of our surveys, just after the 1988 elections (cf. Conway 1991, 10). Several factors influence ministers' interest. Pastors who identify with liberal theological movements are much more interested in politics than others, but fundamentalists are also somewhat more interested; in fact, at the bivariate level theological movement is a much better indicator of interest than is orthodoxy. Reassuringly, our third theological factor works as it should theoretically: conservative eschatology predicts less interest in political matters, especially when general orthodoxy and theological movement are accounted for. Denomination also has some impact, both at the bivariate level and when other factors are controlled: Assemblies and Southern Baptist clergy are more interested in politics than we would predict on the basis of their theological views, while Reformed Church pastors, Presbyterians, and Disciples are less interested. Perhaps recent Christian Right efforts to engage conservative clergy in politics have had some impact in Evangelical denominations, especially among fundamentalists.

To investigate the possibility that interest may differ considerably among Evangelicals, we again turn to the Wheaton religious activist study, with its broad range of Evangelical ministers. There is, in fact, considerable variation—even among these organizational activists—among Evangelical denominations. The strongest political interest is found among Baptists (of all kinds), evangelical Presbyterians (such as the Presbyterian Church in America), and the growing contingent of nondenominational Evangelical Protestants. Considerably less interest is shown by Pentecostals (with the partial exception of the Assemblies of God), Holiness groups (such as the Nazarenes), and the European Free Church groups (such as the Evangelical Covenant). That this pattern conforms to the apparent distribution of clergy and laity in Christian Right organizations suggests that interest is an important precursor (and perhaps product) of political engagement. Thus, not all Evangelical pastors exhibit high political interest, but at least some now match Mainline and modernist clergy.

As we might anticipate from political participation studies, higher education generates greater political interest among clergy, as it does among the mass public. Ministers with college and seminary degrees—and especially those with advanced work—are much more interested in politics. As we might also expect, graduates of the most prestigious colleges and seminaries exhibit more political interest. In addition, a minister's undergraduate major has some impact: those studying the humanities, social sciences, and business administration exhibit more political interest, while those specializing in religion, education, or the natural sciences have less concern for political life. These effects appear even when all other variables are held

Table 8.1
Clergy's Personal Orientations toward Political Activism (Percent)

| | All | Most Orthodox 1 | 2 | 3 | Most Modernist 4 | $r=$ |
|---|---|---|---|---|---|---|
| High level of interest in politics | 79 | 79 | 76 | 77 | 83 | $-.05^{**}$ |
| Would like to be more involved in social and political activities | 55 | 47 | 56 | 58 | 60 | $-.11^{**}$ |
| Ministers have great potential to influence political beliefs of their congregations | 65 | 77 | 64 | 59 | 54 | $.21^{**}$ |
| Difficult for ministers to know the proper political channels to use in accomplishing some goal | 55 | 54 | 57 | 60 | 49 | $-.10^{**}$ |
| Clergy of different faiths need to cooperate more in politics, even if they can't agree in theology | 72 | 69 | 75 | 72 | 72 | $-.02$ |
| Factors encouraging activism | | | | | | |
| Own theological attitudes | 78 | 70 | 78 | 83 | 87 | $-.13^{**}$ |
| Own political attitudes | 74 | 67 | 74 | 77 | 84 | $-.11^{**}$ |
| Denominational leaders | 26 | 18 | 24 | 27 | 54 | $-.19^{**}$ |
| My congregation | 23 | 21 | 25 | 24 | 22 | $.05^{**}$ |
| Other clergy | 20 | 15 | 21 | 24 | 25 | $.01$ |

$^{*}$Pearson correlations between original item and full orthodoxy index significant at $p<.05$; $^{**}$significant at $p<.001$.

constant. Historically, then, educational advantages probably explain much of the political dominance of theological liberals, who had more years of schooling than conservative clergy, but that gap has closed as Evangelicals have enjoyed more extensive secular and theological training.

As among other citizens, political interest among clergy is associated with a sense of partisan and ideological engagement. The stronger the partisan and ideological stances of a minister, the more he or she reports high political interest. Nevertheless, the effects are not symmetrical: strong Democrats report considerably higher levels of interest than strong Republicans, but both exceed that reported by weaker partisans and independents. On the other hand, strong conservatives report much higher levels of interest than strong liberals, who in turn are more concerned with politics than those with more moderate identification. (This same pattern holds on our issue ideology measure from chapter 6.) And those ministers who have become more conservative over the years are also more interested.

Although political interest is not stable and fluctuates with events, the data suggest that conservatives have indeed experienced a considerable increase in political interest, while modernist ministers have retained their traditional concern. The growth of conservative interest is indicated by the fact that on our seven-point scale, the largest proportion choosing point 1 ("Very Interested") are found in the SBC (34 percent) and the Assemblies (24 percent), rather than in the PCUSA (23 percent) or Disciples (20 percent). This high interest is especially evident among younger Evangelical clergy, who have been mobilized by the theological and ideological contests of the 1980s and 1990s. Ironically, among the Mainliners, very high interest is characteristic not of younger clergy but of those in their fifties, whose formative political experiences occurred in the civil rights and Vietnam War era, the heyday of the New Breed or Prophetic Clergy. As we look ahead, then, these findings suggest that further convergence in political interest between Evangelical and Mainline pastors is likely.

## Preference for Involvement

Thus, there has been a considerable narrowing of the gap between orthodox and modernist clergy on interest in politics. But one can be interested in politics without desiring to be engaged. More directly relevant is whether clergy want to "become more involved in political and social action activities." Although interest in politics and a desire to become more involved are positively correlated ($r = .39$), they are clearly different orientations. As Table 8.1 confirms, modernist clergy still report a greater desire to become more involved; but even among the orthodox, almost half the clergy want to be more active. A review of the theological, political, and demographic factors influencing this preference mostly parallels the findings on political interest. When all else is taken into account, adherents to liberal theological movements, strong Democrats, extreme conservatives, and those with advanced secular and seminary degrees want to be more active. Ministers in two Evangelical denominations, the Assemblies of God and the Christian Reformed Church, also exceed expectations in their preferences for more involvement, while clergy in the PCUSA and Disciples are more likely to want somewhat less involvement, once other factors are accounted for, as are strong dispensationalists, who follow theoretical expectations in being somewhat less likely to desire greater political activity. Younger clergy, especially in Evangelical denominations, also prefer more political action. Thus, although this item still reveals a liberal advantage, the results also identify a significant corps of young, theologically orthodox, conservative, and Republican clergy, ready to take political action when the opportunity arises.

The growing desire for political involvement among at least some Evangelical clergy appears clearly in longitudinal data on Southern Baptists. The proportion of Baptist ministers wanting to become more engaged in political and social action activities rose steadily after 1980, from 25 percent in that year to 31 percent in 1984, 41 percent in 1988, and 48 percent in 1992, a level sustained in 1996. This growth was especially visible among the most orthodox clergy and among those identified with fundamentalist or evangelical factions. Although we have no longitudinal data for other Evangelicals, we suspect that a similar pattern would be evident in many denominations. Obviously, those expressing a desire for more involvement are prime candidates for external mobilization (Rosenstone and Hansen 1993).

## Political Efficacy

Other attitudes influencing political involvement fall under the rubric of political efficacy. Citizens who think they can influence the political process are more likely to participate than those who do not (Rosenstone and Hansen 1993, 15–16; cf. Verba, Schlozman, and Brady 1995). Of course, political efficacy has different meanings for those in various occupational roles. For clergy, two kinds of efficacy are relevant: a sense of influence over their congregations and the ability to understand and traverse the political landscape.

Much of the political impact of clergy stems from their role as cue-givers. Indeed, many studies have shown that clergy are perceived as presenting political leadership cues by laity and especially by activists in their congregations, and that most parishioners generally approve of such leadership, although they may not always agree with its direction or with particularly vigorous political action by clergy (see Leege and Kellstedt 1993, 235–254). Certainly, the Christian Right's original strategy in the early 1980s was to mobilize clergy, who would then direct their congregations. And although some contemporary Christian Right organizations, such as the Christian Coalition, prefer to mobilize laity directly, others, such as the Religious Roundtable and the Christian Voters League, still seek to activate orthodox pastors, thereby unleashing "the wealth of political and legislative potential" in the conservative Christian community (Conn 1996).

Obviously, a minister's decision to give political cues depends in part on a perception that such activity will sway parishioners, or at least be well received. As Table 8.1 demonstrates, a strong sense of efficacy is one clear political advantage of the orthodox, who are consistently more convinced that "ministers can have great influence over the social and political views of their congregations." Over half the modernists also agree, but their endorsement is less frequent and much less emphatic. And the factors influencing pastoral efficacy favor the orthodox: efficacy is higher among younger ministers, fundamentalists, those with a conservative eschatology, political conservatives, Republicans, and Assemblies of God and Southern Baptist clergy. Education seems to have little impact; if anything, clergy with the least formal education have a slightly higher sense of efficacy. These findings are certainly consistent with other evidence on the clergy-congregation nexus in Evangelical and Mainline churches. Evangelical laity are most likely to be in the pews on Sunday, are most accepting of clerical pronouncements, put a premium on pastoral leadership, and often regard the minister's "Biblical warrant" for political preaching as definitive (Jelen 1993). As we have also seen, pastor and people usually concur on political and social questions, so the pastor is indeed "preaching to the converted," perhaps a liability in missionary work but a potential political asset. Liberals, on the other hand, face congregations less faithful in attendance, less deferential to pastoral leadership, less compatible in their political views, and probably less receptive to social and political cues (Leege and Kellstedt 1993, 235–254).

Another facet of efficacy is the pastor's self-confidence in negotiating the shoals of politics. We asked whether "it is difficult for ministers to know the proper political channels to use in accomplishing some goal." Presumably those seeing few difficulties are more apt to plunge into politics. As Table 8.1 shows, clergy reactions do not exhibit a simple pattern. The most modernist ministers are slightly less prone to see problems in locating political channels, but their edge over the most orthodox is slight, and the orthodox in turn have only a small advantage over the two middle categories. Denominational data show that Assemblies clergy and Southern Baptists express more doubts about finding the proper political channels than do those in other denominations, while ministers with advanced degrees, strong ideologues, and younger clergy feel somewhat more efficacious. But clearly no theological group is substantially more confident in its ability to pursue the best political strategies. Of course, some theorists argue that efficacy is really a result of participation, rather than a cause; but even if they are correct, the data still evidence a diminishing activism gap between theological groups (cf. Leighly 1995, 186).

## Social Capital: Cooperative Effort

Much scholarly ink has been spilled recently on the role of "social capital" in the political process (Putnam 1993). Social capital is a shorthand concept for the networks and norms that enable political actors to cooperate for common goals. One aspect of social capital that is especially relevant to clergy is willingness to work with potential allies of varying backgrounds. In the United States, with its plethora of interest groups, coalition politics is a prerequisite to success. Groups leery of coalition building may be doomed to failure. There are reasons to expect that the willingness of clergy to engage in coalition building may be distributed unevenly. On the one hand, Mainline churches have long stressed religious cooperation, whether in the form of the National Council of Churches or the ecumenical movement, and usually ignore denominational lines when politicking. Evangelicals, on the other hand, have often been restrained from both religious and political cooperation by particularism, the belief that one's own religious group alone has the true way (Jelen 1991). The Moral Majority's failure to build effective grassroots organizations has often been attributed to the reluctance of its independent Baptist clergy to work with Pentecostals and other conservative Protestants, whom they regarded as theologically deviant (Wilcox 1996, 41). In a similar vein, many Southern Baptists rejected both Falwell's Moral Majority and Pat Robertson's 1988 presidential candidacy not because of political disagreements but out of historic theological and organizational quarrels with independent Baptists and Pentecostals. In recent years, however, groups such as the Christian Coalition have worked to overcome this problem, but perhaps at the cost of de-emphasizing the role of clergy, the natural guardians of theological boundaries.

How do clergy react to "political ecumenism"? We asked whether "clergy of different faiths need to cooperate more in politics, even if they can't agree in theology." Surprisingly, perhaps, we found no statistically significant differences between modernist and orthodox clergy: over two-thirds in each theological group are open to political allies who differ in religious perspective. In fact, the few remaining variations are denominational: many Southern Baptists remain true to their historic "go-it-alone" policy and are significantly less willing to cooperate across theological lines, with some Presbyterians and Disciples following suit. In all three cases, however, there are special situations. Tracing the attitudes of SBC clergy over the period from 1980 to 1996 shows that they are, in fact, moving rapidly toward more cooperative perspectives. Thus, time seems likely to eliminate this denominational distinctive (Guth 1996). On the other hand, the "nonecumenical" attitude among some Disciples is a surprise, given their history of interdenominational involvement. As it turns out, among both Disciples and Presbyterians it is the theologically orthodox who reject political cooperation. This attitude, no doubt, stems from continuing theological battles within these denominations, in which orthodox minorities reject the ecumenical political "liberalism" associated with modernist elites.

## Other Facilitating Attitudes

Finally, we asked clergy in five denominations whether their political participation was encouraged or discouraged by their own theological beliefs, by their political attitudes, by their denomination's officials, by other clergy, and by their congregation. As Table 8.1 indicates, ministers in all groups report that their own theological and political beliefs encourage participation, although modernists are more likely to say this than the orthodox. As we expected, pastors with strong conservative eschatology are most likely to say that their theologies do not encourage political involvement. All this comports well with the patterns we found in earlier chapters. When it comes to prompting from denominational officials, only modernists have a majority reporting such encouragement, and Methodist modernists are especially likely to report positive cues. Clergy are much less likely to feel encouragement from other ministers, although a significant minority of movement liberals do (data not shown), or from their congregations, where at most one-quarter in any orthodoxy group find motivation. Although we must be cautious in this assessment, given that our data are confined to five denominations, it appears that political involvement, at least from the minister's perspective, is motivated primarily by personal theological and political beliefs in ways that still give some advantage to modernist Mainline clergy. And if the Methodist case is representative, modernists may still get the same kind of denominational backing that Quinley's New Breed activists enjoyed a generation ago (1974, 181).

So far, our analysis reveals a mixed picture. Many attitudes advantaging the

New Breed of modernist liberals in the 1960s are still present almost three decades later, but differences are hardly pronounced and probably shrinking. And in a few cases, the orthodox actually have outlooks more conducive to involvement. Modernists still have slightly greater political interest and desire to be involved, but the margins are quite small. The orthodox, on the other hand, sense more ability to influence their congregations on social and political issues, a perception certainly conducive to political effort. And there is remarkably little difference in theological groups' assessment of their ability to locate the correct political channels or their willingness to join coalitions. Modernists still perceive their theological and political beliefs pushing them into politics at a rate slightly higher than do the orthodox, and some modernists see more denominational encouragement, but once again the differences are hardly massive and also seem in the process of transformation.

## PASTORAL APPROVAL OF POLITICAL ACTIVITIES

Of course, political activism means different things to different clergy. For some, it conjures up images of picketing abortion clinics or engaging in civil disobedience to protest U.S. military action in the Persian Gulf. For others, activism means putting campaign signs in the yard, attending political rallies, and endorsing candidates. For yet others, it entails guiding parishioners down the "right" path through asides in sermons, the content of prayers, and the choice of church bulletin inserts.

In Quinley's 1968 survey modernists were far warmer toward almost all kinds of political activity than were orthodox clergy. Given the apparent surge of conservative activity since 1980, however, we need to revisit his findings and consider whether attitudes toward specific actions have changed, especially among the orthodox. Perhaps radical and liberal activists added new activities to the "political repertory" of citizens in the 1960s and 1970s, activities later adopted by conservative movements (Verba, Schlozman, and Brady 1995). Whether or not such previously unconventional activities have been widely diffused among the clergy, we also need to consider the possibility that the orthodox might be more comfortable than before with conventional political activities or, perhaps, those fitting more easily into the traditional religious styles of Evangelical pastors and congregations, possibilities neglected by Hadden and Quinley.

In any event, many studies of both citizens and political elites have discovered a strong connection between approving an action and undertaking that activity (Barnes and Kaase 1979). So, to tap attitudes toward the *appropriateness* of political action by pastors, we asked if they approved of clergy engaging in over twenty different activities. Most items were drawn from Quinley's original battery and were asked in all eight denominations. We also experimented, however, with other questions or variants that evoked the political leadership style of conservative clergy, such as offering prayers about a moral or political issue or praying for a candidate. Although these items were not asked of all clergy, we have responses from two Evangelical churches (the Assemblies of God and Evangelical Covenant) and the largest Mainline body (the United Methodists), providing a full theological range for analysis.

According to Quinley, attitudes of California clergy fell into three dimensions: "Church Leadership," items addressing pastoral activities within the church; "Opinion Leadership," incorporating two items on public statements about issues and candidates; and "Protest Leadership," involving protest and civil disobedience. Our factor analysis of a somewhat larger battery revealed only two dimensions: first, *direct political action,* including items on contacting public officials, joining political organizations, participating in protests, and forming politically related groups within the church; and second, *cue-giving:* taking stands on issues, preaching on political topics, or endorsing candidates—inside or outside the pulpit. Table 8.2 reports the proportion of ministers overall, and in each theological category, who approve of these activities. We have also included alternative items asked in only three denominational surveys with the factor on which they loaded in separate analyses.

### Direct Political Action

Perhaps surprisingly, many ministers have positive attitudes about direct action in politics. Large majorities approve of clergy contacting public officials, forming study groups on public issues in their churches, contributing money to political causes, and organizing political or social action groups in their congregations. Solid majorities also accept participation in protest marches, joining national political organizations, and even running for public office. Only acts of civil disobedience and open campaigning for political candidates fail to gain majority approval, although substantial minorities do endorse such activities.

The historic advantage of modernists still appears, however. Even on items meeting broad acceptance, modernists are more likely to give their endorsement. As the correlation of each item with orthodoxy indicates, theological gaps are largest over study groups in church, civil disobedience, church action groups, and national political organizations. More modest differences occur on contributing money to candidates, participating in protest marches, and running for public office. Only on the very popular activity of contacting public officials and the fairly unpopular one of campaigning for candidates are theological differences relatively modest, albeit still to the modernists' advantage. Overall, orthodoxy correlates with a cumulative direct action approval scale at −.45, capturing the strong tendency for modernists to approve of direct action more than do the orthodox.

While modernist clergy still have considerably more positive attitudes than do the orthodox, there is some evidence of change. A careful comparison shows that the full-sample figures for approval of activities in Table 8.2 are remarkably similar to Quinley's on the same or similar items (1974, 62). The significance of this comparison comes from the fact that his California sample was weighted toward the

Table 8.2
Clergy's Approval of Activities by Orthodoxy (Percent Who "Approve Strongly" or "Approve")

|  | All | Most Orthodox 1 | 2 | Most Modernist 3 | 4 | r= |
|---|---|---|---|---|---|---|
| **Direct action activities** |  |  |  |  |  |  |
| Contact public officials | 91 | 91 | 91 | 92 | 93 | −.05* |
| Form study group in church | 79 | 56 | 78 | 91 | 97 | −.40** |
| Contribute money to candidate | 72 | 58 | 68 | 80 | 87 | −.28** |
| Organize action group in church | 64 | 44 | 61 | 71 | 84 | −.34** |
| Participate in protest march | 60 | 45 | 57 | 66 | 78 | −.27** |
| Join national political organization | 57 | 44 | 51 | 59 | 77 | −.30** |
| Run for public office | 51 | 41 | 47 | 54 | 61 | −.17** |
| Commit civil disobedience | 40 | 24 | 32 | 49 | 63 | −.37** |
| Campaign publicly for candidate | 34 | 32 | 30 | 34 | 46 | −.11** |
| *Approval index for direct action activities* |  |  |  |  |  | *−.45** |
| **Cue-giving activities** |  |  |  |  |  |  |
| Offer public prayer on moral issue | 98 | 99 | 98 | 95 | 95 | .23** |
| Take public stand on political issue | 92 | 88 | 91 | 91 | 95 | −.10** |
| *"Moral issue"†* | *92* | *94* | *93* | *88* | *88* | *.17** |
| *"Political issue"†* | *65* | *61* | *62* | *72* | *83* | *−.16** |
| Preach sermon on controversial issue | 79 | 71 | 75 | 80 | 90 | −.19** |
| Offer public prayer on political issue | 72 | 74 | 68 | 70 | 77 | .02 |
| Public (not pulpit) endorse candidate | 60 | 60 | 55 | 60 | 64 | −.07** |
| Take pulpit stand on political issue | 52 | 49 | 47 | 48 | 64 | −.12** |
| *"Moral issue"†* | *96* | *99* | *96* | *91* | *92* | *.27** |
| *"Political issue"†* | *37* | *38* | *29* | *34* | *51* | *−.07** |
| Offer public prayer for candidate | 35 | 45 | 30 | 28 | 24 | .20** |
| Endorse candidate from pulpit | 7 | 11 | 5 | 5 | 5 | .04* |
| *Approval index for cue-giving activities* |  |  |  |  |  | *−.10** |

*Pearson correlations between original item and full orthodoxy index significant at p<.05; **significant at p<.001.
†Alternative wordings for item used in Assemblies of God, Evangelical Covenant, and United Methodist questionnaires.

modernist and activist end of the denominational spectrum, while our national sample includes a larger (and more representative) contingent of conservative ministers, supposedly more apolitical. That this more conservative sample gives responses similar to Quinley's more liberal pastors suggests a considerable increase of approval among orthodox clergy over the past two decades. The rise of protests and civil disobedience over abortion, pornography, and other social issues led by conservatives may well have bolstered approval ratings for these items, and the direct electoral mobilization by the Christian Right suggests more orthodox support for conventional involvement as well.

Once again, a look at Southern Baptist clergy reveals just such developments. From 1980 to 1992, Baptists warmed considerably toward direct action. For example, the percentage approving protest marches jumped from 21 percent in 1980 to 50 percent in 1992; acceptance of civil disobedience, a hot topic among Baptist prolifers, also rose from just 9 percent in 1980 to over 25 percent in 1992. The almost unanimous rejection of civil disobedience in the 1980 and 1984 surveys was reflected in a typical comment of one Baptist pastor: "There is simply no excuse for civil disobedience; all laws can be changed and all officials replaced." By 1988, however, at the height of Operation Rescue's activities at abortion clinics, a significant minority of pastors adopted a different tone. As one conservative Baptist put it: "All are bound by God's authority to obey civil authority unless it violates God's law or standard. Then, to be truly submissive means to follow God's law, but be willing to endure punishment honorably for disobeying man's law." As we shall see in the next chapter, these changes in attitudes are reflected in changes in pastoral behavior as well.

Although the greatest attitudinal changes among Baptists often occurred with respect to activities that were highly unpopular in 1980, somewhat smaller increases appeared even on more popular activities, such as forming public affairs study groups (57 percent to 72 percent), joining national political organizations (32 percent to 41 percent), and forming action groups (45 percent to 52 percent). On almost all items, even those where approval did not increase, there was a dramatic reduction in "strongly disapprove" responses and a commensurate increase in "not sure" answers. Preliminary results from the 1996 SBC survey show that these more favorable attitudes have persisted. Clearly, Southern Baptist clergy were undergoing a major reorientation of attitudes toward many political activities.

Even more striking is the theological location of the new Southern Baptist attitudes. From 1980 to 1992, approval of political activities rose most dramatically among the most orthodox (using the same metric as in the 1988 sample). Among this large group, slightly more than half the sample in each SBC survey, approval of protest marches rose from 19 percent to 52 percent; of action groups, from 42 percent to 55 percent; and of joining national political organizations, from 31 percent to 42 percent, with similar increases on other items. Among fundamentalists, the increases were even larger. Ironically, theologically moderate and liberal Baptists reversed course, often reducing their approval of political activism, no doubt in vigorous rejection of their opponents' use of these newly accepted political tools (see Guth 1996). And as we might expect, approval of direct action by the orthodox in the SBC is especially concentrated among younger clergy. In fact, differences between older, often antipolitical fundamentalists and their younger theological allies are often dramatic.

Although Southern Baptists may not be typical, they represent one very large orthodox contingent with new understandings of the appropriate political avenues for clergy. Thus, we suspect that our 1988 data capture many Evangelical clergy in transition. No doubt many other clergy, especially in the fastest-growing segments of the Evangelical community, have adopted friendlier attitudes toward political activity. Meanwhile, modernist Mainline Protestant clergy have maintained the enthusiasm for direct action that earned an earlier generation the sobriquets of "New Breed" or "Prophetic Clergy." Thus, we see additional evidence for two-party mobilization in American Protestantism.

## Cue-Giving Activities

In any event, clerical attitudes about cue-giving present a different picture. In providing political direction to their congregations, the orthodox come very close to matching or exceeding the approval rates of modernist ministers. As we shall see, this is especially true where such activities fit the religious styles and political agenda of Evangelical churches. Previous studies have not always offered a full range of cue-giving activities or specified very carefully a representative range of potential issues on which ministers of differing theological orientations might attempt to influence their congregations. In the second half of Table 8.2, we report data on ministers' approval of cue-giving activities. Two findings emerge: first, clergy are quite supportive of most cue-giving leadership; second, on many items, the orthodox compare favorably with modernists, or even exceed them in approval. And, as our experimentation with question form shows, orthodox clergy emphatically support cue-giving on "moral" issues but are less enthusiastic about "political" issues.

As we saw in chapter 5, orthodox and modernist clergy have differing agendas. The orthodox, in particular, argue that moral issues are fit subjects for action, while modernists adopt a more expansive definition of the appropriate public agenda. To test the practical implications of this distinction, in the Assemblies of God, Evangelical Covenant, and United Methodist surveys we deviated from a generic question on approval by introducing a distinction between "moral" and "political," initially qualifying the former as one "such as abortion or divorce" and the latter as one "such as taxes or unemployment." As the data show, this distinction often produces dramatic differences in response. For example, almost all clergy approve "publicly" praying on a moral issue, although, as the correlation shows, the orthodox approve much more strongly on the original five-point scale. When ministers in the other five denominations are asked whether they approve of ministers taking a public stand (but not from the pulpit) on a political or social issue—our usual question—large majorities in all orthodoxy categories approve, with modernists having a very slight advantage. When the two variants are used in three denominations, orthodox clergy are more likely to approve (and approve strongly) on "moral" issues, while modernists respond more warmly to "political" issues. Modernists are considerably more likely to approve of ministers who preach a whole sermon on a controversial social or political issue, but there are only very small differences between theological groups on offering a public prayer on a political issue and endorsing candidates (outside the pulpit).

When asked the generic question, only half the clergy approve of taking stands from the pulpit on "political" issues, with modernists much more supportive. But when "moral" and "political" are substituted in our three-denomination experiment, not only are clergy generally more approving on moral issues, but the orthodox have a considerable edge in strength of approval, while modernists are more supportive of "political" stands. Close to half of the most orthodox approve of offering prayers for candidates—an increasingly popular form of endorsement but one clearly not approved of by most modernists. Finally, only a few clergy—primarily among the most orthodox—accept the idea of endorsing candidates directly from the pulpit. As one very conservative (and very active) Southern Baptist pastor put it, "A minister of the Gospel should never demean the pulpit by endorsing a political candidate from it." Thus, both Jerry Falwell's dreams and the ACLU's nightmares of waves of "election sermons" from Evangelical pulpits are unlikely to materialize.

As the very weak correlation between orthodoxy and our overall cue-giving score indicates, orthodox and modernist clergy match up quite closely on such activities. This outcome obtained even though we were unable to incorporate statistically the "moral leadership" items in the score, as these were used in only three surveys. In calculating analogous cue-giving scores for the Assemblies, Evangelical Covenant, and United Methodist clergy, we find that the orthodox actually have slightly more positive attitudes than do the modernists (data not shown). These findings strongly hint that clerical evaluations of activism are based not only on the specific activity but also in part on which agenda is involved. Thus, the classic studies, focused on the civil rights, antiwar, and other liberal causes of the 1960s, underestimated orthodox clergy's approval of activism. Indeed, while the elite press and social scientists were most impressed by "New Breed" liberals, conservative ministers all over the country were involved in liquor regulation, gambling referenda, attempts to regulate pornography, and many other issues on the moral agenda. Our modest experiment distinguishing "moral" and "political" issues illustrates the importance of ministerial agenda.

To confirm this elemental distinction, we turn again to the Wheaton religious activist study. There we asked whether clergy approved of ministers speaking out on specific issues. Although this simple "yes" or "no" format is not identical with that in the denominational surveys, it should tap the same basic orientations as our "cue-giving" questions. We must also remember that the Wheaton sample is weighted toward organizational activists: all theological groups are inclined to speak out on all the issues listed. Nevertheless, this simple dichotomous question should elicit further empirical illustration of the moral-political distinction (Table 8.3).

Although the expected tendency toward complete activism does appear, orthodox clergy are much more likely to endorse speaking out on the moral reform agenda. Indeed, they not only give strong approval to cue-giving on pornography, sexual behavior, abortion, and school prayer but exceed the modernists' scores by large margins. Even on providing guidance concerning political candidates, slightly more of the most orthodox approve. When the issue falls on the social justice agenda, however, modernists hold a considerable edge, especially on world peace and protection for refugees. Only on church-state and criminal justice issues is there fairly general endorsement of ministerial cue-giving. Conclusions about which clergy are most supportive of cue-giving activism, then, must be carefully qualified by asking, "On what issues?"

Thus, we discover some important differences in attitudes toward political activism among clergy. We find, with Quinley, that the orthodox are still less likely to approve of direct action than their modernist colleagues, but that these attitudes are changing among many Evangelicals, as the Southern Baptist data show. And we

Table 8.3
Clergy's Approval of "Speaking Out" on Various Topics by Orthodoxy,
Wheaton Study Clergy (Percent Who "Approve")

|  | Most Orthodox | | Most Modernist | | | |
|---|---|---|---|---|---|---|
|  | 1 | 2 | 3 | 4 | Diff.[†] | r= |
| Moral reform agenda |  |  |  |  |  |  |
| Pornography | 97 | 83 | 76 | 60 | +37 | .21** |
| Proper sexual conduct | 89 | 85 | 83 | 64 | +25 | .22** |
| Abortion | 89 | 86 | 77 | 66 | +23 | .16** |
| School prayer | 76 | 65 | 55 | 51 | +25 | .12** |
| Social justice agenda |  |  |  |  |  |  |
| World hunger | 65 | 75 | 86 | 93 | −28 | −.19** |
| Housing/homelessness | 62 | 71 | 83 | 90 | −28 | −.18** |
| Peace issues | 52 | 60 | 78 | 85 | −33 | −.23** |
| Sanctuary for refugees | 40 | 49 | 58 | 77 | −37 | −.25** |
| Prison issues | 56 | 63 | 67 | 73 | −17 | −.12** |
| The economy | 48 | 50 | 53 | 62 | −14 | −.11* |
| Common agenda |  |  |  |  |  |  |
| Candidates for office | 35 | 31 | 29 | 30 | +5 | .05 |
| Church-state issues | 73 | 67 | 68 | 71 | +2 | .00 |
| Criminal justice and crime | 69 | 63 | 70 | 70 | −1 | −.04 |

* Pearson correlations between original item and full orthodoxy index significant at $p < .05$;
** significant at $p < .001$.
† Diff. = Difference between approval level of most orthodox and most modernist clergy. A positive figure indicates greater orthodox approval, a negative number, greater modernist approval.

find relatively few and modest differences among theological groups on cue-giving. All this confirms much political stirring among orthodox pastors in recent years. As they become more interested in public affairs and more convinced of the necessity of activism to restore America to her previous moral status, the easiest locus for this attitudinal transformation is in cue-giving activities, where the pastor is on familiar turf, with a congregation that is politically compatible and usually supportive of clerical pronouncements. Once orthodox pastors have exploited these possibilities, some begin to consider more direct political action.

## FACTORS INFLUENCING APPROVAL OF PARTICIPATION

What factors influence ministers' approval of political involvement? Although we have illustrated throughout the previous sections the relationship of Christian orthodoxy to attitudes toward direct action and cue-giving activities, we need to introduce other elements of ministerial belief and identity. A preliminary look at the bivariate relationships among these variables and our direct action and cue-giving scales reveals much stronger relationships with attitudes on direct action than with those on cue-giving. First, approval of direct action is strongly correlated with theological modernism, liberal identification, and nondispensational eschatology, but the associations with cue-giving are much weaker, barely reaching statistical significance. And compared with the entire sample, the Assemblies, Baptist, and Covenant clergy are more disapproving of direct action, the Methodists (again) settle on the mean, and the Presbyterians and Disciples are more positive, as, more surprisingly, are the two Reformed churches. Denomination correlates very weakly with cue-giving, however, with Covenant, Methodist, and Assemblies clergy (in that order) somewhat less approving, while Southern Baptists move to the positive side, along with the Reformed pastors, Presbyterians, and Disciples. As we might expect, communitarians strongly approve direct action but have only a modest edge on cue-giving, while civic gospel adherents are less in favor of direct action but do not differ on cue-giving. Church priorities work as expected. Emphasis on protecting moral standards in America and evangelism are both associated with negative attitudes toward both types of activities, while those stressing political priorities, not surprisingly, are more approving of both.

Agendas and political attitudes also help locate supporters of each type of activism. Extreme liberals, adherents of the social justice agenda, and strong Democrats approve direct action, but only the social justice agenda has a large impact on cue-giving as well. An extensive moral reform agenda discourages direct action but also has a solid positive association with cue-giving. Strong Republicans and conservatives disapprove direct action but do not differ from the sample on cue-giving. And demographic variables are related in predictable ways. Ministers with more education, younger clergy, nonsoutherners, and women are most positive about direct action but are not notably different on cue-giving. Nevertheless, with the exception of years of education, the demographic correlations are not very strong.

As we have seen previously, many of these variables are interrelated: theology, social theology, political agendas, and political beliefs are often connected to each other. To sort out their influence, we incorporated all the variables in multiple regressions, with our direct action and cue-giving measures as the dependent variables. In Table 8.4 we report the beta weights (b) for the influence that our most important measures of theology, social theology, issue agenda, political attitudes, and demographic factors have on ministers' orientation toward political activities.

The most important factors directly influencing a minister's approval of direct action are ideological and theological: extreme liberal ideology and the social justice agenda exhibit a strong influence. Once all other factors are accounted for, the moral reform agenda and Republican partisanship also have a positive influence on approval (this reverses a negative bivariate relationship). Even when political agendas and attitudes are accounted for, the religious variables still have an impact, although the coefficients are quite modest, suggesting that their influence operates indirectly through ideology, agenda, and partisanship. The more orthodox and the more dispensational the clergy, the less the approval of direct action. When entered in the regression as dummy variables with the Assemblies of God representing the suppressed reference group or basis of comparison, the Reformed churches, especially, along with the Presbyterians and Disciples, still exhibit a considerable edge in approval, even with all other variables accounted for, while the Southern Baptist, Covenant, and Methodists do not differ much, once other factors are included.

Our social theology measures also remain as significant predictors, with individualists less likely to approve direct action than communitarians. Interestingly, however, the civic gospel variable reverses signs in the multivariate analysis (in comparison with a negative bivariate correlation), indicating that once other theological measures associated with this ideology—and with political passivity—are accounted for, civic gospel beliefs actually increase approval of direct action. Thus, Christian Right leaders have made some progress in convincing conservative pastors that their orthodox theology does not prohibit political involvement. Note, however, that moral priorities still have a modest negative effect on direct action approval, while political priorities have a similarly modest positive effect.

Finally, demographic variables continue to have some impact. When all else is accounted for, the solid bivariate influence of age actually increases: younger ministers are much more likely to approve of direct action activities, as are ministers with longer education. The historic apolitical bent of southern religion sticks in the multivariate analysis, but barely. Once other factors are accounted for, southern clergy do not differ much from those in other regions. The solid advantage that women clergy have in bivariate terms washes out in the multivariate results. Women clergy are more supportive of direct action because they are younger, less orthodox, and more liberal politically, but their attitudes toward direct action do not differ from those held by comparable men. And a liberal arts major is significant, with humanities and

Table 8.4
Influences on Ministers' Approval of Direct Action
and Cue-Giving Activities

| | Direct Action<br>b | Cue-Giving<br>b |
|---|---|---|
| Theological variables | | |
| Christian orthodoxy | −.11** | −.04 |
| Conservative eschatology | −.06 | .07* |
| Fundamentalist movement | .01 | −.01 |
| Denomination | | |
| Assemblies | † | † |
| Southern Baptist | .04* | .10** |
| Evangelical Covenant | .04* | −.11** |
| Christian Reformed | .28** | .25** |
| Reformed Church | .23** | .18** |
| United Methodist | .01 | −.03 |
| Presbyterian USA | .11** | .11** |
| Disciples of Christ | .08** | .10** |
| Individualist social theology | −.09** | .03 |
| Civic gospel | .20** | .18** |
| Moral priorities | −.08** | −.01 |
| Mission priorities | .03 | −.02 |
| Political priorities | .07** | .10** |
| Political variables | | |
| Social justice agenda | .16** | .20** |
| Issue liberalism | .29** | .16** |
| Democratic identification | .06** | .06* |
| Moral reform agenda | .07* | .10** |
| Issue conservatism | .01 | .12** |
| Republican identification | .05* | .07* |
| Social and demographic variables | | |
| Education | .10** | −.02 |
| Age | −.19** | −.05* |
| Southern residence | −.04* | .01 |
| Female | .00 | −.03* |
| Liberal arts major | .05* | .03 |
| $R^2 =$ | .45 | .21 |

* Coefficient significant at $p < .05$; ** $p < .001$.
† Suppressed reference category for regression.

social science majors more approving of direct action. Overall, the model in Table 8.4 accounts for close to half (45 percent) of the variation in ministers' attitudes toward direct action.

As we can see, modernist liberals still approve more strongly of direct action activities than their orthodox, conservative colleagues, but there are influences that may benefit conservatives in the future: their churches are led increasingly by younger, well-educated ministers with higher levels of political interest. Many are adopting a civic gospel orientation that provides at least some impetus for direct action activities, a powerful conservative agenda is being built that may eventually overcome the depoliticizing impact of traditional orthodoxy and individualist social theology, and the compatible attitudes of Evangelical pastors and congregations may remove one factor constraining activism.

Our multivariate analysis of cue-giving approval confirms that the conservative disadvantage here is rather minimal. A look at the betas suggests that modernists and political liberals have a markedly reduced advantage. When everything is accounted for, there are factors that encourage activity on both sides. While extreme liberals, proponents of the social justice agenda, and Democrats are more approving of cue-giving, so are dispensationalists, adherents of the civic gospel, advocates of the moral reform agenda, and extreme conservatives. Southern Baptist, Christian Reformed, Reformed Church in America, and Presbyterian clergy all are more likely to approve these activities, while the Covenant and Methodist ministers fall on the other side. Younger ministers and male clergy are slightly, but significantly, more likely to approve cue-giving. Nevertheless, cue-giving preferences are not as easily explained as those for direct action. The independent variables together account for only about a fifth of the variance. All this confirms that the forces giving modernists the edge on direct action give them less of a vantage point on cue-giving.


## CONGREGATIONAL REACTION TO MINISTERIAL ACTIVITY

Of course, a minister's personal attitudes are not the only important considerations in predicting involvement. It is also vital to know how his or her congregation responds. As Quinley and Hadden have shown, this is hardly a hypothetical question for those whose livelihood depends upon the goodwill of parishioners. In congregational polities, such as those of the Assemblies of God, Southern Baptists, and Disciples of Christ, the dependence is very direct; but even in more episcopal or connectional polities, such as that of the Methodists, congregational resistance can be a major problem for clergy wanting an active political life, especially if their agenda and views differ from the laity's. As Hadden and Quinley both argued, New Breed activism in the 1960s was eventually halted in large part by congregational resistance (for several specific illustrations, see Balmer 1996).

So, in addition to asking about ministers' approval of clerical actions, we inquired how their congregations would react to each. A quick comparison shows that ministers perceive more congregational support than did Quinley's clergy in 1968. This pattern appears for delivering a sermon on a controversial issue (54 percent support in our sample to 36 percent in Quinley's), publicly taking a stand on an issue (43 percent to 30 percent), organizing a social action group in the church (37 percent to 30 percent), publicly supporting a candidate (24 percent to 17 percent), participating in a protest march (23 percent to 8 percent), and participating in civil disobedience (8 percent to 2 percent). Only on organizing a study group (57 percent to 59 percent) and taking a pulpit stand on a political issue (21 percent to 18 percent) was there no significant difference between the two samples. Clergy today apparently perceive somewhat warmer congregational reactions to ministerial involvement than did their New Breed predecessors, a conclusion also supported by national poll data (Pew Research Center 1996).

Ministers do tend to see their people's reaction through their own preferences; indeed, on many activities over half the pastors claim complete consensus. Interestingly, modernists often view their congregations as more supportive than do orthodox ministers, but primarily on direct action items. The largest gaps appear on forming study groups, for which 81 percent of the most modernist perceive support, compared with 36 percent of the most orthodox, giving money to candidates (61 percent to 31 percent), forming action groups in the church (50 percent to 28 percent), and joining national political organizations (45 percent to 25 percent). On the other hand, the most orthodox clergy perceive more congregational support than do modernists for taking moral issue stands in public (80 percent to 57 percent) and from the pulpit (90 percent to 73 percent), praying for candidates (34 percent to 24 percent), praying on political issues (62 percent to 53 percent), and public endorsements of candidates (33 percent to 13 percent). Just as orthodox clergy tend to prefer cue-giving activities to direct action, they also tend to see their congregations supporting these activities more fully.

Whatever the differences in ministers' perceptions of congregational reactions to specific activities, pastors of all theological stripes generally see their congregations being less supportive of almost all kinds of ministerial politics than they themselves are. To illustrate this pattern, in Table 8.5 we report the mean net differences between pastoral and congregational attitudes on each action in Table 8.2, both for the entire sample and for each orthodoxy category. We have reordered the actions by listing first those on which pastors and congregations agree *least*.

The biggest gaps between ministers and congregations over direct action come, not surprisingly, on the more disruptive acts of protest marching and civil disobedience; ministers perceive their people as even less supportive than they themselves are. A large difference also appears on running for public office, and somewhat smaller ones on more conventional actions generally approved by clergy, such as contributing to candidates, joining political organizations, contacting public officials, and forming study and action groups. And just as the orthodox are more likely to perceive themselves in political agreement with their congregations (see chapter 6), so they are also more likely to perceive minimal differences in their ratings of direct action. As Table 8.5 reports, the most orthodox clergy, on average, report rather small differences, with only running for office approaching a half-point scale difference. In most instances, the gap between ministerial and congregational approval increases as ministers become more liberal theologically; indeed, among the most modernist, differences average anywhere from about a half point to over a full point on protest marches and civil disobedience. On such "unruly" activity, *all* clergy perceive their congregations as quite hostile. On most types of activity, however, the gap has a different composition: modernists actually perceive their congregations as *more supportive* than do orthodox clergy, but their own approval of direct

Table 8.5
Ministers' Perception of Differences between Their Approval of Activities and Their Congregations' by Orthodoxy (Mean Difference on Five-Point Item on Each Activity)

| | All | Most Orthodox 1 | 2 | 3 | Most Modernist 4 | *r= |
|---|---|---|---|---|---|---|
| Direct action activities | | | | | | |
| Participate in protest march | .62 | .23 | .47 | .84 | 1.09 | .34** |
| Commit civil disobedience | .61 | .15 | .40 | .81 | 1.20 | .40** |
| Run for public office | .54 | .46 | .43 | .55 | .62 | .10** |
| Contribute money to candidate | .37 | .27 | .29 | .43 | .53 | .12** |
| Organize action group in church | .34 | .13 | .23 | .42 | .65 | .25** |
| Contact public officials | .32 | .27 | .32 | .29 | .49 | .11** |
| Form study group in church | .32 | .21 | .29 | .38 | .43 | .13** |
| Join national political organization | .28 | .12 | .13 | .29 | .59 | .23** |
| Campaign publicly for candidate | .19 | .07 | .16 | .24 | .59 | .18** |
| Cue-giving activities | | | | | | |
| Preach sermon on controversial issue | .59 | .43 | .48 | .60 | .72 | .13** |
| Take public stand on political issue | .49 | .52 | .46 | .70 | .80 | .16** |
| *"Moral issue"[†]* | *.37* | *.27* | *.36* | *.43* | *.61* | *.15**￼* |
| *"Political issue"[†]* | *.35* | *.14* | *.35* | *.61* | *.70* | *.27**￼* |
| Take pulpit stand on political issue | .49 | .26 | .31 | .47 | .73 | .19** |
| *"Moral issue"[†]* | *.25* | *.24* | *.22* | *.21* | *.39* | *.08**￼* |
| *"Political issue"[†]* | *.21* | *.08* | *.12* | *.37* | *.60* | *.23**￼* |
| Public (not pulpit) endorse candidate | .41 | .25 | .29 | .45 | .70 | .20** |
| Offer public prayer on political issue | .20 | .13 | .18 | .29 | .37 | .14** |
| Offer public prayer on moral issue | .16 | .15 | .17 | .13 | .16 | .02 |
| Offer public prayer for candidate | .09 | .08 | .04 | .15 | .17 | .07* |
| Endorse candidate from pulpit | .01 | +.08 | +.07 | +.02 | .14 | .13** |

* Pearson correlation between score and full orthodoxy index significant at *p* < .05; ** significant at *p* < .001.
† Alternative wordings for item used in Assemblies of God, Evangelical Covenant, and United Methodist questionnaires.

action "outruns" that higher congregational tolerance, creating the larger "gaps" seen in Table 8.5.

The situation is somewhat different with cue-giving. For these activities, once again, modernist ministers consistently perceive larger differences in approval of clerical action between themselves and their congregations. Indeed, for the most modernist clergy, the differences are fairly consistent at about three-quarters of a point for cue-giving activities, whether from the pulpit or outside. Only on a few of the least popular items, such as offering prayers for candidates, do they and their congregations agree (in disapproval). Once again, the gaps between orthodox congregations and their clergy are modest, especially when "moral" rather than "political" questions are involved. When this division is made, ministers and people are in greater agreement, especially in their willingness to allow clergy to act on issues of moral importance.

When modernists' approval of political activity differs from that of their congregations, it is almost always the pastor who has more positive attitudes. But another kind of discrepancy exists for some orthodox clergy. Although, as we have seen, the orthodox usually agree with their parishioners, on several items some conservatives actually perceive their people to be *more* supportive of action than they themselves are. For example, about a fifth of the orthodox say their congregations' approval exceeds their own on pulpit and public endorsements of candidates, running for public office, campaigning for candidates, and joining national political organizations. A slightly smaller group sees similar backing for protest marches, study groups, action groups, financial contributions to candidates, and political sermons. Here, then, we see congregational pressure on some conservative ministers to become more active politically. And although this may not exactly represent a new kind of "gathering storm" in Evangelical churches, such expectations have become a part of the job description for clergy in some congregations (cf. Dobson 1996).

Thus, our look at ministers' perception of potential congregational reaction to activism suggests several conclusions. First, ministers in the 1990s see a good bit more congregational support for activism than did their 1960s predecessors. Second, modernists perceive more support for direct action than do the orthodox, while the latter find their congregations more supportive of cue-giving than do modernists. Finally, ministers generally see their congregations as less tolerant of most political actions than they themselves are, indicating that for many potential activists among the clergy, the congregation may act as a restraint. Still, it is important to note that a majority of ministers tend to agree with their parishioners in evaluating many items. Modernists are more likely to confront a major gap between their own strongly positive feelings about involvement and a less positive reaction by the congregation, while some of the orthodox actually perceive some pressure from the congregation to be more active than they want to be. In any event, the smaller gaps between the orthodox and their congregations open up opportunities for mobilization of pastors by Christian Right organizations.

## CONCLUSIONS

In this chapter we have revisited the findings of Jeffrey Hadden, Harold Quinley, and other scholars on the basic orientation of Protestant ministers toward various kinds of political activities. Like those studies, we find that modernist, liberal clergy possess many beliefs and attitudes that produce a more positive role orientation toward at least some actions that ministers have historically undertaken to influence the governmental process. They have slightly higher levels of political interest, want to be more involved in social and political action, and point to their own theological and political beliefs as important sources of motivation, while perceiving at least some denominational encouragement for such action.

When it comes to approval of specific activities, modernists are still substantially more supportive of both the direct action that gave the "New Breed" its name in the 1960s—protest, civil disobedience, joining national movements—and more conventional political acts, such as contributing to candidates, running for public office, or working in a political campaign. They also maintain a slight advantage in cue-giving, especially on issues remote from the traditional moral concerns of conservative clergy and parishioners. On both direct action and cue-giving the theological, political, and educational advantages of modernist liberals might seem to preserve a solid advantage in attitude and orientation.

And yet, positive attitudes about political involvement are on the rise among orthodox ministers, especially when the researcher is careful to use the terms and contexts within which such involvement is most appropriate. Thus, the recent Christian Right mobilization is buttressed by basic attitudinal changes among Evangelical clergy. Orthodox ministers have closed the gap in political interest, have a considerable desire for greater involvement in social and political action, are more confident about their ability to influence their parishioners, and are almost as willing as their modernist brethren to join hands across previously unbreachable theological boundaries for good political purposes. While they generally remain somewhat less enamored of direct action as an avenue for clerical involvement, their attitudes toward traditional leadership roles are just as positive as those of modernists, especially when the issue is defined as "moral"—not an infinitely expandable category but an elastic one nevertheless in the hands of Evangelical elites. And in addition to finding themselves in general agreement with their people on most political issues, orthodox clergy also find themselves in closer agreement with their congregations on appropriate political roles for ministers.

Where we have longitudinal data available, as in the Southern Baptist case, we find massive changes over the past two decades, changes that extended beyond our 1988 study. Although not all Evangelicals have experienced the same politicization, evidence suggests that the largest and fastest-growing segments of the orthodox Protestant community have become much more accepting of political involvement: Baptists generally, nondenominational Protestants, various Evangelical Presbyterian groups, and the Assemblies of God (but not all Pentecostals). On the other hand, many traditional Evangelical clergy in churches such as Pentecostal, Holiness, and some formerly ethnic denominations (such as the Evangelical Covenant in this study) cling to more traditional apolitical stances.

These differences in the Evangelical community are worth stressing for several reasons, not the least of which is the relative size of the politicized and less politicized elements. Although we have weighted our denominational samples equally for purposes of analysis, we should remember that "politicized" Evangelicals include not only the largest and most rapidly growing lay contingents but the largest group of clergy. The SBC alone has about as many ordained clergy as all four Mainline churches in this study combined, and almost as many members. The point is simple: although the average political attitudes of Evangelical clergy may still not be as conducive to political action as those of Mainliners, the absolute number of conservative clergy predisposed to approve political activity is large and growing, and probably exceeds that of activist liberals. Whether and how those clergy become active is the story of the next chapter.

# 9
# Petitioning Caesar: Political Involvement by Ministers

The final question we consider is this: How active are Protestant clergy in politics? On this issue there is much room for scholarly debate. The classic studies found theologically modernist and politically liberal clergy more engaged in public life than their orthodox and conservative counterparts, but as we have seen, these studies may have distorted the clergy's political role. Written at the height of protest against racial injustice, poverty, and the Vietnam War, they understandably focused on such activities. They not only ignored activism on conservative issues but also neglected conventional acts, especially of the kind befitting the style of theological traditionalists. And they assumed that the liberal advantage in activism was a permanent feature of ministerial politics, rather than a reflection of the politics of the 1960s (Beck and Jennings 1979). Today clergy from both ends of the political spectrum engage in a wide range of political actions. We want to explain not only why some clergy are more active than others but also why certain clergy prefer specific kinds of political activities.

In this chapter we review the involvement of Protestant clergy in the late 1980s and early 1990s, finding that modernists continue to dominate some forms of political expression common during the 1960s heyday of the New Breed but also that orthodox ministers have closed the gap on others. In addition, orthodox clergy have their own preferred forms of involvement, in which they sometimes exceed the modernists. Then we seek to explain ministerial involvement in eight different participation modes, testing perspectives drawn from the scholarly literature on participation and from earlier clergy studies. We find that socioeconomic status, psychological engagement, and organizational mobilization all influence certain forms of activism, but that ministerial role orientations and ideological mobilization provide the most powerful explanations. Finally, we assess the factors influencing overall activism, both during a minister's career and in 1988.

## POLITICAL ACTIVISM BY CLERGY: CAREER PATTERNS AND 1988

How active were orthodox and modernist ministers in the late 1980s? Were the relative levels of activism changing? Did different clergy vary in kind of activity? Had the repertory of routine clerical actions expanded to include activities that were once exceptional? To answer these and other questions, we asked ministers in five denominations (the Assemblies of God, Southern Baptists, Methodists, Presbyterians, and Disciples of Christ) two questions: first, whether they had *ever* engaged in particular political actions and, second, whether they had undertaken these *in 1988*. Ministers' answers to the first set of queries provide us with data on what we will call their *career participation,* while answers to the second supply information on *current* or election-year activism. We expect that career participation will reflect past patterns of political activism, while the data from the election year of 1988 should capture contemporary patterns and influences. Thus, in the following tables we report both sets of responses. Altogether, we listed twenty-three political acts, but not all items were used in all denominations. A few were asked only of Assemblies and Methodist pastors (and in the 1992 Covenant study), while others appeared only in the Baptist, Presbyterian, and Disciples surveys. For most questions, however, we have data from all five church bodies. On every item, however, we have responses from pastors representing the full theological range, from most orthodox to most modernist, giving us considerable confidence in the results. In addition, we use the 1992 surveys of Covenant and Southern Baptist clergy to confirm and extend the analysis.

We find that ministerial activism falls into eight participatory modes: *political pronouncement, moral pronouncement, candidate endorsement, electoral campaigning, joining, church action, contacting,* and *protest* (see appendix B for details). In the next section, we look at the frequency of ministerial activity, considering both career participation and activism in 1988 by theological groups, for comparison with the findings of earlier studies. Once again, we report in the tables the correlations between our full orthodoxy scale and each activity as a rough measure of differences between theological groups.

### Speaking the Word: Political and Moral Pronouncement

For Protestant clergy, the "power of the Word" has always been a distinguishing characteristic, and the centrality of sermons and verbal guidance has been stressed in studies of clerical politics. Although the role of sermons in conveying pastoral cues has often been noted, clergy have many opportunities to pronounce on social and political issues, sometimes to more effect than in a sermon. As one CRC pastor told us, "You often have more productive conversation in Sunday school, Bible classes, and youth group meetings than comes from the pulpit." In any event, clergy have varied styles of providing verbal cues.

One stylistic difference uncovered by earlier studies is the proclivity of modernists to preach entire sermons on political issues, while orthodox clergy prefer to insert political commentary in sermons on biblical themes. Indeed, Koller and Retzer (1980) argue that when such insertions are accounted for, the differences Quinley found between modernist and orthodox are greatly reduced. As we shall see, this finding is only partially confirmed here. As Table 9.1 shows, touching on issues is common among clergy; but contrary to Koller and Retzer, modernists still have an edge in both the career and the 1988 data. Only 74 percent of the orthodox reported touching on an issue in 1988, compared with 86 percent of modernists. Koller and Retzer's contention that modernists preach more political sermons is borne out, however; both in the past and in 1988, the data reveal a much wider gap among theological groups.

When ministers are asked about public pronouncements on political issues outside the pulpit, however, theological differences vanish or are sharply reduced—depending on the wording of the question. In the version used for the Southern Baptists, Presbyterians, and Disciples (which did not specify what a "political issue" was), there is little difference among theological groups in career behavior or in 1988, where the most orthodox and most modernist are both slightly more vocal than more moderate colleagues. When "political issue" is defined as it was in the Assemblies/Methodist surveys as issues like "taxes and unemployment" (i.e., found on the social justice agenda), modernists are slightly more likely to be vocal, although in 1988 the most orthodox group comes in a close second.

Modernists are also more likely to have offered a public prayer on a political issue during their career, although the moderately modernist and moderately orthodox both exceed the activity of their more extreme brothers and sisters. (Perhaps they viewed prayers as a less confrontational way of raising issues in religious venues.) But by 1988 the differences in the frequency of political prayer are statistically insignificant. And while fewer ministers take pulpit stands on political issues, once again modernists have a substantial career advantage and a slightly smaller one in 1988. All in all, Quinley's findings on the participatory advantage of modernists still hold on some kinds of political pronouncements, although the gaps are seldom very large and, in the case of public stands outside the pulpit and public prayers on political issues, have closed entirely.

Even the few remaining theological differences vanish when the issue is defined as moral. Orthodox ministers are actually more likely than modernists to have offered a prayer on a moral issue during their careers, and in 1988 as well, although the latter difference is not statistically significant. Orthodox and modernist clergy are equally prone to pulpit pronouncements and public statements on moral issues. Thus, the process by which issues become defined as "moral" is critical to pastoral activity among theological conservatives. It was not without reason that early Christian Right leaders sought to cast political controversies within a framework of Christian morality (Wuthnow 1983). To the extent that they succeeded in tying political activity to the "moral agenda," they unleashed additional clerical resources.

Table 9.1
Clergy's Political Activities by Orthodoxy: Political and Moral Pronouncement
(Percent Undertaking Action)

| | All | Most Orthodox 1 | 2 | Most Modernist 3 | 4 | *r= |
|---|---|---|---|---|---|---|
| **Political pronouncement** | | | | | | |
| Touched on issue in sermon[‡] | | | | | | |
| Career | 97 | 95 | 95 | 98 | 99 | .11** |
| In 1988 | 79 | 74 | 73 | 76 | 86 | .15** |
| Public stand on political issue[‡] | | | | | | |
| Career | 93 | 92 | 91 | 92 | 95 | .05* |
| In 1988 | 65 | 67 | 61 | 60 | 69 | .05 |
| (Alternate version)[†] | | | | | | |
| Career | 77 | 74 | 75 | 83 | 85 | .12** |
| In 1988 | 45 | 45 | 38 | 44 | 55 | .08* |
| Preached whole sermon on issue[§] | | | | | | |
| Career | 79 | 60 | 68 | 76 | 84 | .19** |
| In 1988 | 40 | 29 | 32 | 31 | 47 | .18** |
| Prayed publicly on political issue[†] | | | | | | |
| Career | 71 | 68 | 73 | 80 | 75 | .08* |
| In 1988 | 45 | 43 | 45 | 44 | 49 | .06 |
| Pulpit stand on political issue[†] | | | | | | |
| Career | 56 | 51 | 54 | 61 | 68 | .16** |
| In 1988 | 30 | 29 | 26 | 26 | 39 | .10** |
| **Moral pronouncement** | | | | | | |
| Prayed publicly on moral issue[†] | | | | | | |
| Career | 96 | 97 | 94 | 97 | 92 | −.09** |
| In 1988 | 78 | 79 | 79 | 74 | 76 | −.03 |
| Pulpit stand on moral issue[†] | | | | | | |
| Career | 95 | 94 | 97 | 95 | 95 | .00 |
| In 1988 | 80 | 82 | 80 | 80 | 78 | −.02 |
| Public stand on moral issue[†] | | | | | | |
| Career | 94 | 92 | 94 | 97 | 97 | .08* |
| In 1988 | 72 | 74 | 70 | 68 | 72 | −.01 |

*p<.05; **p<.001.
[†] Alternative forms of question used in the Assemblies of God and United Methodist surveys.
[‡] Question asked only of Southern Baptists, Presbyterians, and Disciples of Christ ministers.
[§] Question asked only of Presbyterian and Disciples of Christ ministers.

## Candidate and Campaign Activity

While Hadden and Quinley ignored ministers' electoral activities, Beatty and Walter (1989) found their 1983 sample of ministers to be quite active in voting, persuading others to vote for candidates, giving money to candidates, attending rallies, and working in campaigns. Combining these items into a single index, they concluded that modernists had only a small advantage over more traditionalist ministers. We used very similar items but excluded voting from consideration because it is almost universal among clergy. Our analysis shows that electoral actions are better understood as parts of *two* separate participatory modes, *candidate endorsement* and *campaigning,* each preferred by different clergy (see Table 9.2).

Ministers are certainly not reticent about endorsing candidates, at least outside the pulpit: *in 1988 fully two-fifths of all clergy made a public endorsement of a*

Table 9.2
Clergy's Political Activities by Orthodoxy: Candidate and Campaign Activities
(Percent Undertaking Action)

|  | All | Most Orthodox 1 | 2 | 3 | Most Modernist 4 | *r= |
|---|---|---|---|---|---|---|
| Candidate activity |  |  |  |  |  |  |
| Publicly endorsed candidate |  |  |  |  |  |  |
| Career | 66 | 66 | 60 | 66 | 70 | .05* |
| In 1988 | 41 | 44 | 36 | 35 | 44 | .02 |
| Prayed publicly for candidate[+] |  |  |  |  |  |  |
| Career | 36 | 47 | 31 | 23 | 20 | −.22** |
| In 1988 | 16 | 25 | 14 | 8 | 8 | −.18** |
| Endorsed candidate from pulpit |  |  |  |  |  |  |
| Career | 10 | 16 | 9 | 6 | 6 | −.13** |
| In 1988 | 3 | 6 | 2 | 2 | 2 | −.09** |
| Campaign activity |  |  |  |  |  |  |
| Campaigned for candidate[+] |  |  |  |  |  |  |
| Career | 33 | 30 | 27 | 38 | 49 | .17** |
| In 1988 | 10 | 11 | 8 | 10 | 10 | .00 |
| Presidential campaign activity |  |  |  |  |  |  |
| In 1988 presidential primaries | 18 | 16 | 13 | 16 | 23 | .10** |
| In 1988 presidential election | 29 | 27 | 23 | 25 | 35 | .09** |
| Ran for public office[+] |  |  |  |  |  |  |
| Career | 8 | 4 | 7 | 8 | 10 | .09** |
| In 1988 | 1 | 0 | 1 | 2 | 2 | .05* |

*p<.05; **p<.001.
[+]Question in Assemblies of God and United Methodist questionnaires only.
[+]Question in Southern Baptist, Presbyterian, and Disciples questionnaires only.

*political candidate.* Modernists and the orthodox are in rough parity, with both out-performing more theologically centrist clergy. Some pastors did not confine their imprimaturs to secular settings, as about one in six prayed publicly for a candidate, an increasingly popular mode of blessing among the most orthodox, one-quarter of whom report such prayers in 1988. Indeed, almost one-half of this group have prayed for a candidate sometime during their ministry. Such action has become so popular, in fact, that a leading Christian Right figure felt impelled to warn during the 1996 presidential campaign that "religious conservatives must resist the temptation to pray in explicitly political terms" (Reed 1996, 262). The warning seems not to have impressed all orthodox clergy: preliminary results from a postelection survey of Southern Baptists show that almost 50 percent of the most orthodox report public prayers for a candidate in 1996. A similar conservative edge appears in the least fre-quent action, pulpit endorsements. All in all, in candidate endorsement the orthodox match or exceed modernists.

Campaigning for candidates reveals a more complex pattern. In a question asked only of Assemblies and Methodist clergy, modernists show a substantial ca-reer advantage in working in political campaigns, with almost half having such ex-perience, compared with fewer than a third of the orthodox. This margin disappears in 1988, however, as about one of ten ministers in each category did campaign work. Unfortunately, the Assemblies and Methodist clergy may not be entirely representa-tive of either orthodox or modernist clergy; as we saw in chapter 7, they were the least active of the five denominations during the 1988 presidential primary and gen-eral election campaigns. A better assessment of campaign involvement comes from analysis of 1988 presidential election activity, which demonstrates, first, that clergy were extraordinarily active compared with other citizens, with almost a fifth partici-pating in the primaries and close to a third in the general election, and, second, that liberals still had a slight advantage, although the most orthodox clergy were not the least active in either 1988 campaign.

We must caution that our activism questions certainly do not pick up the ratio-nale for campaigning. Some clergy clearly hope to influence their congregations through the visibility of their own activity, while others abjure any such intent. Per-haps an extreme example of the latter posture is a Southern Baptist minister who noted, "While on vacation from my church field, I wore a campaign button and placed a Bush bumper sticker on my car. Both were removed after returning home. I hold the view that all ministers should develop a keen interest in politics and gov-ernment—yet not toward the leading of his people in a partisan way." A liberal Dis-ciples minister, on the other side of the political fence, did not hide his active support of Michael Dukakis from his congregation but didn't hope to influence them, either: "I don't sense that it has compromised my ability to be a leader/pastor. Converting people to the Democratic Party has never been on my agenda." For other clergy, however, providing just such electoral guidance is paramount to their involvement (cf. Shie 1991, 154).

One electoral activity that does show a continuing modernist advantage is running for office: the few clergy seeking official positions are disproportionately modernist. Note that such action does not correlate highly with any other kind of ministerial activity. Indeed, few factors other than the attitudes of the minister and congregation about running for office have any influence over such decisions. Despite the high visibility of clergy candidacies in recent years, including the 1988 Jackson and Robertson campaigns, many clergy argue that there is an incompatibility between their calling and the demands of public office, restraining the easy movement from profession to public office that occurs among businesspeople, lawyers, and educators. Conservative clergy are the most emphatic on this point, often rejecting the possibility of being simultaneously a minister of the gospel and an elected official (cf. Shie 1991, 181–183). As one Southern Baptist put it, "A pastor should encourage qualified Christians to run for public office, but he should *never* step down from his calling." Or as a Baptist colleague put it flatly, "Pat and Jesse are simply wrong!" (Indeed, in response to such criticisms, Robertson gave up his ordination before the 1988 GOP primaries.)

Even theological liberals seeing fewer inherent contradictions in the roles of minister and politician strongly sense the practical constraints of time, energy, and congregational resistance when considering a run for public office. Many clergy argued that they simply had no time for even part-time office. And as previous studies have shown, congregational reaction may be especially strong here. One liberal Presbyterian was forced to resign the pastorate when he campaigned for the state senate, not because he was running for office but because he was running as a Democrat. (He was sure he would have kept his job if he had chosen the Republican ticket!) A liberal Southern Baptist pastor had no prima facie objection to ministers holding public office, but had reservations based on experience:

> My minister of music ran for public office and was elected to the city council. He has served well, even though he has had to make some tough, hard decisions which have affected some of our church members. So as a result of these decisions, I, as pastor, have spent way too much time in the ministry of reconciliation. I really feel that I have saved his ministry here on many occasions. Naturally, I have some mixed emotions about the church staff holding political office.

Given such reservations and experiences, it is not surprising that so few clergy use their many politically relevant skills to run for public office, despite their strong political interest and considerable concern with public issues.

Overall, these findings suggest that conservative and liberal clergy both seek to influence elections, but through somewhat different means. Conservatives, with more receptive congregations, prefer to work within traditional religious forms and structures. A few choose to invoke the authority of the pulpit to make candidate pronouncements, but others use less direct, but equally effective, vehicles such as prayers for candidates or other public statements. Modernist liberals, on the other hand, often leading conservative congregations that may disapprove of high-visibility ministerial activism, frequently participate as individuals in election campaigns. As we shall see later, their educational characteristics and organizational situations also encourage this outlet.

## Organizational Activity: Joining and Church Activity

Ever since the days when Alexis de Tocqueville marveled at the social networks pervading American communities, associational activity has been a distinct feature of American social and political life. Like other well-educated professionals, ministers often are enmeshed in organizations. Some are religious in orientation, others may be purely secular. For the politically interested, there are a host of groups that seek to advance their political objectives. As Table 9.3 shows, many clergy have contributed money to a party organization, political action committee, or candidate committee, while others have joined national political organizations.

These activities, without doubt, are the special province of modernist liberals. While almost three-fifths of the clergy have donated money at some point, only two-fifths of the orthodox have done so, compared with three-quarters of the modernists. In 1988, the ratio was still almost two to one. Fewer clergy report joining national political organizations, but once again the pattern favors the modernists, especially in career activism. Joining, then, has been a distinctly liberal mode of participation and seems destined to remain so, despite persistent Christian Right efforts to mobilize clerical activists. Perhaps the recent shift of the Christian Coalition toward recruiting conservative laity, in preference to clergy, is rooted in the continuing reluctance of orthodox ministers to join outside political organizations (Reed 1996, 121). There is some evidence, however, that Christian Right groups may have made some progress in attracting clergy during the early 1990s, after the time of most of our surveys (cf. Berkowitz and Green 1996; Guth 1996).

A related participation mode is in-church organization. (Indeed, such activities have a moderately high correlation with joining organizations and formed a single loose dimension in the original factor analysis.) Our two indicators here are ministers' past and current efforts to address public issues by forming political or social issue study groups, or—going even further—by setting up an action group on public affairs. Both acts were regarded by Quinley as types of the aggressive political activity favored by the New Breed of the 1960s. Certainly, Table 9.3 would not require revision of that assessment almost thirty years later. Only one-quarter of the orthodox have ever formed a church study group, compared with four-fifths of the modernists. The gap in 1988 is almost four to one. Slightly fewer clergy have ever started an action group, and the advantage remains with the modernists on career activity, although in 1988 the orthodox had closed some of the gap. Nevertheless, these differences survived, if in somewhat attenuated form, even after 1988 (see later discussion).

These persistent patterns are somewhat puzzling, especially given the reports of rampant political organizing in conservative churches. Why the continued gap in

Table 9.3
Clergy's Political Activities by Orthodoxy: Joining, Church, Contacting, and Protest
(Percent Undertaking Action)

| | All | Most Orthodox 1 | 2 | Most Modernist 3 | 4 | *r= |
|---|---|---|---|---|---|---|
| Joining organizations | | | | | | |
| Contributed money to political committee | | | | | | |
| Career | 57 | 42 | 51 | 65 | 74 | .28** |
| In 1988 | 28 | 20 | 21 | 31 | 39 | .19** |
| Joined national political organization | | | | | | |
| Career | 40 | 28 | 35 | 40 | 57 | .26** |
| In 1988 | 17 | 14 | 14 | 15 | 25 | .13** |
| In-church activity | | | | | | |
| Formed study group in church | | | | | | |
| Career | 53 | 24 | 47 | 64 | 81 | .47** |
| In 1988 | 17 | 8 | 14 | 19 | 29 | .23** |
| Organized action group in church | | | | | | |
| Career | 42 | 23 | 34 | 47 | 62 | .47** |
| In 1988 | 14 | 10 | 9 | 16 | 20 | .15** |
| Contacting influentials | | | | | | |
| Circulated petition[+] | | | | | | |
| Career | 94 | 91 | 94 | 94 | 95 | .06* |
| In 1988 | 57 | 62 | 57 | 51 | 56 | −.04 |
| Contacted public officials | | | | | | |
| Career | 85 | 79 | 85 | 87 | 92 | .15** |
| In 1988 | 47 | 44 | 44 | 48 | 53 | .09** |
| Wrote letter to editor[+] | | | | | | |
| Career | 63 | 50 | 57 | 64 | 72 | .19** |
| In 1988 | 18 | 13 | 18 | 18 | 21 | .08* |
| Protesting | | | | | | |
| Participated in protest march | | | | | | |
| Career | 32 | 18 | 21 | 33 | 53 | .33** |
| In 1988 | 6 | 8 | 4 | 5 | 7 | .02 |
| Committed civil disobedience | | | | | | |
| Career | 11 | 4 | 5 | 12 | 22 | .25** |
| In 1988 | 2 | 1 | 1 | 2 | 2 | .04* |

* p<.05; ** p<.001.
[+] Question in Southern Baptist, Presbyterian, and Disciples questionnaires only.

group formation? There are several possibilities. Perhaps the Evangelical pastor's authority discourages the notion that issues should be studied by laity, rather than resolved on the basis of his biblical warrants (Jelen 1993). Or else the complex informal structure of Evangelical churches, with Bible study and prayer groups, Sunday school classes, mission organizations, and so on, makes additional groups superfluous. Or, as is often the case, study and action groups are formed by lay activists, freeing the pastor for "religious" activities and avoiding controversy, an approach recommended by many Christian Right leaders (Reed 1996, 121). One CRC minister noted that study and action groups were often a good idea, but "only if formed and supported by the consistory." Whatever the explanation, few Evangelical ministers instigate these groups.

Another approach is to focus on the other side: Why do modernists employ such devices? Perhaps clergy aware of political differences with their congregation may prefer gentle consciousness-raising through study groups to more direct persuasion. Or a pastor unsure of the congregation's response to a pressing political issue may diffuse responsibility by creating an action group. Unfortunately, the data do not support these conjectures: among liberal clergy, it is those who are closest to their parishioners politically, or only modestly more liberal, who are most likely to form study and action groups, not those perceiving the biggest gap. Indeed, some very liberal pastors argue that a wide chasm precludes the strategy entirely. ("If you are going to form a social action group in the church," wrote an RCA minister, "there should be more than just one of you.") A more plausible explanation may be that group and committee formation is a characteristic liberal strategy, inculcated in Mainline seminaries (Carroll and Marler 1995, 12) and honed by experience in denominational bureaucracies. As a Methodist minister told us, "The most common response of a Methodist preacher to any problem is 'Let's form a task force on that.'" Whatever the explanation, reliance on group formation remains one distinctive trait of modernist political style.

## Going Inside and Going Outside: Contacting and Protesting

A time-honored way to influence the political process is to contact influentials, either directly or through the media. Verba and Nie (1972) found that communicating with government officials on public issues was part of a *communal* factor, which they called "social contacting." In Table 9.3 we report the proportion of clergy engaged in three forms of contacting: circulating petitions, contacting public officials, and writing letters to the editor.

Virtually all clergy have at some time signed or circulated a petition, although modernists have a very slight advantage. Indeed, well over half the clergy engaged in petitioning in 1988 alone, but the most orthodox had a slight, statistically insignificant edge. A slightly smaller majority have contacted a public official at some time; almost half did so during 1988, with the liberal advantage in career activism declining to a relatively small annual difference. A similar pattern appears on writing letters to the editor, a less popular technique in which highly educated liberals have a considerable career advantage and a slightly smaller one for 1988. Altogether, though, the modernist bias on contacting in 1988 is very small.

Contacting community influentials is, of course, a quintessential "insider" activity, used by those who expect notables to be responsive to citizen demands. Protest activities, such as marches, demonstrations, and especially civil disobedience, are often regarded as the "resource of the resourceless" for those who have found the "system" unresponsive (Lipsky 1968). If more recent observers are correct, however, such "unruly" activities are now more widely accepted. Certainly, the 1980s and 1990s saw many incidents of clergy protests over abortion, treatment of refugees, American economic sanctions against Cuba, and many other public issues. As we saw in chapter 8, however, not all clergy perceive protests as appropriate avenues for political expression and even fewer think their laity approve. In fact, protesting remains distinctly uncommon among clergy. Only a third have ever marched in protest, although the number rises to over half among the most modernist, who are quite distinct even from the moderately modernist. The 1988 data augur a theological reversal, however, as the orthodox are actually more involved, although the difference is not statistically significant. A closer look at the age of protesters confirms our suspicions. Among clergy over forty-five years old, the proportion of the most modernist group ever having protested is much higher than among the most orthodox clergy, no doubt reflecting the experiences of the 1960s and early 1970s, when these age cohorts were entering the ministry. In 1988, however, protest is more common among those under forty-five, but the most orthodox outprotest the most modernist by 14 to 8 percent.

The rise of antiabortion activism no doubt accounts for this change, especially in 1988, when Operation Rescue was trying to mobilize Evangelical clergy and, through them, their congregations, in protests at the time of the Republican and Democratic national conventions. After peaking in 1988, however, clergy engagement in abortion protests diminished, reflecting several factors. The clergy pioneering these protests were disappointed by the failure of most parishioners to follow their lead, as opposition to such tactics came from many other Evangelical leaders. To some extent, peaceful protest may have become a domesticated technique, allowing clergy of all sorts to consider action, but such decisions will remain the exception, not the rule, of orthodox clerical politics.

Of course, antiabortion "rescues" quickly moved from legal protest to civil disobedience. The rejection of civil disobedience by clergy is even clearer than their reluctance to engage in legal protest. Only one minister in ten, mostly older modernists, reports ever having engaged in civil disobedience. Few participated in 1988, with only 1 or 2 percent in each theological category. While a handful of conservatives report arrests in "rescue" operations, they were indeed "prophetic," at least in the biblical tradition of being few in number and largely unheeded. Indeed, by the mid-1990s this wave of clerical activism had receded, leaving antiabortion militants lamenting "The Silence of the Shepherds," that is, the lack of ministerial leadership for aggressive action (Maxwell 1995). Tougher police tactics and legal constraints also reduced the viability of "rescue" operations as a vehicle for clerical politics (Hooten 1996).

Clearly, no issues of the late 1980s elicited the massive protests characteristic of the 1960s heyday of the civil rights and antiwar movements. Thus, we find a different sort of "convergence" between orthodox and modernist clergy: very few ministers in any group engage in "unruly" activity. The orthodox still reject such techniques, and modernists have abandoned them. If legal protests are becoming almost conventional among Americans, as Verba, Schlozman, and Brady (1995) suggest, civil disobedience at least is still not "normal" for clergy.

## EXPLAINING MODES OF CLERICAL ACTIVISM

We have learned that some of the disparity in activism between orthodox and modernist clergy still persists, but that differences appear to be diminishing. Furthermore, any evaluation of overall political involvement depends on the activity being considered. Modernists still dominate in joining political groups, organizing within churches, and, to a lesser extent, campaigning, but orthodox clergy have recently pulled even on many activities, ranging from political and moral pronouncements to candidate endorsements—and, perhaps, legal protest. But the amount of each activity is only one concern. We also want to explain why ministers choose a particular mode, using theoretical perspectives derived from the participation literature, and some insights from previous clergy studies.

Given the rich variety of influences on ministerial behavior, we did a good bit of exploration to identify key variables for the analysis. We found that our theological, social theology, and church role measures had little direct influence on activity, once the political variables they produce were included. Their influence, then, is indirect, shaping ministers' political worldviews in many ways but having very little direct impact on participation. Nevertheless, theological measures such as orthodoxy are often correlated with ministerial action, as the preceding tables show, and the reader is reminded of their fundamental, if indirect, role in shaping political activity. In the following section, then, we turn to a multivariate analysis of the modes of participation, testing perspectives that stress (1) the socioeconomic and (2) psychological variables influencing activism; (3) clerical role expectations regarding particular types of participation; (4) ideological mobilization; and (5) organizational mobilization. In each section to follow, we present a brief review of the bivariate relationships between each mode of activity and the important predictors suggested by the five theoretical perspectives, then turn to the results of a series of multiple regressions, with each participatory mode as the dependent variable, and all the independent variables entered simultaneously. As we will discover, each theoretical approach has some merit in predicting clerical activism, but not for all modes. Nevertheless, the results confirm several predictions of participation theory.

## Socioeconomic Status

First we turn to the oldest strand of participation theory, the socioeconomic status, or SES, model. As we observed in chapter 1, this perspective stresses the influence of education, income, and social status resources in encouraging or facilitating political participation in the mass public (Verba and Nie 1972). Does it also explain differences in participation in clerical activity? For the most part, the SES variables have only very modest bivariate correlations with most modes of activity (data not shown), and only a few survive the multiple regression in Table 9.4. Higher education (measured by a factor score incorporating length and quality of secular and seminary education) has a modest bivariate association with most modes but has independent influence only in encouraging political pronouncements, in-church activities, and campaigning. Thus, ministers with extended education, at the most selective colleges and seminaries, and with liberal arts majors are slightly more likely to engage in these activities but not others. Of course, higher education has an important indirect impact on participation by encouraging political interest, creating a sense of political efficacy, fostering ideological thinking, and increasing ministerial approval of political involvement (see chapter 8). Nevertheless, the weak relationship between education and activism today suggests either that orthodox clergy have greatly reduced the education gap or that they have compensated in other ways, such as developing new ideological incentives or superior mobilization techniques.

Other personal traits of ministers are even less relevant. Although we have no direct data on current income, ministerial salaries in all denominations are closely related to church size, which we use as a proxy here. As Table 9.4 shows, pastors in large churches are slightly more likely to engage in in-church organizing, contacting, protesting, and moral pronouncements. Some of these tendencies may be tied to church size itself, of course, rather than to pastoral income. Large churches may provide more scope for in-church organizing, or more necessity for it, while ministers of large congregations may have more occasions to deal with government officials. Time in the ministry also has some effect: those new to their calling tend to make more political and moral pronouncements and engage in in-church organizing, while more experienced pastors tend to campaign, paralleling the usual political science findings about the greater conventional activism of older citizens.

We should comment on some socioeconomic and demographic variables that are missing from Table 9.4. Our inspection of the bivariate correlations showed that region, size of community, gender, and the social class of the minister's family of origin have virtually no significant influence on any participatory modes, a finding confirmed by the multivariate analysis. For reasons of space, then, we have excluded them from the table. On the whole, demographic variables provide relatively little assistance in understanding the participatory modes of Protestant clergy.

## Psychological Engagement

Unlike the status resources themselves, the psychological engagement often associated with higher status exhibits more influence. Not surprisingly, interest in politics

Table 9.4
Determinants of Pastoral Activism: Multiple Regression Analysis

| Variables | Political | Moral | Candidate | Campaign | Joining | Church | Contacting | Protest |
|---|---|---|---|---|---|---|---|---|
| SES |  |  |  |  |  |  |  |  |
| Education | .14* | -.01 | .02 | .07** | .04 | .07* | .01 | .02 |
| Church size | .01 | .06* | .01 | -.01 | -.01 | .11** | .06* | .05* |
| Years in ministry | -.10** | -.08** | -.04 | .05** | .00 | -.06* | -.03 | -.03 |
| Psychological |  |  |  |  |  |  |  |  |
| Interest in politics | .07* | .11* | .10** | .13** | .09** | .06* | .07* | -.02 |
| Political efficacy | .00 | .00 | .06* | .05* | .04* | .04 | .05* | .04* |
| Role orientation |  |  |  |  |  |  |  |  |
| Approve action | .40** | .23** | .32** | .16** | .31** | .25** | .18** | .27** |
| Ideological |  |  |  |  |  |  |  |  |
| Justice agenda | .18** | .21** | .09** | .13** | .11** | .13** | .12* | .04 |
| Moral agenda | .08* | .04 | .08* | .04 | .03 | .04 | .12* | .02 |
| Liberalism | .04 | .05 | .01 | .07* | .06* | .08* | .07 | .06 |
| Conservatism | .13* | .01 | .14** | .14** | .04 | -.02 | .03 | .09* |
| Democratic | -.02 | -.03 | .09** | .20** | .11** | -.01 | -.04 | .03 |
| Republican | .03 | .07 | .10** | .17** | .11** | -.02 | .01 | .02 |
| Organizational |  |  |  |  |  |  |  |  |
| Church approves | .16** | .09* | .10** | .04* | .03 | .14** | .02 | .07** |
| Tenure length | .08* | .06 | .02 | -.01 | .07** | .05* | .03 | .04* |
| More liberal than church | .06 | .13* | .03 | -.04 | -.08* | -.11** | -.08 | -.06 |
| More conservative | .00 | .04 | -.01 | -.03 | .02 | .04* | .02 | .02 |
| Liberal group | .06* | .00 | .01 | .04* | n.a. | .03 | .06* | -.01 |
| Conservative group | -.01 | .07* | .00 | .05* | n.a. | .02 | .07* | .11** |
| Assemblies of God | .12* | -.05 | -.15** | -.17** | -.01 | .02 | n.a. | .08* |
| Southern Baptist | n.a. | n.a. | -.11** | -.04 | -.11** | -.08* | -.05 | -.01 |
| United Methodist | + | + | -.19** | -.23** | -.02 | .13** | n.a. | .07* |
| Adjusted $R^2$ | .33 | .16 | .26 | .24 | .23 | .23 | .13 | .13 |

* $p < .05$; ** $p < .001$.
+ Suppressed reference category.

has a solid positive bivariate correlation with every mode of activism, while politi-cal efficacy also has universally positive correlations: ministers who think they can influence the political attitudes of their parishioners make political and moral pro-nouncements and, especially, endorse candidates, while those who understand the proper political channels tend to campaign, join political organizations, contact of-ficials, and protest (data not shown). As Table 9.4 reveals, in the regression political interest retains considerable influence on almost all modes, except for protest, but political efficacy is reduced to a marginal, if still significant, role in most cases (cf. Verba, Schlozman, and Brady 1995). Our guess is that interest and efficacy have al-ways been correlates of pastoral activism, though neglected by earlier studies. The implications of these findings are suggested by our discovery in chapter 8 that ortho-dox and modernist ministers differ little on these variables today.

## Ministerial Role Orientations

Not surprisingly, ministers' role orientations are strongly associated with actual participation. To test the impact of role conceptions, we calculated scales for minis-terial approval of the specific activities in each mode. All the bivariate correlations are quite strong, with the largest coefficient between attitudes on political pro-nouncement and that activity, followed by joining and candidate endorsements. Ac-tions that many clergy approve but less often undertake, such as campaigning, con-tacting, and protesting, have somewhat smaller correlations (data not shown). In the regression, approval of political activity remains a powerful influence, usually pre-senting the largest beta coefficient for most participation modes. The data demon-strate how powerfully ministerial role conceptions shape clerical behavior: those who approve of a political act in theory are much more likely to undertake it. Thus, as more Evangelical clergy develop supportive attitudes toward direct political ac-tion and cue-giving activities, as we predicted in the last chapter, we can expect to see additional activism from the "private" party.

## Ideological Mobilization

A first look at the ideological mobilization variables presents a more varied and in-teresting picture. A bivariate analysis shows that ministers with an extensive moral reform or social justice agenda are more active on almost every mode of activity but in somewhat varying ways. Both agendas influence political and moral pronounce-ment, but those high on social justice concerns make more political pronounce-ments, while those stressing moral reform are understandably more prone to moral statements. High scores on both agendas are associated with candidate endorse-ment, but social justice concerns predominate in political campaigning. Joining and church organizing are preferred by social justice activists, who have an advantage, but not a monopoly, on contacting and protesting as well (data not shown). As Table 9.4 reports, the social justice agenda retains a large influence when all variables are taken into account, encouraging every type of participation, with only the coefficient for protest missing statistical significance. Concern with the moral reform agenda also has universally positive coefficients, but most are small, and only those for contacting, candidate endorsement, and political pronouncement are statistically significant. We also considered whether our findings might be an artifact of ministers' concentration on two or three salient issues, rather than the size of their agenda, as captured by the social justice and moral reform scales. But no single issue—not abortion, social welfare, concern with the environment, or any other—matches the power of the overall indices. Thus, activism is associated with commitment to a broad range of concerns, whether moral reform or social justice.

We also found that our issue ideology score was a stronger correlate of participation than attitudes on any single issue or set of issues. We thus included it in the analysis, bifurcating it at the midpoint to produce the liberalism and conservatism scores presented in Table 9.4. At the bivariate level, we found that liberal views had a positive association with greater activity on every mode except moral pronouncements, while conservatism encouraged moral pronouncements, candidate endorsement, and protest but was negatively related to both organizational modes (data not shown). When entered in the multiple regression, however, some of these effects shift (Table 9.4). Ironically, although our earlier analysis showed that the social justice agenda outperformed the moral agenda, conservative ideology usually has a larger independent effect than liberal attitudes, especially on candidate endorsement, campaigning, political pronouncement—and on protest. Thus, ministers with the most conservative views have some advantage in activity related to electoral politics, perhaps reflecting the ideological climate of the 1988 election year.

As in other studies (Rosenstone and Hansen 1993, 130), strength of partisanship is also associated with political participation. We computed two measures of Republican and Democratic affiliation, respectively, scoring pure Independents as "0," partisan leaners as "1," weak partisans as "2," and strong identifiers as "3." Strong Republican identification produces candidate endorsements but works against in-church organizing, while Democrats excel in campaigning, joining, and in-church activism. Interestingly, partisanship has at best weak bivariate associations with political and moral pronouncements, contacting, or protest activity. Thus, while strong party ties are obviously most related to electoral and organizational activities, Republican and Democratic clergy differ in overall participatory styles. Do these tendencies survive the regression? As Table 9.4 demonstrates, strong partisanship has independent influence almost exclusively on candidate endorsement, campaigning, and joining—three activity modes related closely to the party system. Thus, ministers behave very much like other citizens in responding to the opportunities presented by the electoral process—strong partisans are much more active.

## Organizational Mobilization

What about the organizational variables? Certainly the most crucial part of the pastor's organizational life is the congregation. Several ministers reported that political activity had at some point in their careers led to loss of members or to adverse feedback from parishioners. One RCA minister, strongly committed to a voucher system for church-related schools, noted that his advocacy had prompted "three families to leave our church. Antagonism toward Christian schools among the congregation prevents me from playing a more active role." As ministers tend to see their congregations' reactions through the lenses of their own, we used a congregational approval score that isolated the unique "congregational" component from shared attitudes. Our review of the bivariate relationships showed that congregational support has a positive, though modest, association with most types of activism, notably with in-church activities, political pronouncements, candidate endorsements, and protest actions (data not shown). These are activities on which minister and congregation may disagree and which are quite visible to active parishioners, creating the potential for congregational influence. On the other hand, congregational approval has little association with moral pronouncements, which may elicit more agreement from a sympathetic church, or joining national political organizations, essentially an individual activity, perhaps invisible to most parishioners.

Despite these relatively weak bivariate correlations, the relationships persist and in a few cases actually increase in the regressions reported in Table 9.4. Church approval is most important in encouraging political pronouncements and in-church organizing, but it also influences candidate endorsements, protest, and other activities. Only on joining and contacting, two modes less subject to congregational scrutiny, does the congregation not have an impact. This finding has important practical significance. Recent studies have suggested that congregational support for ministerial activity may be growing in the United States, especially among Evangelicals (Guth 1996; Pew Research Center 1996). Certainly some ministers sense this trend: from 1980 to 1992, Southern Baptist clergy perceived increasingly greater congregational approval for ministerial involvement, even taking the increases in their own approval into account. Thus, some of the rise in ministerial activity on the right in recent years has been facilitated or even encouraged by changing congregational attitudes. On the other hand, the larger gap between liberal clergy and their churches may constrain some activities but encourage others, such as campaigning, joining, and contacting, which are less affected by congregational attitudes.

According to conventional wisdom among clergy, ministerial freedom also depends on tenure: the longer pastors serve a congregation, the more they can "politic" (Sapp 1975). A Disciples minister put it succinctly, in speaking of aggressive action such as running for public office: "This depends on length of service in a congregation—the longer the ministry, the more the openness of the congregation to consider this." But his hypothesis receives only modest support from the bivariate data. Length of time at the current church is indeed positively associated with all forms of activism, but only the correlations for joining, candidate endorsement, and campaigning reach statistical significance (data not shown). Even this minimal relationship may reflect factors other than the "credit" a minister builds with his or her congregation. Ministers, like other Americans, may be more active in electoral politics the longer they live in a specific community. Thus, the positive associations of electoral activities with tenure may actually reflect longer residence in one locality rather than time at a particular church. But the multivariate results conform more closely to the conventional wisdom than do the bivariate data. When all else is accounted for, ministers long entrenched at their current church are more prone to make political pronouncements, join organizations, do in-church organizing, and engage in protest, thus providing some support for the "building credit" theory.

The ideological compatibility or contrast between pastor and congregation is also associated with certain modes of activity. Clergy who are more liberal than their congregation are less prone to endorse candidates but more likely to organize, inside and outside the church. Candidate endorsement is a favorite, on the other hand, of pastors who are more conservative than their parishioners; these latter clergy also have a slight tendency to avoid in-church organizing (data not shown). Here again, the multivariate analysis provides a slightly different picture. As Table 9.4 reports, ministers who are more liberal than their church are slightly more likely to make moral pronouncements, once everything else is controlled, but are less likely to join political organizations, do in-church organizing, or (although the coefficients miss statistical significance) engage in contacting, protest, and campaigning. Being more conservative than one's church has fewer independent effects, enhancing slightly the prospects of in-church organizing.

We also looked at other organizational variables. As the participation literature would suggest, members of political organizations are slightly more active than nonmembers. The participatory pattern has a familiar face: members of liberal groups prefer political pronouncement, campaigning, in-church organizing, and contacting, while those in conservative groups excel in moral pronouncement, endorsements, contacting, and protest (data not shown). In the multivariate analysis, most of these tendencies survive: membership generally encourages campaign activity and contacting for both liberals and conservatives, political pronouncements for liberals, and moral statements and protest activities among conservatives.

Of course, we cannot be sure which way causation runs: organizations may activate their members, or, alternatively, political activists may join organizations. We suspect that both effects are real. That mobilization does occur, however, is strongly suggested by the 1992 Southern Baptist data in which ministers who were members of outside organizations not only were more active politically but also were usually engaged most heavily in the very mode of activity stressed by each group: clergy who were members of the American Family Association "petitioned" and "boycotted," Focus on the Family and Christian Coalition members "campaigned," and pastors in Bread for the World "contacted" public officials (Guth 1996). These differences strongly hint that organizations do "elicit" more activism than would otherwise occur, even among politically interested clergy, and channel that activity into favorite modes of involvement.

We also considered whether activity was associated with a series of contextual organizational factors: closeness of the 1988 presidential election, competitiveness of the state party system, strength of state Christian Right organizations, and other variables that might tap indirectly the outside mobilization of clergy in 1988. None had significant correlations with any mode of participation, with the possible exception of the closeness of the 1988 presidential race in each state, which approached a significant relationship with campaigning (data not shown). Once again, clerical mobilization is more a matter of personal and congregational influence than of political context.

As we have seen previously, ministers from specific denominations may be shaped in distinct ways by their church's history, doctrines, and organization. The historic church-state separationism of the Southern Baptists, encouragement of social activism by Methodist bureaucracies, and other similar distinctives have appeared earlier. And although we expect that most differences in the political attitudes and behavior of ministers in different denominations have eroded, unique influences may remain.

Are there some distinct denominational contributions to participatory modes? We included dummy variables for Assemblies of God, Southern Baptists, and United Methodists in Table 9.4. (Methodists are the suppressed reference category for the pronouncement variables, while PCUSA and Disciples ministers form the comparison category for other measures.) In several instances, denomination adds explanatory power: Assemblies clergy are more likely to make political pronouncements than their scores on other variables would predict. On the other hand, Assemblies, Southern Baptist, and especially Methodist clergy are less likely to make candidate endorsements than Presbyterians and Disciples. As we saw earlier, Assemblies and Methodist ministers participate much less in political campaigns than Presbyterians and Disciples, but Southern Baptists are not significantly less active. Southern Baptists (but not Assemblies and Methodist ministers) are less likely to join organizations. Similarly, Baptists do less in-church organizing and Methodists do much more, while both Assemblies and Methodists are more likely than Presbyterians and Disciples to engage in protest, once other factors are controlled. Obviously, denominational cultures still influence clerical activity.

Thus we find at least some support for all four perspectives on clerical participation in political life. Although some socioeconomic variables, especially education, have a modest direct impact, they influence participation indirectly by shaping ministers' psychological orientations, role expectations, and political attitudes. Psychological resources, especially interest in politics, have a pervasive influence, although political efficacy is less important. A minister's understanding of the propriety of various activities has an enormous effect on action, as do a variety of ideological factors, including agenda, beliefs, and partisanship. On the whole, the organizational context is a good bit less important, but the congregation, denomination, and even external interest groups may promote or discourage various kinds of activities. All in all, the models predict respectable amounts of the variation in participation, ranging from 33 percent on political pronouncements to 13 percent for contacting and protesting.

## A MEASURE OF GENERAL ACTIVISM

Although we have argued that ministerial activism is best approached by asking, "Which ministers are active in different kinds of activities?" we will conclude by assessing the factors that influence overall activity. Although a single index of participation can be somewhat misleading because the common items in our surveys tend to fall into the modes favored by modernists, the results are still instructive, if interpreted cautiously. We first constructed an eleven-item career participation index to measure lifetime involvement by clergy. The results strongly confirm Quinley's findings. The mean number of lifetime acts for the entire sample was 4.88, with a steady increase as one moves from the orthodox (3.91) through the moderately orthodox (4.35) and moderately modernist (5.13) to the most active group, the modernists (6.11). By denomination, the Assemblies and Southern Baptists were least active (mean acts = 3.94 and 3.78), while Methodist, Presbyterian, and Disciples clergy were much more experienced (5.18, 5.72, and 5.75 acts, respectively). The figures for the campaign year of 1988 alone, however, suggest a narrowing gap. Modernists were still most active (3.51 acts), but the orthodox and the moderate modernists were quite close (2.69 and 2.74, respectively), with the moderate orthodox now bringing up the rear (2.44). As we might expect, denominational differences are reduced as well. Assemblies ministers averaged 2.54 acts; Baptists, 2.49; Methodists, 2.77; Presbyterians, 3.33; and Disciples, 3.37. Note that, in 1988, Methodist participation rates are actually closer to those of the Evangelicals than to those of Mainline ministers.

What factors best explain overall activism? Table 9.5 summarizes the results of two multiple regressions. The comparison of the career activism coefficients with those for the election year of 1988 is illuminating. Career activism is clearly influenced by socioeconomic status factors: the better the education, bigger the church, and longer the career, the more a minister has participated in the political process. (Of course, older ministers obviously have had more years to be involved.) In 1988, however, only church size still has a (barely) significant impact on participation. While status factors are less important in 1988, political interest and a sense of political efficacy play a larger role in predicting who is active. As we noted in chapter 8, on these factors, conservative clergy are at only a modest disadvantage, if any, in contemporary clerical politics.

Not surprisingly, role orientations predict both career and 1988 activism, but the relative power has shifted somewhat from the direct action score to the cue-giving measure, on which conservative clergy match up very well. Were there more pronouncement activities included in either activism scale, this measure might prove even more important. The ideological measures also detect the shifting determinants of activism. Whereas the social reform agenda overwhelms the moral reform agenda as a predictor of career activism, the balance is much closer in 1988, with high scores on both producing greater activity. And while ideological liberalism and conservatism both miss independent impact on career activity when other factors are accounted for, conservatism becomes a strong factor in 1988. In the same vein, Democratic partisanship has a modest predictive power for career involvement, but both Democratic and Republican identifications are major forces in 1988.

The influence of organizational factors also shifts. Not surprisingly, a minister's *current* context matters more for activism in 1988 than for that over an entire clerical career. Thus, ministers with congregational support and longer tenure are more involved in 1988. On the other hand, ideological contrasts with the congrega-

Table 9.5
Determinants of Overall Pastoral Activism:
Multiple Regression Analysis

|  | Career | 1988 |
|---|---|---|
| Socioeconomic status |  |  |
| Education | .09** | .05 |
| Church size | .07** | .05* |
| Years in ministry | .09** | −.01 |
| Psychological |  |  |
| Interest in politics | .11** | .15** |
| Political efficacy | .00 | .05* |
| Role orientation |  |  |
| Approve direct action | .35** | .28** |
| Approve cue-giving | .09** | .12** |
| Ideological |  |  |
| Justice agenda | .22** | .17** |
| Moral agenda | .06* | .11** |
| Liberalism | .05 | .05 |
| Conservatism | .05 | .11** |
| Democratic | .07** | .14** |
| Republican | .02 | .14** |
| Organizational |  |  |
| Church approves | .05* | .07** |
| Tenure length | .01 | .06** |
| More liberal than church | .03 | −.06* |
| More conservative | .03 | .05* |
| Liberal group | .05* | .05* |
| Conservative group | .04* | .08* |
| Assemblies of God | −.04 | −.07* |
| Southern Baptist | −.17** | −.14** |
| United Methodist | −.02 | −.08** |
| Adjusted $R^2$ | .53 | .41 |

*$p<.05$; **$p<.001$.

tion work in opposite ways. Ministers who are more liberal than their people are less active, everything else being equal, while those who are more conservative than their parishioners are more involved. Membership in liberal and conservative organizations is also associated with activity, both over ministers' careers and in 1988, with conservative organization membership having a bigger effect in that year.

Finally, denominational context does matter. When all other influences are accounted for, Southern Baptists were still much less active over their careers than might be expected, but Assemblies and Methodist clergy were not significantly different than their other traits would predict. In 1988, however, the Assemblies, Baptists, and Methodists were all less active (in comparison to the Presbyterians and Disciples) than other variables would predict. Thus, there were residual factors connected to denominational history, tradition, and context that still constrained political involvement in these churches.

## AFTERWORD ON 1992 AND CONCLUSIONS

What can we conclude about clerical politics at the end of the 1980s? First, modernist liberals still had a participatory edge, but that advantage was clearly eroding. Modernists still excelled in joining political organizations, organizing within the church, and contacting influentials, but their advantage was small or nonexistent on political and moral pronouncements, candidate and campaign activity, and protesting. Second, orthodox and modernist clergy do have varying styles, preferring different political activities. And although a mode preferred by one side may eventually be adopted by the other, as protest activity was tried by conservatives in the 1990s, increased involvement by either clerical "party" is usually channeled into their preferred modes.

This conjecture is supported by surveys of Evangelical Covenant and Southern Baptist ministers in 1992. Although both denominations are predominantly Evangelical, they differ politically. As we have shown elsewhere, Southern Baptist political activity grew markedly from 1988 to 1992 (Guth 1996). We have no baseline data for the Covenant clergy, but they were clearly less active in most ways in 1992 than were Southern Baptists. In both denominations, however, activity among orthodox and modernist ministers occurred in modes emphasized in the past. In both these predominantly conservative churches, modernists still excelled in joining, in-church activities, and contacting public officials directly, but orthodox clergy in 1992 were clearly more active than modernists in political pronouncements, moral pronouncements, candidate endorsements, campaign activities, mounting petition drives, and sponsoring boycotts. Certainly, political momentum seemed to be with the conservatives.

Of course, such comparisons are confined to two orthodox denominations. Perhaps modernists there behave differently than those in Mainline churches. As we have no data from any Mainline Protestant church in 1992, we cannot be sure that their modernists did not exceed the activity of orthodox clergy. But a comparison of the most orthodox Southern Baptists in 1992 (well over half the sample) with the most modernist clergy in the 1988 study strongly suggests a new equivalence of activity. Based on the same index used in 1988, the most orthodox Southern Baptists in 1992 matched the 1988 score of the most active groups—modernist Presbyterians and Disciples (mean acts = 5.30).

Although the Baptists did not catch up in joining, church organizing, and some forms of contacting (they didn't even narrow the gap), they compensated with superior performance in the modes previously favored by conservatives and increases in selected direct action activities. They beat the modernists' 1988 scores in several categories: preaching a whole sermon on a political issue (58 to 47 percent), taking a public stand on a political issue (79 to 69 percent), public endorsement of a candidate (71 to 44 percent), presidential primary involvement (33 to 23 percent), and presidential general election activity (67 to 35 percent). Interestingly, 12 percent of the most orthodox Baptists also reported protesting in 1992, compared with 7 percent of the most modernist clergy in 1988. Fifty-four percent also engaged in a boycott based on a political or social issue, a figure for which we have no comparison for modernists in 1988 but which seems unlikely to be surpassed by that theological group. Of course, Southern Baptist clergy are not entirely typical of orthodox ministers, and it is possible that Mainline modernists stepped up their activism in 1992 as well, but the data suggest that we have reached a rough parity in political competition between the two historic "parties" in Protestantism. In the next chapter, we will take a final look at the various groups of clergy, noting their political tendencies and projecting some possibilities for the future of clerical activism in American political life.

# 10
# Conclusion:
# The Present and Future
# of Clerical Politics

*John Morrow, pastor of the Living Word Christian Center in Lincoln, Nebraska, a life-long Republican, went to a sparsely attended GOP county convention during the early 1980s. "I didn't hear much of substance so I thought that if we showed up with at least 50 people we ought to at least get debate going on issues that are important." For Morrow and like-minded pastors, that meant abortion. After becoming a delegate and recruiting others for a couple of years, Morrow and other leaders of the "Conservative Coalition" were about to add pro-life language to the party platform, which had not previously addressed the topic. He urged fellow pro-lifers to work within the GOP: "If we were going to have an effect on this state and nation, it would be best to work within the established system. It's not practical to talk about [starting] third and fourth political parties." Within a few years, the forces led by Morrow and his supporters had shown considerable impact in the Lancaster County Republican Party.*

(Based on Russo and Knapp 1994, 10)

*Richard Morse was busy cleaning the bathroom in his church in Kirkland, Washington, when a message came inviting him to attend the National Prayer Breakfast. Morse, a Disciples of Christ pastor, regards the trip as one of "the highlights of his life." As acting president of the Interfaith Alliance in the state of Washington, Morse has become a controversial figure in his area for the past year for his "outspokenness." "There is a need for religious people to stand up and be counted on issues of religious plurality," he stated. "We like to remind a certain group here in Washington [state] that it is a Christian coalition, not the Christian Coalition." Morse defends the separation of church and state, and opposes the introduction of prayer in the schools. Under his leadership, the Washington Interfaith Alliance fought "extremist" candidates in local school board races and determined to publish voter guides "to have a major impact on the 1996 elections." In this regard, he has had the strong support of his congregation, who initially feared that he would leave the church to work full-time with the Interfaith Alliance, but Morse has no such plans. He continues to want to serve his church: "I could see where the genius of faith is—in making a difference in people's lives."*

(Based on Neiberger 1996; Interfaith Alliance Homepage)

185

Pastors Morrow and Morse have more in common than the similarity of their names: they are both political activists, embodying the two faces of contemporary ministerial politics in the United States. Pastor Morrow personifies the Christian Right as it has burst upon the scene in the past two decades. If the classic studies of pastoral politics are any indication, his species did not exist a generation ago, but it is certainly proliferating at the end of the twentieth century. On the other hand, Pastor Morse leads an organization created to combat the Christian Right, directed primarily at clergy of a more liberal stripe. Clearly, pastoral activity has changed in many ways since the appearance of the New Breed in the 1960s, and yet there may be underlying continuities with ministerial politics of the past.

This book has explored the roots of these competing forces in contemporary American religious politics. In this final chapter, we tie our findings together into a coherent package, speculate about the future of pastoral politics, and, finally, raise some questions about the appropriate role for pastors in the political process.

## A TYPOLOGY OF PROTESTANT CLERGY

To reduce the complexity in clerical politics to a manageable state, we conclude by reviewing a typology of ministerial politics in the contemporary United States. To accomplish this, we used a procedure known as cluster analysis to put ministers of similar ideological orientations and activity levels into coherent groups. We found that a six-group solution worked very well in summarizing the political tendencies of clergy in our sample. We have used descriptive labels for these groups to capture both their general position on the political spectrum and their activist orientation: the *Christian Right* (9.7 percent of the weighted sample), *Conventional Conservatives* (28.2 percent), the *Old Breed* of inactive conservatives (20.2 percent), *Quiescent Liberals* (11.9 percent), *Conventional Liberals* (20.5 percent), and the *New Breed* of liberal activists (9.7 percent). The results of our analysis are presented in Table 10.1, which places our types in their denominational, theological, and political locations.

Virtually all the denominations have at least some representation of each type of clergy, but there are clear differences in the proportion of their clergy who fall into each cluster (the percentages in this section of Table 10.1 add to 100 on each line). The Assemblies of God have a minority of Christian Right activists, a large body of conventional conservatives, a significant group of Old Breed inactives, and a mere handful of liberals of any kind. Southern Baptists are almost identical, except for slightly smaller proportions in each conservative group and noticeable minorities of liberals. Both the Evangelical Covenant and the Christian Reformed Church ministers cover more of the spectrum, but they lean toward conservatism and toward either conventional or inactive political status. The Mainline churches vary somewhat but have liberal majorities with significant numbers of Conventional Liberals or members of the New Breed. Note, however, that even in the PCUSA and Disciples only one in five clergy falls under the latter rubric. In sum, the fit between the six clusters and denomination is good but not perfect.

Does theology differentiate these groups? The data in the table should come as no surprise to the reader. Theologically, the Christian Right clergy are located in the most orthodox quartile of the sample, while the New Breed is overwhelmingly concentrated in the most modernist. In addition, both activist groups draw disproportionately from among clergy who think of themselves as part of two historic religious movements, fundamentalism and liberalism—the polar categories on our religious movement scale—a tendency that is emphatic in the case of the New Breed, two-thirds of whom call themselves theological liberals. Interestingly, the only theological measure that does not clearly distinguish among the groups is dispensationalism, which is almost equally characteristic of all the conservative clusters and equally uncharacteristic of the liberals (data not shown). This suggests that the old dispensationalist bias toward political passivity no longer has the power it once did in clerical politics. On the whole, though, it is obvious that activism in "two-party" Protestantism is most characteristic of clergy on the polar extremes of Christian orthodoxy, who also identify with the historic religious movements of fundamentalism and liberalism.

Both our social theology measures also serve to distinguish among the political groups. New Breed liberals are extremely close to the communitarian end of our individualism scale, while the Christian Right pastors adhere quite strongly to the new civic gospel, as well as to classic religious individualism. Less active ministers are characterized by somewhat lower scores on each measure: Conventional and Quiescent Liberals are less communitarian than the New Breed, and Conventional Conservatives and the Old Breed are less attached to the civic gospel than is the Christian Right. Overall, the social theology measures seem to put a chasm between the conservative and liberal groups, even deeper than that cut by theology. Almost none of the conservative groups contain any communitarians, and none of the liberal groups have much sympathy for the civic gospel. The data provide more empirical evidence of the "theological" culture war among Protestant clergy.

The political agendas of each group are quite consistent with their social theologies. As we would expect, the Christian Right activists score high on the moral reform agenda, followed by Conventional Conservatives and Old Breed pastors—at considerable distance. On the liberal side, New Breed liberals are distinguished even more clearly by their extensive concern with social justice issues, with a breadth of agenda that puts them far out in front of even their Conventional Liberal colleagues, and very much out of line with the Quiescent Liberals. These findings suggest that the New Breed clergy may not have the full backing of fellow liberals for the broad range of issue concerns they address, while the Christian Right has somewhat more support from Conventional Conservatives on the moral reform agenda, and even a modicum of help from the inactive Old Breed.

The clusters are also quite distinctive in ideological and partisan terms. We di-

Table 10.1
Typology of Clergy

| | Christian Right | Conventional Conservatives | Old Breed | Quiescent Liberals | Conventional Liberals | New Breed |
|---|---|---|---|---|---|---|
| Percent of sample | 9.5% | 28.2% | 20.2% | 11.9% | 20.5% | 9.7% |
| Denomination | | | | | | |
| Assemblies of God | 16 | 47 | 35 | 1 | 1 | 0 |
| Southern Baptist | 14 | 42 | 29 | 7 | 7 | 1 |
| Evangelical Covenant | 11 | 35 | 23 | 13 | 15 | 3 |
| Christian Reformed | 10 | 36 | 17 | 14 | 18 | 5 |
| Reformed Church | 8 | 24 | 15 | 13 | 30 | 10 |
| United Methodist | 7 | 21 | 16 | 16 | 29 | 13 |
| Presbyterian USA | 5 | 12 | 10 | 18 | 33 | 22 |
| Disciples of Christ | 5 | 12 | 9 | 17 | 37 | 19 |
| Theology | | | | | | |
| Most orthodox | 62 | 58 | 49 | 3 | 3 | 2 |
| Most modernist | 3 | 3 | 4 | 47 | 57 | 70 |
| Fundamentalist | 32 | 29 | 27 | 2 | 3 | 1 |
| Liberal | 1 | 1 | 1 | 31 | 44 | 64 |
| Social theology | | | | | | |
| High communitarian | 8 | 10 | 11 | 57 | 64 | 78 |
| High civic gospel | 78 | 68 | 58 | 6 | 6 | 2 |
| Political agenda | | | | | | |
| High moral issue | 61 | 46 | 20 | 1 | 5 | 7 |
| High social reform | 10 | 2 | 1 | 4 | 19 | 51 |
| Issue ideology and party | | | | | | |
| Most liberal | 1 | 1 | 1 | 42 | 58 | 83 |
| Most conservative | 58 | 46 | 35 | 0 | 0 | 0 |
| Strong Republican | 50 | 31 | 22 | 3 | 2 | 3 |
| Strong Democrat | 1 | 1 | 3 | 18 | 28 | 52 |
| Activist orientations | | | | | | |
| Very high interest | 79 | 56 | 36 | 39 | 59 | 83 |
| Political efficacy | 85 | 73 | 64 | 49 | 56 | 67 |
| Cooperation | 75 | 67 | 60 | 61 | 70 | 76 |
| Strongly approve of activism | 73 | 41 | 21 | 50 | 75 | 95 |
| Mean acts, 1988 (of 12 possible) | 5.7 | 2.6 | .6 | .6 | 2.9 | 6.4 |

vided the issue ideology score (derived in chapter 6) into quintiles for presentation purposes. The New Breed is easily identifiable by its position: 83 percent fell into the most liberal quintile, compared with only 58 percent of Conventional Liberals. On the other side, the Christian Right was not quite as distinct, with only 58 percent in the most conservative quintile and the next group, the Conventional Conservatives, not that far behind. Nevertheless, our measure of issue ideology is one of the best discriminators among the groups, predicting a pastor's position better than almost any other variable. Of course, ideology is increasingly being transformed into partisanship, but party identification does not present quite so strong a contrast. Still, half the Christian Right pastors are "strong" Republicans, and half of the New Breed are "strong" Democrats, with such partisanship falling off dramatically toward the middle of the table.

These clusters also differ on many of the prerequisites to political activism, whether among citizens or clergy. There is, first of all, a striking variation in the level of political interest expressed by the groups. After calculating the proportion of each group choosing the two highest positions on a seven-point political interest item, we found that the Christian Right and New Breed clergy have extremely high political interest, followed at a respectable distance by their conventional and, then, inactive brethren. Of course, high political interest is usually associated with more extensive agendas, as well as strong ideological and partisan stances, as political scientists well know. These findings help explain why Christian Right and New Breed activists are more sharply distinguished politically from their inactive colleagues than theological similarity might predict—they are simply far more interested. Political efficacy follows the same U-shaped pattern, although the conservative groups have somewhat more confidence in their ability to influence congregations than do their liberal counterparts, perhaps reflecting greater political compatibility with the laity. And the Christian Right and New Breed score highest on willingness to cooperate with other clergy, regardless of theology, but the other groups are not far behind in this measure of "social capital."

As we should expect, the six clusters differ in willingness to approve ministerial activism. For the table we used an overall approval rating, including both direct action and cue-giving. While the Christian Right strongly endorses ministerial activism, it still trails the New Breed and has less support from the other two conservative groups than the New Breed has from the liberals. As the discerning reader could guess, this results from a continuing reluctance of many conservatives, especially the Old Breed, to endorse direct action. And, given the link between approval of activism and activism itself, we expect that these groups will have distinctive activity profiles. Here again we see a mirror image, with the Christian Right and New Breed looking much alike and activism falling dramatically with movement from each pole to the middle groups. The conservative groups were slightly less active than their liberal counterparts in 1988, but this gap may be an artifact of bias in the items used in the common batteries. Overall, the mean scores may not even capture the full difference between the two extreme clusters and the other four groups. Christian

Right and New Breed pastors are "hyperactive," involved in politics at rates far higher than those of the small number of activists found in national studies of the mass public. In contrast, the Conventional Liberals and Conventional Conservatives resemble citizens who are sometimes involved beyond voting, while the Old Breed and Quiescent Liberals are like most Americans, who vote but do little else in politics—Verba and Nie's (1972) "voting specialists."

Although theological, ideological, and political measures differentiate these groups, only a few demographic or personal traits make much difference, primarily educational experience (Table 10.2). Although the liberal clusters have more years of education than the three conservative groups, among the latter the Christian Right has more college graduates and clergy with additional graduate work. New Breed clergy are quite distinctive in several ways, however: they attend far more prestigious undergraduate institutions, with over half matriculating at highly selective colleges, compared with only 11 percent for the Christian Right. Similar figures obtain for theological education, where almost half of the New Breed attend the most prestigious divinity schools. Finally, the New Breed is also much more likely to major in the social sciences and humanities.

Other demographic factors show fewer differences. Almost half the Christian Right is southern, compared with only a third of the New Breed. There are some social class differences, with the conservative groups more likely to come from blue-collar or farm backgrounds, while the liberal groups tend to have origins in business or professional homes. Although all Protestant clergy tend to be drawn from non-metropolitan places, pastors in the conservative groups were more often brought up in rural areas and in smaller towns than the liberals, but the Christian Right is the least rural of the conservatives (especially in current residence), and the New Breed is from slightly larger urban areas than the other liberal groups. Interestingly, the inactive Old Breed is even more concentrated today in smaller places (data not shown), suggesting that its political passivity may be due in part to lack of stimulation by the hot-button agenda issues or opportunity for activism present in urban communities. The Christian Right clergy are also younger, while the New Breed is the oldest of the political groups. This difference reflects the mobilization of different age cohorts: the New Breed in the political controversies of the 1960s and early 1970s, and the Christian Right in those of the 1980s. Fully one-quarter of the Christian Right activists are under thirty-five years old, compared with only 15 percent of the New Breed, a good omen for the growth, and persistence, of the Christian Right.

The groups also differ by gender and family situation: only 2 percent of the Christian Right clergy are women, but 10 percent of the New Breed and Conventional Liberals are; 94 percent of the Christian Right report being in "traditional" family situations (i.e., married once), compared with 78 percent of the New Breed, which has many more single, divorced, or divorced and remarried pastors. All in all, the distinctive ideological and activity profiles of each cluster do have some basis in differing personal and social situations, especially their differing educational backgrounds.

Table 10.2
Typology of Clergy: Selected Demographic Characteristics

| | Christian Right | Conventional Conservatives | Old Breed | Quiescent Liberals | Conventional Liberals | New Breed |
|---|---|---|---|---|---|---|
| Percent of sample | 9.5% | 28.2% | 20.2% | 11.9% | 20.5% | 9.7% |
| College education | | | | | | |
| Some college or less | 24 | 30 | 31 | 6 | 5 | 4 |
| College degree | 50 | 48 | 52 | 72 | 68 | 57 |
| Graduate work | 26 | 22 | 17 | 22 | 27 | 39 |
| Highly selective college | 11 | 11 | 11 | 36 | 45 | 53 |
| Social science or humanities major | 36 | 32 | 32 | 52 | 57 | 65 |
| Seminary education | | | | | | |
| None | 29 | 27 | 29 | 4 | 3 | 0 |
| Some | 10 | 13 | 13 | 4 | 4 | 3 |
| Seminary degree | 39 | 43 | 42 | 66 | 58 | 49 |
| Graduate work | 22 | 17 | 15 | 27 | 35 | 48 |
| Prestige seminary | 22 | 17 | 15 | 27 | 35 | 48 |
| Southern residence | 48 | 41 | 43 | 37 | 37 | 35 |
| Blue-collar or farm | 60 | 61 | 63 | 47 | 45 | 45 |
| Childhood community | | | | | | |
| Under 50,000 | 63 | 64 | 67 | 53 | 57 | 50 |
| Over 50,000 | 27 | 26 | 23 | 47 | 43 | 50 |
| Age | | | | | | |
| Under 35 | 24 | 21 | 16 | 16 | 15 | 15 |
| Married, never divorced | 94 | 93 | 96 | 84 | 78 | 78 |
| Female | 2 | 1 | 2 | 8 | 9 | 9 |

Nevertheless, the critical differences among political groups are ideational: issues of theology, social theology, and political attitudes. Although it would be dangerous to extrapolate too much from our sample, we think the evidence points clearly to the existence of a "two-party system" in American Protestantism, one that extends beyond the theological meaning Martin Marty intended with this coinage, into the real "two-party" world of politics and government. True, the metaphor may work best for the Christian Right and the New Breed, somewhat less well for the two conventional groups, and poorly for the two "spectator" groups in the middle, the Old Breed and Quiescent Liberals. But in one sense it replicates the party system in the larger electorate, driven by hyperactive partisans with strong ideological commitments, who seek to mobilize less activist identifiers, and even sway sympathetic spectators.

This clerical two-party system is very competitive. Christian Right activists and their fellow travelers among Conventional Conservatives have probably become as numerous and almost as involved as their liberal counterparts. True, a somewhat larger proportion of conservatives remain faithful to the old Evangelical warnings against mixing religion and politics, but these are concentrated among older clergy, destined to be replaced by younger, better-educated, more politically conscious ministers. If this happens, religious conservatives may be mobilized even more effectively. Of course, it is always dangerous to project current trends in ministerial politics into the future; the New Breed of activist liberals are still with us, but they were not the wave of the future envisioned by Harvey Cox and others a generation ago (Garrett 1973). Just as congregational resistance cut the heart out of the New Breed, national events, ministerial fatigue, or lay opposition may limit the future impact of conservative Christian clergy. We should expect, however, that whenever national issues engage the theological sensitivities of the clergy, left or right, some will resort to the "bully pulpit," as they have done repeatedly throughout American history.

## THE FUTURE OF MINISTERIAL POLITICS

As we look ahead, then, we project that the high level of pastoral activism we have seen in the 1980s and 1990s is likely to persist. First, political agendas with theological underpinnings are likely to have a staying power that some secular agendas may not. In the same vein, specific policy preferences similarly derived are likely to persist. As long as religious people, including their leaders, sense a discontinuity between core values and public policy, religious activism can be expected. This is especially true in an era when many conservative religious people have acquired the education, psychological orientations, financial resources, and civic skills to participate effectively.

Of course, not all religious politics will be pastor-led. As we have seen, many religious organizations in politics have purposefully circumvented clergy, preferring to work through religious laity. This often reflects their frustration in mobilizing Old Breed conservatives and Quiescent Liberals, fear of running afoul of various legal restrictions on political activities by churches, and perhaps recognition of the many constraints that pastors face in undertaking institutional action. Nevertheless, clergy on both sides of the ideological divide are well-educated citizens, prominent and respected members of their communities. As such we expect to find them engaged as individuals, as they have been throughout American history. And their more subtle, but perhaps more pervasive and effective, role as cue-givers will persist as long as Protestant churches survive.

Whether inevitable or not, pastoral activism has been subjected to much criticism in recent years, despite its ancient American pedigree. In part, such criticism reflects a natural tendency of those who disagree with positions advanced to shift the argument to another level. For example, the media elites and academics who applauded the New Breed's battles against racial injustice, poverty, and the Vietnam War are less enamored of the Christian Right's fights against abortion, pornography, and gay rights, often claiming that these actions violate the separation of church and state. And, ironically, attacks on clerical politics often come from ministers themselves, who agree more than ever on the propriety of involvement but are starkly divided by the causes they defend and, often, by the techniques they regard as legitimate. The fact that many controversial issues have been nationalized and opened to greater media exposure, and that both sides are now well equipped with money, skilled leadership, and strong organization, makes controversy over the pastoral role more heated than ever.

What should be the role of religious leaders in politics? Our empirical inquiry gives us no special insight, but it has certainly made us conscious of the dilemmas confronting professional clergy. Perhaps referring back to the minister's roles mentioned in chapter 1 will be helpful. First, clergy are citizens with the same rights and responsibilities as others to participate. And in many ways clergy are model citizens: very interested, well informed, highly principled, and willing to be active on community concerns. Such participation is to be applauded. This is not to say that such citizen activism may not create problems for clergy in their professional roles, but that is a difficulty faced by people in many occupations. We have no sympathy for any modern, informal version of the clergy disability provisions in some early state constitutions that deprived ministers of various political rights, despite the appeal this notion has to some secular opinion leaders and activists.

When we move from minister as citizen to pastor as religious professional, things become more complicated. The continuing religious character of American society and the esteem in which clergy are held mean that they will often play a key role in connecting the fundamental religious values of their traditions with contemporary public policy (Fetzer 1992). Not to do so may indeed render religious faith arid and irrelevant to parishioners. As American clergy instruct their flocks about theological matters, they will inevitably convey a vision of the human community, the means to improve that community, and the critical questions confronting it. Serious consideration of religious values will inevitably lead some pastors to favor smaller government and to oppose abortion, while others seek to expand government help for the poor. These forays are to be expected and even encouraged. Without these moral cues, we would indeed have a "naked public square" (Neuhaus 1984), a public life devoid of moral content. We prefer, however, that pastors who enter this minefield do so with prophetic boldness—and with civility and tolerance. This is an unusual combination: prophets are not usually exemplars of either civility or tolerance, but in a democratic society prophetic vision may be as necessary as civility and tolerance. Remember the abolitionists, often long on vision but short on civility.

We are more hesitant when the political world engages the pastor as institutional leader. We know that denominations, local church councils, and even individual churches often take official positions on public issues. While tax laws and other legal restrictions may dampen enthusiasm for institutional action, many pastors still see the political mobilization of their congregation or denomination as a part of their role as institutional leader. And the civil rights movement reminds us that such mobilization often achieves valuable results. Still, here is where political activity most often raises the hackles of other citizens and, sometimes, members of the church itself, who may not share the pastor's views. We think that such political activities, whether in the form of pulpit endorsements of candidates, campaign fund-raising in churches, or political pronouncements by church bodies, should be rare, whatever their legal status.

Of course, these distinctions are artificial. In real life pastors play their roles as citizen, religious professional, and institutional leader simultaneously, and it is often difficult to separate them. Consider a not-so-hypothetical pastor who leads a large, established upper-middle-class Mainline church in a metropolitan area. He would be considered a "traditionalist" within his increasingly liberal denomination. His sermon themes are religious ones that express a social theology that we would call "individualist," but he seldom mentions his views on any political issue in the sermon, prayers, or other parts of the service. In many ways, he fits the 1960s stereotype of an Old Breed pastor. On the other hand, his wife is a member of a well-known Christian Right organization and active in a pro-life caucus within the denomination, and the pastor himself is a strong, devoted Republican. In election years, his lawn at the parsonage, next door to the church, is festooned with Republican campaign posters, easily visible from the street and from the church. Has he violated our rules for pastors? In which role? The complexities of this question are faced by every American Protestant minister who has to decide whether and how to employ the real "bully pulpit."

# Appendix A:
# Methodology of the Studies

The data for the study were gathered by national mail surveys of over 5,000 ministers from eight denominations, originally conducted with some coordination by seven investigators in four separate studies. The first survey focused on the Southern Baptist Convention, the Presbyterian Church in the U.S.A., and the Christian Church (Disciples of Christ), and was conducted by James Guth and Helen Lee Turner of Furman University as part of a larger study of the Disciples of Christ. These surveys were administered in the fall and winter of 1988–89. The Assemblies of God and United Methodist Church surveys were conducted by John Green and Margaret Poloma of the University of Akron during the summer of 1989. The surveys of the Christian Reformed Church and the Reformed Church in America were done by Corwin Smidt and James Penning of Calvin College, also during the summer of 1989. We added a survey of another denomination, the Evangelical Covenant Church, following the 1992 presidential election. This survey was conducted by Richard Dodson, with the assistance of John Green of the University of Akron. The number of ministers surveyed in each denomination varied considerably; for the purposes of analysis, we have weighted each sample equally, to prevent sample size from distorting the results.

Because the survey instruments were developed originally for somewhat varying purposes, they are not entirely identical but contain several core batteries on ministers' theological, social, and political characteristics. The surveys also included unique items on issues raised in denominational meetings and on several political questions that surfaced during the 1988 presidential campaign. And most inquired about ministers' votes and involvement (if any) in that campaign. Response rates varied: Assemblies of God (52 percent), Southern Baptists (47 percent), Christian Reformed and Reformed Church (both 66 percent), Methodists (54 percent), and Presbyterians and Disciples (both 64 percent). The response rate for the 1992 ECC survey was 52 percent. Although these response rates are generally good for mail surveys, we were concerned about the possibility of response bias, especially in the Assemblies, Southern Baptist, and Evangelical Covenant samples. A variety of tests comparing respondents with the overall demographic characteristics of the clergy, as drawn from denominational sources, revealed very few systematic differences. Among Assemblies and Southern Baptists, the respondents may be slightly better educated than the clergy as a whole, but the main difference appears to be in current tenure at a church, as respondents are somewhat more sedentary than the clergy as a whole. This bias no doubt reflects the relatively frequent movement of clergy and the vagaries of forwarding orders at local post offices. We also suspected that political interest might prompt a higher response rate, but an analysis of responses by date of return in three of the denominations (the SBC, PCUSA, and Disciples of Christ) shows very few differences among those replying quickly to the first mailing and those who answered more reluctantly in the second, third, and fourth mailings.

# Appendix B:
# Modes of Participation

As earlier studies have discovered, most political actions by clergy are part of a generalized political activity factor. In other words, clergy who are active in one way tend to participate in others. But as various types of clergy differ somewhat in the sort of activism they undertake, conclusions about which clergy are "more active" politically depend in part on which specific actions are included in a general index. If, for example, we use only Quinley's activity items, included in all five 1988 surveys, we might decide that theologically modernist, liberal clergy still have a sizable political advantage over orthodox, conservative ministers, albeit a declining one. If we use broader batteries of items, including activities more characteristic of the political style of conservatives, such as those located in either alternative battery, we find that contemporary differences between theological groups are quite modest.

Although we are interested in overall activity, we think a better approach is first to ask: "What kinds of ministers engage in which activities?" Thus, in the text we look in detail at specific modes of participation. As Verba and his colleagues suggest, such modes may characterize not only average citizens but also specific occupational and professional groups. To identify modes of participation among clergy, we used data on involvement in 1988, a presidential election year. Although this results in a slightly different typology than that produced by looking at career activism, and the configuration of forces influencing political behavior certainly differs from year to year, we think the 1988 data best represent the contemporary form of clerical activities.

Although our experimentation with alternative question form has produced important insights in chapter 8, such variation complicates the analysis of participation. Because not all items were available in all five surveys, we could not rely solely on a simple factor analysis to isolate modes. After much exploration, we found that the most representative classification was produced by the following procedure. We subjected the most extensive battery (the twenty Assemblies/Methodist items) to a factor analysis with oblique rotation to determine the basic structure of ministerial activity. (Oblique rotation was used because we expected the factors to be distinct but also intercorrelated.) This procedure produced four significant factors that made intuitive sense, along with an "orphan" item on contacting public officials. Inspection of the loadings suggested that two of the original factors, a "pronouncement" factor and an "organization" factor, could each be profitably split into two, a decision confirmed by a secondary factor analysis.

When this exercise was complete, we calculated additive indices for eight modes of activity: *political pronouncement, moral pronouncement, candidate endorsement, electoral campaigning, joining, in-church action, contacting,* and *protest.* Each scale was calculated for all ministers asked the items constituting that scale. For *candidate endorsement* and *campaigning,* a relevant item found only in the Assemblies/Methodist battery was dropped to permit construction of a scale across all five denominations. The resulting two-item variables, however, are almost identical with three-item alternatives calculated for those two determinations ($r = .89$ for candidate endorsement and .97 for campaigning). The orphan *contacting* item formed an acceptable scale with two items found only in the Baptist/Presbyterian/Disciples battery, namely, circulating petitions on public issues and writing letters to the editor; as a result, this full index is available only for these three denominations. A few questions asked of only one or two denominations were discarded for purposes of scale construction but are included in the tables for illustration.

To summarize: five of the eight scales *(candidate endorsement, electoral campaigning, joining, church action,* and *protest)* include all five denominations; two scales are based on the Assemblies and Methodist samples alone *(political pronouncement* and *moral pronouncement);* and one is based on the SBC, Presbyterian, and Disciples samples only *(contacting).*

We are quite confident, however, that very much the same results would appear had we asked all items of all clergy. This is confirmed by the Wheaton religious activist study. There we had only general activism items, plus a different battery of questions on whether pastors had "spoken out" on various issues. Despite variations in wording and format and the absence of questions on civil disobedience, joining national political organizations, and in-church organizing, a factor analysis produced six factors parallel to those here; only the in-church organizing factor is understandably missing, and *protest* and *contacting* items load on a single loose factor, reflecting the absence of other militant activity items that might have isolated a distinct *protest* factor. But the striking comparability of results in our denominational sample and this sample of activist clergy is very reassuring.

# References

Abell, Aaron I. 1962. *The Urban Impact on American Protestantism.* Hamden, Conn.: Archon.

Adams, James. 1970. *The Growing Church Lobby in Washington.* Grand Rapids, Mich.: Eerdmans.

Ahlstrom, Sydney E. 1975. *A Religious History of the American People.* 2 vols. Garden City, N.Y.: Doubleday.

Alvis, Joel L., Jr. 1994. *Religion and Race: Southern Presbyterians, 1946–1983.* Tuscaloosa: University of Alabama Press.

Ammerman, Nancy Tatom. 1990. *Baptist Battles.* New Brunswick, N.J.: Rutgers University Press.

Andersen, Kristi. 1976. "Generation, Partisan Shift, and Realignment: A Glance Back to the New Deal." In *The Changing American Voter,* by Norman H. Nie, Sidney Verba, and John R. Petrocik, 74–95. Cambridge, Mass.: Harvard University Press.

Balmer, Randy. 1996. *Grant Us Courage: Travels Along the Mainline of American Protestantism.* New York and Oxford: Oxford University Press.

Barnes, Samuel H., and Max Kaase. 1979. *Political Action: Mass Participation in Five Western Democracies.* Beverly Hills, Calif.: Sage.

Bates, Stephen. 1993. *Battleground: One Mother's Crusade, the Religious Right, and the Struggle for Control of Our Classrooms.* New York: Poseidon Press.

Beatty, Kathleen Murphy, and Oliver Walter. 1989. "A Group Theory of Religion and Politics: The Clergy as Group Leaders." *Western Political Quarterly* 42:129–158.

Beck, Paul Allen, and M. Kent Jennings. 1979. "Political Periods and Political Participation." *American Political Science Review* 73:737–750.

Bellah, Robert N., Richard Madsen, William M. Sullivan, Ann Swidler, and Steven M. Tipton. 1985. *Habits of the Heart: Individualism and Commitment in American Life.* Berkeley: University of California Press.

———. 1991. *The Good Society.* New York: Knopf.

199

Benson, Peter L., and Dorothy L. Williams. 1982. *Religion on Capitol Hill: Myths and Realities*. San Francisco: Harper and Row.

Berkowitz, Laura A., and John C. Green. 1996. "Charting the Coalition: The Local Chapters of the Ohio Christian Coalition." Paper presented at the Conference on the Christian Right in Comparative Perspective, Calvin College, Grand Rapids, Michigan, October 4–5.

Bibby, John F. 1987. *Politics, Parties and Elections in America*. Chicago: Nelson Hall.

Billingsley, K. L. 1990. *From Mainline to Sideline: The Social Witness of the National Council of Churches*. Washington, D.C.: Ethics and Public Policy Center.

Blumhofer, Edith L. 1993. *Restoring the Faith: The Assemblies of God, Pentecostalism, and American Culture*. Urbana: University of Illinois Press.

Bouma, Gary D. 1984. *How the Saints Persevere: Social Factors in the Vitality of the Christian Reformed Church*. Clayton, Australia: Monash University.

Boyer, Paul. 1992. *When Time Shall Be No More: Prophecy Belief in Modern American Culture*. Cambridge, Mass.: Harvard University Press.

Bratt, James D. 1984. *Dutch Calvinism in Modern America*. Grand Rapids, Mich.: Eerdmans.

————. 1992. "Adam, Eve and the Christian Reformed Church." *Christian Century* 109: 805–808.

Bratt, James D., and Ronald Wells. 1997. "Piety and Progress: A History of Calvin College." In *Models for Christian Higher Education: Strategies for Survival and Success in the Twenty-First Century*, ed. Richard T. Hughes and William B. Adrian, 141–162. Grand Rapids, Mich.: Eerdmans.

Buzzard, Lynn. 1989. "The 'Coming Out' of Evangelicals." In *Contemporary Evangelical Political Involvement*, ed. Corwin E. Smidt, 133–146. Lanham, Md.: University Press of America.

Campbell, Angus, Philip E. Converse, Warren E. Miller, and Donald E. Stokes. 1960. *The American Voter*. New York: Wiley.

Campolo, Tony. 1995. *Can Mainline Denominations Make a Comeback?* Valley Forge, Pa.: Judson Press.

Carnett, Shelia. 1993. "Modern Day Crusader: Pastor's Causes Draw Praise, Criticism." *Greenville (S.C.) News*, August 15, 1B.

Carroll, Jackson W., and Penny Long Marler. 1995. "Culture Wars? Insights from Ethnographies of Two Protestant Seminaries." *Sociology of Religion* 56:1–20.

Chiles, Robert E. 1965. *The Theological Tradition in American Methodism 1790–1935*. New York: Abingdon.

Coalter, Milton J., John M. Mulder, and Louis B. Weeks. 1992. *The Re-forming Tradition: Presbyterians and Mainstream America*. Louisville, Ky.: Westminster/John Knox.

Conn, Joseph. 1996. "Pyramid Power." *Church and State* 49 (March):11.

Conover, Pamela Johnston, and Stanley Feldman. 1986. "Morality Items on the 1985 Pilot Study." National Election Study Report, Ann Arbor, Michigan.

Converse, Philip. 1964. "The Nature of Belief Systems in Mass Publics." In *Ideology and Discontent*, ed. David E. Apter, 206–261. New York: Free Press.

Conway, M. Margaret. 1991. *Political Participation in the United States*. Washington, D.C.: CQ Press.

Cornell, George. 1992. "Southern Baptists Top Denomination in 1,322 Counties." *Greenville (S.C.) News*, July 18, 12A.

Dahlstrom, Kendall. 1996. Telephone interview with James L. Guth, September 12.

Dobson, Edward G. 1996. "Taking Politics Out of the Sanctuary." *Christianity Today,* May 20, 16–17.

Dodson, Richard S. 1995. "A Survey of the Political Attitudes of Evangelical Covenant Pastors." Thesis option paper, Department of Political Science, University of Akron.

Downs, Donald A. 1989. *The New Politics of Pornography.* Chicago: University of Chicago Press.

Dudley, Carl S., and Thomas Van Eck. 1992. "Social Ideology and Community Ministries." In *Yearbook of American and Canadian Churches, 1992,* ed. Kenneth B. Bedell and Alice M. Jones, 5–14. Nashville, Tenn.: Abingdon.

Eighmy, John Lee. 1972. *Churches in Cultural Captivity.* Knoxville: University of Tennessee Press.

Ellingsen, Mark. 1993. *The Cutting Edge: How Churches Speak on Social Issues.* Grand Rapids, Mich.: Eerdmans.

Evangelical Covenant Church Website. 1996. Http://www.npcts.edu/cov/index.htm.

Fetzer, Joel. 1992. "The Role of the Local Pastor in Shaping Evangelicals' Attitudes on the Morality of War." Paper presented at the annual meeting of the Society for the Scientific Study of Religion, Washington, D.C., November 6–8.

Findlay, James F., Jr. 1993. *Church People in the Struggle: The National Council of Churches and the Black Freedom Movement, 1950–1970.* New York: Oxford University Press.

Finke, Roger, and Rodney Stark. 1992. *The Churching of America 1776–1990: Winners and Losers in Our Religious Economy.* New Brunswick, N.J.: Rutgers University Press.

Flanigan, William H., and Nancy H. Zingale. 1994. *Political Behavior of the American Electorate.* 8th ed. Washington, D.C.: CQ Press.

Fowler, Robert Booth. 1995. *The Greening of Protestant Thought.* Chapel Hill: University of North Carolina Press.

Frame, Randy. 1989. "Assemblies of God Celebrates 75 Years." *Christianity Today,* September 22, 45.

Friedly, Robert L., and D. Duane Cummins. 1987. *The Search for Identity: Disciples of Christ—The Restructure Years.* St. Louis: CBP Press.

Gaddy, C. Welton. 1996. *Faith and Politics: What's a Christian to Do?* Macon, Ga.: Peake Road.

Gamwell, Franklin I. 1996. "Faith and Politics: Details and Designs." *Christian Century* 113:604–606.

Garrett, William R. 1973. "Politicized Clergy: A Sociological Interpretation of the 'New Breed.'" *Journal for the Scientific Study of Religion* 12:384–399.

Goldman, Ari. 1991. *The Search for God at Harvard.* New York: Times Books.

Green, John C., and James L. Guth. 1986. "Big Bucks and Petty Cash: Party and Interest Group Activists in American Politics." In *Interest Group Politics,* 2d ed., Allan Cigler and Burdett Loomis, 91–113. Washington, D.C.: CQ Press.

———. 1991a. "An Ideology of Rights: Support for Civil Liberties Among Politial Activists." *Political Behavior* 12:321–344.

———. 1991b. "Who's Right and Who's Left? Activist Coalitions in the Reagan Era." In *Do Elections Matter?* 2d ed., ed. Benjamin Ginsberg and Alan Stone, 32–56. Armonk, N.Y.: M. E. Sharpe.

———. 1993. "From Lambs to Sheep: Denominational Change and Political Behavior." In *Rediscovering the Religious Factor in American Politics,* ed. David C. Leege and Lyman A. Kellstedt, 100–117. Armonk, N.Y.: M. E. Sharpe.

————. 1996. "Methodist Opinion: Diversity at Century's End," *Circuit Rider* 20 (November): 9–11.

Green, John C., James L. Guth, and Cleveland R. Fraser. 1991. "Apostles and Apostates? Religion and Politics Among Party Activists." In *The Bible and the Ballot Box: Religion and Politics in the 1988 Election,* ed. James L. Guth and John C. Green, 113–136. Boulder, Colo.: Westview Press.

Green, John C., James L. Guth, Corwin E. Smidt, and Lyman A. Kellstedt. 1996. *Religion and the Culture Wars: Dispatches from the Front.* Lanham, Md., and London: Rowman and Littlefield.

Greer, Bruce A. 1991. "Active and Inactive Disciples, Presbyterians, and Southern Baptists: A Comparative Socioeconomic, Religious, and Political Profile." In *A Case Study of Mainstream Protestantism: The Disciples' Relation to American Culture, 1880–1989,* ed. D. Newell Williams, 386–415. Grand Rapids, Mich.: Eerdmans.

Guth, James L. 1985–86. "Political Converts: Partisan Realignment Among Southern Baptist Ministers." *Election Politics* 3(1):2–6.

————. 1996. "The Political Mobilization of Southern Baptist Clergy, 1980–1992." In *Religion and the Culture Wars: Dispatches from the Front,* ed. John C. Green, James L. Guth, Corwin E. Smidt, and Lyman A. Kellstedt, 146–173. Lanham, Md., and London: Rowman and Littlefield.

Guth, James, Cleveland R. Fraser, John C. Green, Lyman A. Kellstedt, and Corwin E. Smidt. 1996. "Religion and Foreign Policy Attitudes: The Case of Christian Zionism." In *Religion and the Culture Wars: Dispatches from the Front,* ed. John C. Green, James L. Guth, Corwin E. Smidt, and Lyman A. Kellstedt, 330–360. Lanham, Md., and London: Rowman and Littlefield.

Guth, James L., John C. Green, Lyman A. Kellstedt, and Corwin E. Smidt. 1995. "Onward Christian Soldiers: Political Activists in Five Religious Interest Groups." In *Interest Group Politics,* 2nd edition, ed. Allan Cigler and Burdett Loomis, 55–76. Washington, DC: CQ Press.

Guth, James, Lyman A. Kellstedt, Corwin E. Smidt, and John C. Green. 1994. "Cut from the Whole Cloth: Antiabortion Mobilization among Religious Activists. In *Abortion Politics in the United States and Canada,* ed. Ted G. Jelen and Marthe A. Chandler, 107–129. Westport, Conn.: Praeger.

Hadden, Jeffrey K. 1969. *The Gathering Storm in the Churches.* Garden City, N.Y.: Doubleday.

————. 1987. "Religious Broadcasting and the New Christian Right." *Journal for the Scientific Study of Religion* 26:1–24.

Harding, Susan. 1994. "Imagining the Last Days: The Politics of Apocalyptic Language." In *Accounting for Fundamentalisms,* ed. Martin E. Marty and R. Scott Appleby, 57–78. Chicago: University of Chicago Press.

Harwell, Jack U. 1993. "Southern Baptists Attack President Clinton." *Baptists Today,* June 29, 1–3.

Hatch, Nathan O. 1989. *The Democratization of American Christianity.* New Haven, Conn.: Yale University Press.

————. 1994. "The Puzzle of American Methodism." *Church History* 63:175–189.

Hertzke, Allen D. 1988. *Representing God in Washington: The Role of Religious Lobbies in the American Polity.* Knoxville: University of Tennessee Press.

————. 1991. "An Assessment of the Mainline Churches Since 1945." In *The Role of Reli-*

*gion in the Making of Public Policy,* ed. James E. Wood Jr. and Derek Davis, 43–79. Waco, Tex.: J. M. Dawson Institute of Church-State Studies.

———. 1993. *Echoes of Discontent: Jesse Jackson, Pat Robertson, and the Resurgence of Populism.* Washington, D.C.: CQ Press.

Hessel, Dieter T. 1993. *The Church's Public Role.* Grand Rapids, Mich.: Eerdmans.

Himmelstein, Jerome. 1990. *To the Right: The Transformation of American Conservatism.* Berkeley: University of California Press.

Hofrenning, Daniel J. B. 1995. *In Washington but Not of It.* Philadelphia: Temple University Press.

Hoge, Dean R. 1976. *Division in the Protestant House: The Basic Reasons Behind Intra-Church Conflicts.* Philadelphia: Westminster Press.

Honey, Charles. 1995. "Pastoral Politics." *Grand Rapids Press,* December 4, B1.

Hooten, Jeff. 1996. "Whatever Happened to Clinic Protests?" *Citizen,* August 26, 1–3.

Hudson, Winthrop S. 1961. *American Protestantism.* Chicago: University of Chicago Press.

Hunt, Earl G., Jr. 1987. *A Bishop Speaks His Mind: A Candid View of United Methodism.* Nashville, Tenn.: Abingdon.

Hunter, James D. 1991. *Culture Wars: The Struggle to Define America.* New York: Basic Books.

Hunter, James D., and Kimon Howland Sargeant. 1993. "Religion and the Transformation of Public Culture." *Social Research* 60:545–570.

Ice, Martha Long. 1995. *Clergy Worldviews: Now the Men's Voices.* Westport, Conn.: Praeger.

Iyengar, Shanto. 1991. *Is Anyone Responsible?* Chicago: University of Chicago Press.

Iyengar, Shanto, and Donald R. Kinder. 1987. *News That Matters.* Chicago: University of Chicago Press.

Jankowski, Thomas B., and John M. Strate. 1995. "Modes of Participation over the Adult Life Span." *Political Behavior* 17:89–106.

Jeffries, Vincent, and Clarence E. Tygart. 1974. "The Influence of Theology, Denomination, and Values upon the Positions of Clergy on Social Issues." *Journal for the Scientific Study of Religion* 13:309–324.

Jelen, Ted G. 1991. *The Political Mobilization of Religious Beliefs.* Westport, Conn.: Praeger.

———. 1993. *The Political World of the Clergy.* Westport, Conn.: Praeger.

Johnson, Benton. 1966. "Theology and Party Preference Among Protestant Clergymen." *American Sociological Review* 31:200–208.

———. 1967. "Theology and the Position of Pastors on Public Issues." *American Sociological Review* 32:433–442.

Johnson, Robert. 1990. "Heavenly Gates: Preaching a Gospel of Acquisitiveness, A Showy Sect Prospers." *Wall Street Journal,* December 11, Al.

Jorstad, Erling. 1970. *The Politics of Doomsday: Fundamentalists of the Far Right.* Nashville, Tenn.: Abingdon.

Keith, Bruce E., David B. Magleby, Candice J. Nelson, Elizabeth Orr, Mark C. Westlye, and Raymond E. Wolfinger. 1992. *The Myth of the Independent Voter.* Berkeley: University of California Press.

Kellstedt, Lyman A., and John C. Green. 1993. "Knowing God's Many People: Denominational Preference and Political Behavior." In *Rediscovering the Religious Factor in American Politics,* ed. David C. Leege and Lyman A. Kellstedt, 53–71. Armonk, N.Y.: M. E. Sharpe.

Kingdon, John W. 1984. *Agendas, Alternatives, and Public Policies.* Boston: Little, Brown.

Kinnamon, Michael. 1992. "Restoring Mainline Trust: Disagreeing in Love." *Christian Century* 109 (July 1–8):645–648.

Kirkpatrick, Jeane. 1976. *The New Presidential Elite: Men and Women in National Politics.* New York: The Russell Sage Foundation and the Twentieth Century Fund.

Kleppner, Paul. 1970. *The Cross of Culture: A Social Analysis of Midwestern Politics 1850–1900.* New York: Free Press.

Koller, Norman B., and Joseph D. Retzer. 1980. "The Sounds of Silence Revisited." *Sociological Analysis* 41:155–161.

Ladd, Everett Carll, Jr., and Charles D. Hadley. 1975. *Transformations of the American Party System: Political Coalitions from the New Deal to the 1970s.* New York: Norton.

Ladd, Everett Carll, Jr., and Seymour Martin Lipset. 1975. *The Divided Academy: Professors and Politics.* New York: Norton.

Langenbach, Lisa, and John C. Green. 1992. "Hollow Core: Evangelical Clergy and the 1988 Robertson Campaign." *Polity* 25:147–158.

Leege, David C., and Lyman A. Kellstedt, eds. 1993. *Rediscovering the Religious Factor in American Politics.* Armonk, N.Y.: M. E. Sharpe.

Lehman, Edward C., Jr. 1993. *Gender and Work: The Case of the Clergy.* Albany: State University of New York Press.

Leighley, Jan E. 1995. "Attitudes, Opportunities and Incentives: A Field Essay on Political Participation." *Political Research Quarterly* 48:181–209.

Lerner, Robert, Stanley Rothman, and S. Robert Lichter. 1989. "Christian Religious Elites." *Public Opinion* 11 (March/April):54–58.

Levine, Jeffrey, Edward G. Carmines, and Robert Huckfeldt. 1997. "The Rise of Ideology in the Post–New Deal Party System." *American Politics Quarterly* 25:19–34.

Lienesch, Michael. 1993. *Redeeming America: Piety and Politics in the New Christian Right.* Chapel Hill: University of North Carolina Press.

Lipsky, Michael. 1968. "Protest as a Political Resource." *American Political Science Review* 62:1144–1158.

Longfield, Bradley J. 1991. *The Presbyterian Controversy: Fundamentalists, Modernists, and Moderates.* New York: Oxford University Press.

Lowi, Theodore J. 1995. *The End of the Republican Era.* Norman: University of Oklahoma Press.

Luidens, Donald A. 1993. "Between Myth and Hard Data: A Denomination Struggles with Identity." In *Beyond Establishment: Protestant Identity in a Post-Protestant Age,* ed. Jackson Carroll and Wade Clark Roof, 248–269. Louisville, Ky.: Westminster/John Knox.

Luidens, Donald A., and Roger J. Nemeth. 1989. "After the Storm: Closing the Clergy-Laity Gap." *Review of Religious Research* 31:183–195.

McClosky, Herbert, Paul Hoffman, and Rosemary O'Hara. 1960. "Issue Conflict and Consensus Among Party Leaders and Followers." *American Political Science Review* 54:406–427.

McEllhenney, John G., Frederick E. Maser, Charles Yrigoyen Jr., and Kenneth E. Rowe. 1992. *United Methodism in America.* Nashville, Tenn.: Abingdon.

McKinney, William, and Daniel V. A. Olson. N.d. "Protestant Church Leaders: A Preliminary Overview." Unpublished manuscript.

Maddox, William S., and Stuart A. Lilie. 1984. *Beyond Liberal and Conservative.* Washington, D.C.: Cato Institute.

Manis, Andrew M. 1987. *Southern Civil Religions in Conflict.* Athens: University of Georgia Press.

Marsden, George M. 1980. *Fundamentalism and American Culture: The Shaping of Twentieth-Century Evangelicalism, 1870–1925.* New York: Oxford University Press.

Martin, William. 1996. *With God on Our Side: The Rise of the Religious Right in America.* New York: Broadway Books.

Marty, Martin. 1970. *Righteous Empire: The Protestant Experience in America.* New York: Dial Press.

———. 1997. "Where Do You Draw the Line? Negotiating with Modernity." *Christian Century* 114:38–39.

Maxwell, Joe. 1995. "The Silence of the Shepherds." *World,* January 21, 12–17.

May, Henry F. 1949. *Protestant Churches and Industrial America.* New York: Harper.

Meier, Kenneth J. 1994. *The Politics of Sin: Drugs, Alcohol and Public Policy.* Armonk, N.Y.: M. E. Sharpe.

Menendez, Albert J. 1977. *Religion at the Polls.* Philadelphia: Westminster Press.

———. 1996. *Evangelicals at the Ballot Box.* Amherst, N.Y.: Prometheus Books.

Miller, Warren E., and J. Merrill Shanks. 1996. *The New American Voter.* Cambridge, Mass.: Harvard University Press.

Mooney, Carolyn J. 1995. " 'Cleaning Up the Seminaries': Doctrinal Strife Wanes as Conservatives Control Southern Baptist Convention." *Chronicle of Higher Education,* July 7, A13.

Mooney, Christopher Z., and Mei-Hsien Lee. 1995. "Legislating Morality in the American States: The Case of Pre-*Roe* Abortion Regulation Reform." *American Journal of Political Science* 39:599–627.

Murphy, Andrew. 1992. "The Mainline Confronts the Persian Gulf War: Assessing the Present Moment in Liberal Protestantism." Paper presented at the annual meeting of the American Political Science Association, Chicago, September 3–6.

National and International Religion Report. 1993. "Restructuring, Magazine Revamping and Reconsideration of Laity." *National and International Religion Report,* June 28, 5.

Neiberger, Ami. 1996. "Activist Profile: Rev. Richard Morse." *Freedom Writer Magazine,* June, 12–15.

Nelsen, Hart, and Sandra Baxter. 1981. "Ministers Speak on Watergate: Effects of Clergy Role During Political Crisis." *Review of Religious Research* 23:150–166.

Nesmith, Bruce. 1994. *The New Republican Coalition: The Reagan Campaigns and White Evangelicals.* New York: Peter Lang.

Neuhaus, Richard J. 1984. *The Naked Public Square: Religion and Democracy in America.* Grand Rapids, Mich.: Eerdmans.

———. 1992. "Presbyterians: Where Have All the People Gone?" *First Things,* no. 28 (December):66–68.

Nie, Norman H., Sidney Verba, and John Petrocik. 1976. *The Changing American Voter.* Cambridge, Mass.: Harvard University Press.

Niebuhr, Gustav. 1995. "Preaching Love Where Hate Has Found a Home." *New York Times,* October 29, 1995, 10.

———. 1996. "Christian Split: Can Nonbelievers Be Saved?" *New York Times,* August 22, A1.

Niebuhr, H. Richard. 1929. *The Social Sources of Denominationalism.* New York: World Publishing.

Novak, Michael. 1982. *The Spirit of Democratic Capitalism.* New York: Simon and Schuster.

Olson, Daniel V. A., and Jackson W. Carroll. 1992. "Religiously Based Politics: Religious Elites and the Public." *Social Forces* 70:765–786.

Olson, Laura R. 1994. "The Implications of Issue Definition Among Protestant Clergy." Paper presented at the annual meeting of the Social Science History Association, Atlanta, October 13–16.

Olsson, Karl A. 1985. *Into One Body . . . by the Cross*. 2 vols. Chicago: Covenant Press.

Parham, Robert. 1996. "Honest Speech in Church." *Ethics Report* 4(3): 1–3.

Parry, Pam. 1996. *On Guard for Religious Liberty: Six Decades of the Baptist Joint Committee*. Macon, Ga.: Smyth and Helwys.

Petrocik, John. 1981. *Party Coalitions: Realignments and Decline of the New Deal Party System*. Chicago: University of Chicago Press.

Pew Research Center. 1996. "The Diminishing Divide: American Churches, American Politics." Washington, D.C.: Pew Research Center for the People and the Press.

Piepkorn, Arthur C. 1978. *Profiles in Belief: The Religious Bodies of the United States and Canada*. 4 vols. San Francisco: Harper and Row.

Plowman, Edward E. 1988. "United Methodist Church Warns Against Political Activity." *National and International Religion Report,* March 28, 2.

Poloma, Margaret M. 1989. *The Assemblies of God at the Crossroads: Charisma and Institutional Dilemmas*. Knoxville: University of Tennessee Press.

Poloma, Margaret M., and John C. Green. 1992. "Pentecostal Preachers and Politics: The Case of the Assemblies of God." Paper presented at the annual meeting of the Society for the Scientific Study of Religion, Washington, D.C., November 6–8.

Presley, Sue Anne. 1995. "A Left Jab to the Religious Right in Texas" *Washington Post National Weekly Edition,* November 13–19, 34.

Putnam, Robert D. 1993. *Making Democracy Work: Civic Traditions in Modern Italy*. Princeton, N.J.: Princeton University Press.

Quinley, Harold E. 1974. *The Prophetic Clergy: Social Activism Among Protestant Ministers*. New York: Wiley.

Reed, Ralph. 1996. *Active Faith: How Christians Are Changing the Soul of American Politics*. New York: Free Press.

Reichley, A. James. 1985. *Religion in American Public Life*. Washington, D.C.: Brookings.

Richardson, David. 1996. Interview with James L. Guth, Grand Rapids, Michigan, October 4.

Roof, Wade Clark, and William McKinney. 1987. *American Mainline Religion: Its Changing Shape and Future*. New Brunswick, N.J.: Rutgers University Press.

Roozen, David A., William McKinney, and Jackson W. Carroll. 1984. *Varieties of Religious Presence: Mission in Public Life*. New York: Pilgrim Press.

Rosenstone, Steven, and John Hansen. 1993. *Mobilization, Participation, and Democracy in America*. New York: Macmillan.

Rozell, Mark J., and Clyde Wilcox. 1996. *Second Coming: The New Christian Right in Virginia Politics*. Baltimore, Md.: Johns Hopkins University Press.

Russo, Ed, and Fred Knapp. 1994. "Religion, Politics, Mix in Some Churches." *Lincoln Journal,* September 6, 10.

Sapp, William D. 1975. "Factors in the Involvement of Southern Baptist Pastors in Governmental Decision-Making." Ph.D. diss., Southern Baptist Theological Seminary, Louisville.

Schneider, Robert A. 1989. "Voice of Many Waters: Church Federation in the Twentieth

Century." In *Between the Times: The Travail of the Protestant Establishment in America, 1900–1960*, ed. William R. Hutchison, 95–121. Cambridge: Cambridge University Press.

Schuller, David S., Merton P. Strommen, and Milo L. Brekke, eds. 1980. *Ministry in America.* San Francisco: Harper and Row.

Shafer, Byron E., and Williain J. M. Claggett, 1995. *The Two Majorities: The Issue Context of Modern American Politics.* Baltimore, Md., and London: Johns Hopkins University Press.

Shie, Paul C. J. 1991. "Why the Robertson Campaign Failed: A Study of Political Mobilization of Evangelical Ministers in the 1988 Republican Presidential Primaries." Ph.D. diss., University of Kansas.

Shipp, Julian. 1996. "Greensboro Presbyterians Jubilant over New Agreement Ratified by Kmart Workers." News Release 3769 of *PCUSA News,* August 14.

Smith, Tom. 1980. "America's Most Important Problem: A Trend Analysis, 1946–1976." *Public Opinion Quarterly* 44:164–180.

Solomon, Burt. 1996. "Christian Soldiers." *National Journal,* February 24, 410–415.

Spittler, Russell P. 1994. "Are Pentecostals and Charismatics Fundamentalists?" In *Charismatic Christianity as a Global Culture,* ed. Karla Poewe, 103–116. Columbia: University of South Carolina Press.

Stark, Rodney. 1980. "Comment: On Buying Back Youthful Daubings." *Sociological Analysis* 41:162–163.

Stark, Rodney, Bruce D. Foster, Charles Y. Glock, and Harold Quinley. 1970. "Sounds of Silence." *Psychology Today,* April, 11.

———. 1971. *Wayward Shepherds: Prejudice and the Protestant Clergy.* New York: Harper and Row.

Sullivan, John L., James Piereson, and George E. Markus. 1982. *Political Tolerance and American Democracy.* Chicago: University of Chicago Press.

Thompson, James J., Jr. 1982. *Tried as by Fire: Southern Baptists and the Religious Controversies of the 1920s.* Macon, Ga.: Mercer University Press.

Tocqueville, Alexis, de. 1945. *Democracy in America.* 2 vols. New York: Random House.

Thomas, George M. 1989. *Revivalism and Cultural Change: Christianity, Nation Building, and the Market in the Nineteenth-Century United States.* Chicago: University of Chicago Press.

Turner, Helen Lee. 1992. "Fundamentalism in the Southern Baptist Convention: The Crystallization of a Millennialist Vision." Ph.D. diss., University of Virginia.

Turner, Helen Lee, and James L. Guth. 1989. "The Politics of Armageddon: Dispensationalism Among Southern Baptist Ministers." In *Religion and Political Behavior in the United States,* ed. Ted G. Jelen, 187–208. Westport, Conn.: Praeger.

Van Deth, Jan W. 1990. "Interest in Politics." In *Continuities in Political Action,* ed. M. Kent Jennings and J. W. Van Deth, 275–312. New York: Walter de Gruyter.

Verba, Sidney, and Norman Nie. 1972. *Participation in America: Political Democracy and Social Equality.* New York: Harper and Row.

Verba, Sidney, Kay Lehman Schlozman, and Henry E. Brady. 1995. *Voice and Equality: Civic Voluntarism in American Society.* Cambridge, Mass.: Harvard University Press.

Wald, Kenneth. 1997. *Religion and Politics in the United States.* 3d ed. Washington, D.C.: CQ Press.

Wald, Kenneth, Dennis E. Owen, and Samuel S. Hill Jr. 1988. "Churches as Political Communities." *American Political Science Review* 82:531–548.

Warner, R. Stephen. 1988. *New Wine in Old Wineskins: Evangelicals and Liberals in a Small-Town Church*. Berkeley: University of California Press.

———. 1993. "Work in Progress: Toward a New Paradigm for the Sociological Study of Religion in the United States." *American Journal of Sociology* 98:1044–1093.

Watson, David K. 1982. "A History of the Political Attitudes of CRC People." Unpublished paper, Calvin College, Grand Rapids, Michigan.

Weber, Timothy P. 1987. *Living in the Shadow of the Second Coming: American Premillennialism, 1875 to 1982*. Chicago: University of Chicago Press.

Wells, David. 1993. *No Place for Truth, Or Whatever Happened to Evangelical Theology?* Grand Rapids, Mich.: Eerdmans.

Wilcox, Clyde. 1996. *Onward Christian Soldiers: The Religious Right in American Politics*. Boulder, Colo.: Westview Press.

Wilcox, Clyde, Ted G. Jelen, and Sharon G. Linzey, 1991. "Reluctant Warriors: Premillennialists and Politics in the Moral Majority." *Journal for the Scientific Study of Religion* 30:245–258.

Williams, D. Newell, ed. 1991. *A Case Study of Mainstream Protestantism: The Disciples' Relation to American Culture, 1880–1989*. Grand Rapids, Mich.: Eerdmans.

Willimon, Will. 1996. "Reformer and Hand-Wringer." *Christian Century* 113:533–534.

Witham, Larry. 1996. "Hillary Speaks to Fellow Methodists." *Washington Times,* April 25, A9.

Wuthnow, Robert. 1983. "The Political Rebirth of American Evangelicals." In *The New Christian Right: Mobilization and Legitimation,* ed. Robert C. Liebman and Robert Wuthnow, 168–185. New York: Aldine.

———. 1988. *The Restructuring of American Religion*. Princeton, N.J.: Princeton University Press.

Zaller, John R. 1992. *The Nature and Origins of Mass Opinion*. New York: Cambridge University Press.

Zipperer, John. 1994. "Against All Odds." *Christianity Today,* November 14, 58–62.

# Index

209

clerical, 24, 173, 180–181
education and, 174
measurement of, 20–21
model of, 21
modes of, 163
SES and, 174
Partisan change, analysis of, 122–126, 123
(table)
Partisanship, 131, 182
analysis of, 116–117, 121, 122–126, 176
attitudes/personal traits and, 124
clerical, 117–119, 118 (table), 120–122,
122 (table), 134–137
cognitive, 117
conative, 117
ideological, 117, 119–122
ideology and, 17–18, 124, 131
influences on, 123 (table)
orthodoxy and, 123
self-conscious identification and, 116
theology and, 121
two-party system and, 116
Party images
analyzing, 126–128
clerical (by orthodoxy), 127 (table)
Party voting, analysis of, 128–131
Pastor's Conference (SBC), 49
Pastors for Life, 1
Pastors' Forum (SBC), 49
PCUS. See Presbyterian Church in the
United States
PCUSA. See Presbyterian Church in the
United States of America
"Peace with Justice" statement (1981), 41
"Pelvic politics," 16, 83
Pentecostalism, 11, 27, 48
individual gospel and, 13
politics and, 160, 161
social capital and, 144
theological movements and, 49
Perot, Ross, 133
Piereson, James, political tolerance and, 69
Pluralism, 37, 39, 42, 103
Political action, 169
appropriateness of, 146
clerical approval of, 148 (table)
See also Direct action

Political activities, 18–19
approval of, 146–153, 159, 160
clerical, 138–139, 165 (table), 166
(table), 170 (table)
enhancing/inhibiting, 139
limitations/dangers of, 61
See also Activism
Political attitudes, 12, 23, 191
clergy-laity gap in, 113 (table)
clerical, 133 (table)
empirical studies of, 96
political beliefs and, 117, 154
of Protestant clergy, 98 (table), 101
(table)
theological perspective and, 100
Political efficacy, 175, 188
Political interest, 139–142
clergy and, 194
Political issues, 157
attention for, 73, 78
clergy-laity gap on, 114
cue-giving on, 150, 151
moral issues and, 88
praying about, 146, 151, 164
Political pronouncements, 163–164, 165
(table), 180, 183
congregational approval for, 178
Politics
clerical, 8, 42, 96, 138, 145, 192–194
priorities for, 72
religion and, 61, 73–74
theology and, 73, 77, 105, 154
transformation of, 108
Poloma, Margaret, ix
Pornography, 2, 86, 89, 90, 91, 97, 98
civil disobedience over, 148
conservatism on, 100
cue-giving on, 151, 152
party identification and, 132
"Postmaterialism" (Inglehart), 67
Postmillennialism, 46, 47
Premillennialism, 10, 34, 44, 46–47, 48,
56
Pentecostalism and, 27
politics and, 73, 76
theology and, 75
Presbyterian Church in America, 140